World Facts

The Earth

AREA: 196,938,000 sq mi (510,066,000 sq km)

LAND: 57,393,000 sq mi (148,647,000 sq km)— 29.1%

WATER: 139,545,000 sq mi (361,419,000 sq km)— 70.9%

POPULATION: 6,624,528,000 people

The Continents

	AREA (sq mi)	AREA (sq km)	Percent of Earth's Land
Asia	17,208,000	44,570,000	30.0
Africa	11,608,000	30,065,000	20.2
North America	9,449,000	24,474,000	16.5
South America	6,880,000	17,819,000	12.0
Antarctica	5,100,000	13,209,000	8.9
Europe	3,841,000	9,947,000	6.7
Australia	2,970,000	7,692,000	5.2

Highest Point On Each Continent

	feet	meters
Mount Everest, Asia	29,035	8,850
Cerro Aconcagua, South America	22,834	6,960
Mount McKinley (Denali), N. America	20,320	6,194
Kilimanjaro, Africa	19,340	5,895
El'brus, Europe	18,510	5,642
Vinson Massif, Antarctica	16,067	4,897
Mount Kosciuszko, Australia	7,310	2,228

Lowest Point On Each Continent

	feet	meters
Dead Sea, Asia	-1,380	-421
Lake Assal, Africa	-512	-156
Laguna del Carbón, South America	-344	-105
Death Valley, North America	-282	-86
Caspian Sea, Europe	-92	-28
Lake Eyre, Australia	-52	-16
Bentley Subglacial Trench, Antarctica (ice covered)	-8,383	-2,555

Ten Longest Rivers

	LENGTH miles	kilometers
Nile, Africa	4,241	6,825
Amazon, South America	4,000	6,437
Yangtze (Chang Jiang), Asia	3,964	6,380
Mississippi-Missouri, North America	3,710	5,971
Yenisey-Angara, Asia	3,440	5,536
Yellow (Huang), Asia	3,395	5,464
Ob-Irtysh, Asia	3,362	5,410
Amur, Asia	2,744	4,416
Lena, Asia	2,734	4,400
Congo, Africa	2,715	4,370

Ten Largest Lakes

	AREA (sq mi)	AREA (sq km)	Greatest Depth (feet)	(meters)
Caspian Sea, Europe-Asia	143,254	371,000	3,363	1,025
Superior, N. America	31,701	82,100	1,332	406
Victoria, Africa	26,836	69,500	269	82
Huron, N. America	23,013	59,600	751	229
Michigan, N. America	22,318	57,800	922	281
Tanganyika, Africa	12,587	32,600	4,823	1,470
Baikal, Asia	12,163	31,500	5,371	1,637
Great Bear, N. America	12,086	31,300	1,463	446
Malawi, Africa	11,159	28,900	2,280	695
Great Slave, N. America	11,043	28,600	2,014	614

Ten Largest Islands

	AREA (sq mi)	AREA (sq km)
Greenland, North America	836,000	2,166,000
New Guinea, Asia-Oceania	306,000	792,500
Borneo, Asia	280,100	725,500
Madagascar, Africa	226,600	587,000
Baffin, North America	196,000	507,500
Sumatra, Asia	165,000	427,300
Honshu, Asia	87,800	227,400
Great Britain, Europe	84,200	218,100
Victoria, North America	83,900	217,300
Ellesmere, North America	75,800	196,200

The Oceans

	AREA (sq mi)	AREA (sq km)	Percent of Earth's Water Area
Pacific	65,436,200	169,479,000	46.8
Atlantic	35,338,500	91,526,400	25.3
Indian	28,839,800	74,694,800	20.6
Arctic	5,390,000	13,960,100	3.9

Deepest Point In Each Ocean

	feet	meters
Challenger Deep, Mariana Trench, Pacific	-35,827	-10,920
Puerto Rico Trench, Atlantic	-28,232	-8,605
Java Trench, Indian	-23,376	-7,125
Molloy Deep, Arctic	-18,599	-5,669

Ten Largest Seas

	AREA (sq mi)	AREA (sq km)	Average Depth (feet)	(meters)
Coral Sea	1,615,260	4,183,510	8,107	2,471
South China Sea	1,388,570	3,596,390	3,871	1,180
Caribbean Sea	1,094,330	2,834,290	8,517	2,596
Bering Sea	972,810	2,519,580	6,010	1,832
Mediterranean Sea	953,320	2,469,100	5,157	1,572
Sea of Okhotsk	627,490	1,625,190	2,671	814
Gulf of Mexico	591,430	1,531,810	5,066	1,544
Norwegian Sea	550,300	1,425,280	5,801	1,768
Greenland Sea	447,050	1,157,850	4,734	1,443
Sea of Japan (East Sea)	389,290	1,008,260	5,404	1,647

Earth's Extremes

HOTTEST PLACE: Dalol, Danakil Desert, Ethiopia; annual average temperature— 93°F (34°C)

COLDEST PLACE: Plateau Station, Antarctica; annual average temperature— -70°F (-57°C)

WETTEST PLACE: Mawsynram, Assam, India; annual average rainfall— 467 in (1,187 cm)

DRIEST PLACE: Atacama Desert, Chile; rainfall barely measurable

HIGHEST WATERFALL: Angel Falls, Venezuela— 3,212 ft (979 m)

LARGEST HOT DESERT: Sahara, Africa— 3,475,000 sq mi (9,000,000 sq km)

LARGEST ICE DESERT: Antarctica— 5,100,000 sq mi (13,209,000 sq km)

LARGEST CANYON: Grand Canyon, Colorado River, Arizona; 277 mi (446 km) long along river, 600 ft (180 m) to 18 mi (29 km) wide, about 1.1 mi (1.8 km) deep

LONGEST REEF: Great Barrier Reef, Australia— 1,429 mi (2,300 km)

GREATEST TIDAL RANGE: Bay of Fundy, Nova Scotia, Canada— 52 ft (16 m)

MOST PREDICTABLE GEYSER: Old Faithful, Wyoming, U.S.; annual average interval— 66 to 80 minutes

LARGEST CAVE SYSTEM: Mammoth Cave, Kentucky, U.S.; over 330 mi (530 km) of passageways mapped

Abbreviations

COUNTRY NAMES

ARM. .... Armenia
AZERB. .... Azerbaijan
B. & H.; BOSN. & HERZG.
.... Bosnia and Herzegovina
BELG. .... Belgium
CRO. .... Croatia
EST. .... Estonia
HUNG. .... Hungary
KOS. .... Kosovo
LATV. .... Latvia
LIECH. .... Liechtenstein
LITH. .... Lithuania
LUX. .... Luxembourg
MACED. .... Macedonia
MOLD. .... Moldova
MONT. .... Montenegro
N.Z. .... New Zealand
NETH. .... Netherlands
SLOV. .... Slovenia
SWITZ. .... Switzerland

U.A.E. .... United Arab Emirates
U.K. .... United Kingdom
U.S. .... United States

PHYSICAL FEATURES

I.-s. .... Island-s
L. .... Lake
Mt.-s. .... Mont, Mount-ain-s
R. .... River

OTHER

ALA. .... Alabama
ARK. .... Arkansas
CONN. .... Connecticut
D.C. .... District of Columbia
Eq. .... Equatorial
FLA. .... Florida
ILL. .... Illinois
IND. .... Indiana
KY. .... Kentucky

LA. .... Louisiana
MASS. .... Massachusetts
MD. .... Maryland
MINN. .... Minnesota
MISS. .... Mississippi
N.H. .... New Hampshire
N.Y. .... New York
PA. .... Pennsylvania
P.E.I. .... Prince Edward Island
Pop. .... Population
Rep. .... Republic
R.I. .... Rhode Island
St.-e .... Saint-e
TENN. .... Tennessee
VA. .... Virginia
VT. .... Vermont
WASH. .... Washington
WIS. .... Wisconsin
W.VA. .... West Virginia
& .... and

NATIONAL GEOGRAPHIC

STUDENT ATLAS OF THE WORLD

THIRD EDITION

YOU are the world!

NATIONAL GEOGRAPHIC

WASHINGTON, D.C.

TABLE OF CONTENTS

North America:
Floods, page 68

South America:
Three-toed sloth,
page 78

Asia:
Terraced rice
fields, page 90

Antarctica: Whale, page 123

Africa: Giraffe, page 108

BACK OF THE BOOK

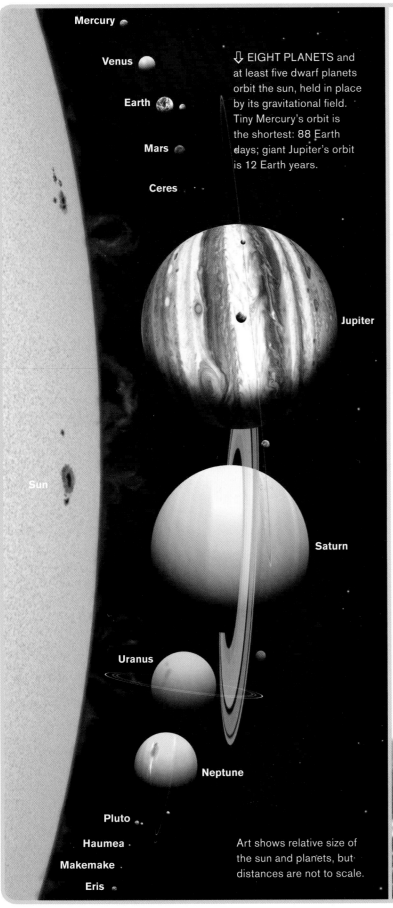

Mercury

Venus

Earth

Mars

Ceres

⇩ EIGHT PLANETS and at least five dwarf planets orbit the sun, held in place by its gravitational field. Tiny Mercury's orbit is the shortest: 88 Earth days; giant Jupiter's orbit is 12 Earth years.

Jupiter

Sun

Saturn

Uranus

Neptune

Pluto

Haumea

Makemake

Eris

Art shows relative size of the sun and planets, but distances are not to scale.

Earth in Space

A̱t the center of our solar system is the sun, a huge mass of hot gas that is the source of both light and warmth for Earth. Third in a group of 13 planets that revolve around the sun, Earth is a terrestrial, or mostly rocky, planet. So are Mercury, Venus, and Mars. Earth is about 93 million miles (150 million kilometers) from the sun, and its journey, or revolution, around the sun takes 365¼ days. Farther away from the sun, four more planets—Jupiter, Saturn, Uranus, and Neptune (all made up primarily of gases)—plus at least five "dwarf" planets (Ceres, Pluto, Haumea, Makemake, and Eris) complete the main bodies of our solar system. The solar system, in turn, is part of the Milky Way galaxy.

⇐ SPRING
Northern Hemisphere

⇨ WINTER
Northern Hemisphere

EARTH'S SEASONS change throughout the year because the planet tilts 23.5° on its axis as it revolves around the sun. For example, when the Northern Hemisphere is tilted toward the sun, summer occurs there; when it's tilted away from the sun, it experiences winter.

⇐ SUMMER
Northern Hemisphere

⇨ FALL
Northern
Hemisphere

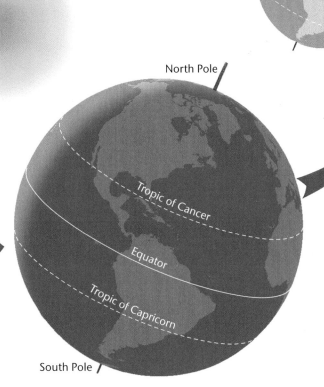

North Pole

Tropic of Cancer

Equator

Tropic of Capricorn

South Pole

⇩ AN ENVELOPE OF AIR surrounds Earth. Called the atmosphere, it is made up of a mix of nitrogen, oxygen, and other gases. It is 300 miles (483 km) thick. The troposphere, which extends upward as much as 10 miles (16 km) from Earth's surface, is called the zone of life. The combination of gases, moderate temperatures, and water in this layer supports plants, animals, and other forms of life on Earth.

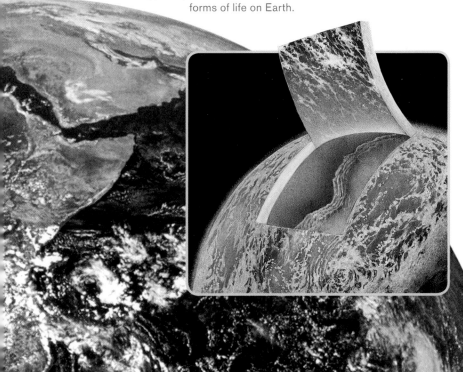

⇧ EARTH ROTATES WEST TO EAST on its axis, an imaginary line that runs through Earth's center from Pole to Pole. Each rotation takes 24 hours, or one full cycle of day and night. One complete rotation equals one Earth day. One complete revolution around the sun equals one Earth year.

Map Projections

Maps tell a story about physical and human systems, places and regions, patterns and relationships. This atlas is a collection of maps that tell a story about Earth.

Understanding that story requires a knowledge of how maps are made and a familiarity with the special language used by cartographers, the people who create maps.

Globes present a model of Earth as it is—a sphere—but they are bulky and can be difficult to use and store. Flat maps are much more convenient, but certain problems result from transferring Earth's curved surface to a flat piece of paper, a process called projection. There are many different types of projections, all of which involve some form of distortion: area, distance, direction, or shape.

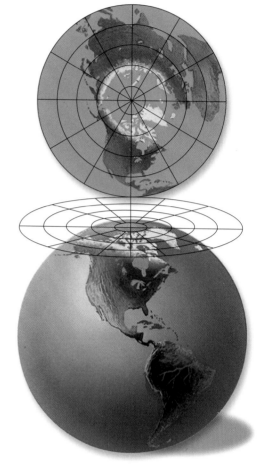

⇧ AZIMUTHAL MAP PROJECTION. This kind of map is made by projecting a globe onto a flat surface that touches the globe at a single point, such as the North Pole. These maps accurately represent direction along any straight line extending from the point of contact. Away from the point of contact, shape is increasingly distorted.

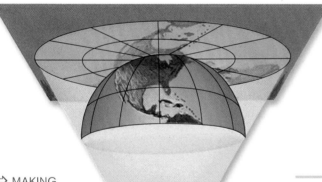

⇨ MAKING A PROJECTION. Imagine a globe that has been cut in half as this one has. If a light is shined into it, the lines of latitude and longitude and the shapes of the continents will cast shadows that can be "projected" onto a piece of paper, as shown here. Depending on how the paper is positioned, the shadows will be distorted in different ways.

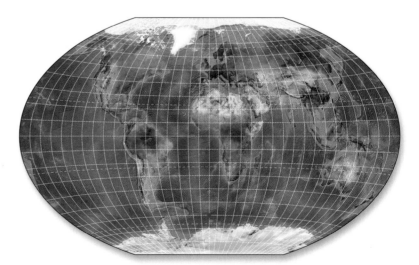

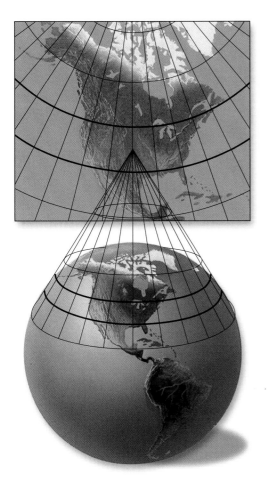

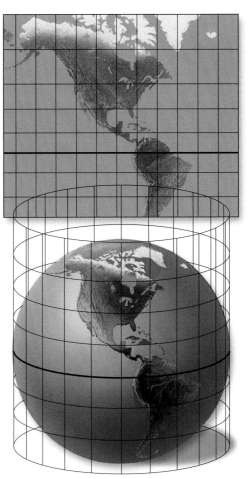

⇧ CONIC MAP PROJECTION. This kind of map is made by projecting a globe onto a cone. The part of Earth being mapped touches the sides of the cone. Lines of longitude appear as straight lines; lines of latitude appear as parallel arcs. Conic projections are often used to map mid-latitude areas with great east-west extent, such as North America.

⇧ CYLINDRICAL MAP PROJECTION. A cylindrical projection map is made by projecting a globe onto a cylinder that touches Earth's surface along the Equator. Latitude and longitude lines on this kind of map show true compass directions, which makes it useful for navigation. But there is great distortion in the size of high-latitude landmasses.

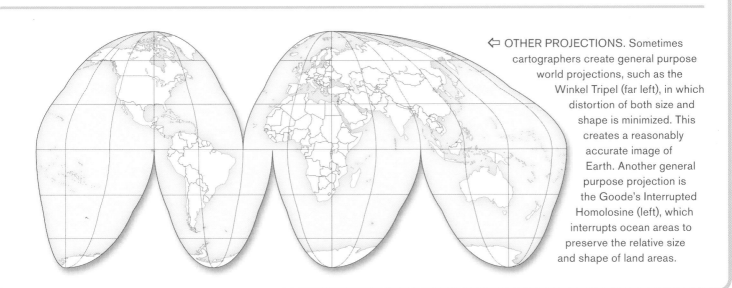

⇦ OTHER PROJECTIONS. Sometimes cartographers create general purpose world projections, such as the Winkel Tripel (far left), in which distortion of both size and shape is minimized. This creates a reasonably accurate image of Earth. Another general purpose projection is the Goode's Interrupted Homolosine (left), which interrupts ocean areas to preserve the relative size and shape of land areas.

Reading Maps

People can use maps to find locations, to determine direction or distance, and to understand information about places. Cartographers rely on a special graphic language to communicate through maps.

An imaginary system of lines, called the global grid, helps us locate particular points on Earth's surface. The global grid is made up of lines of latitude and longitude that are measured in degrees, minutes, and seconds. The point where these lines intersect identifies the absolute location of a place. No other place has the exact same address.

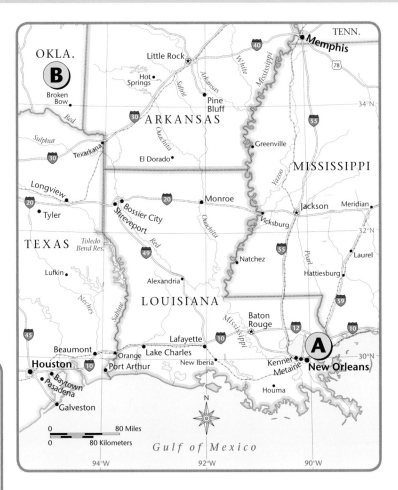

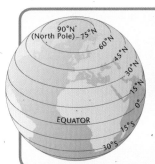

LATITUDE. Lines of latitude—also called parallels because they are parallel to the Equator—run east to west around the globe and measure location north or south of the Equator. The Equator is 0° latitude.

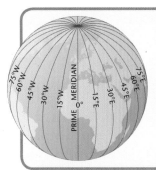

LONGITUDE. Lines of longitude, also called meridians, run from Pole to Pole and measure location east or west of the prime meridian. The prime meridian is 0° longitude, and it runs through Greenwich, near London, England.

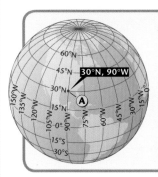

GLOBAL GRID. When used together, latitude and longitude form a grid that provides a system for determining the exact, or absolute, location of every place on Earth. For example, the absolute location of point A is 30°N, 90°W.

⇧ DIRECTION. Cartographers put a north arrow or a compass rose, which shows the four cardinal directions—north, south, east, and west—on a map. On this map, point **B** is northwest (NW) of point **A**. Northwest is an example of an intermediate direction, which means it is between two cardinal directions. Grid lines can also be used to indicate north.

⇨ SCALE. A map represents a part of Earth's surface, but that part is greatly reduced. Cartographers include a map scale to show what distance on Earth is represented by a given length on the map. Scale can be graphic (a bar), verbal, or a ratio.

To determine how many miles point **A** is from point **B**, place a piece of paper on the map above and mark the distance between **A** and **B**. Then compare the marks on the paper with the bar scale on the map.

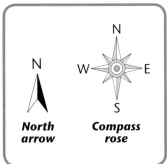

North arrow

Compass rose

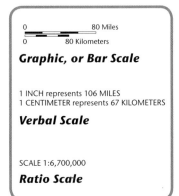

0 ⊢ 80 Miles
0 ⊢ 80 Kilometers

Graphic, or Bar Scale

1 INCH represents 106 MILES
1 CENTIMETER represents 67 KILOMETERS

Verbal Scale

SCALE 1:6,700,000

Ratio Scale

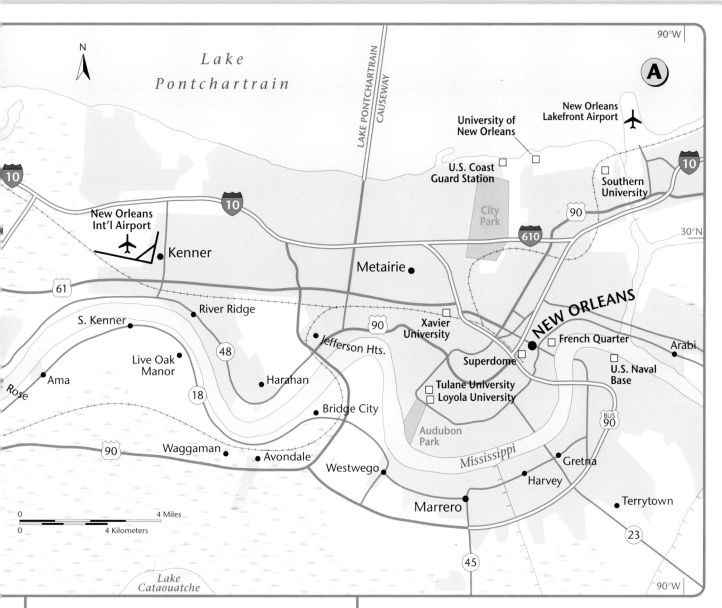

⬇ SYMBOLS. Finally, cartographers use a variety of symbols, which are identified in a map key or legend, to tell us more about the places represented on the map. There are three general types of symbols:

● ● · POINT SYMBOLS show exact location of places (such as cities) or quantity (a large dot can mean a more populous city).

LINE SYMBOLS show boundaries or connections (such as roads, canals, and other trade links).

AREA SYMBOLS show the form and extent of a feature (such as a lake, park, or swamp).

Additional information may be coded in color, size, and shape.

⬆ PUTTING IT ALL TOGETHER. We already know from the map on page 8 which states A and B are located in. But to find out more about city A, we need a larger scale map—one that shows a smaller area in more detail (see above).

MAP LEGEND

▨ Metropolitan area		▬▬	Road
▢ Lake or river		⊦⊦⊦⊦	Railroad
▨ Park		∖__∕	Runway
▢ Swamp		✈	Airport
⊥⊥⊥ Canal		▢	Point of interest
▬▬ Highway		● ● ·	Town

Types of Maps

This atlas includes many different types of maps so that a wide variety of information about Earth can be presented. Three of the most commonly used types of maps are physical, political, and thematic.

A **physical map** identifies natural features, such as mountains, deserts, oceans, and lakes. Area symbols of various colors and shadings may indicate height above sea level or, as in the example here, ecosystems. Similar symbols could also show water depth.

A **political map** shows how people have divided the world into countries. Political maps can also show states, counties, or cities within a country. Line symbols indicate boundaries, and point symbols show the locations and sometimes sizes of cities.

Thematic maps use a variety of symbols to show distributions and patterns on Earth. For example, a choropleth map uses shades of color to represent different values. The example here shows the amount of energy consumed each year by various countries. Thematic maps can show many different things, such as patterns of vegetation, land use, and religions.

A **cartogram** is a special kind of thematic map in which the size of a country is based on some statistic other than land area. In the cartogram at far right, population size determines the size of each country. This is why Nigeria—the most populous country in Africa—appears much larger than Sudan, which has more than double the land area of Nigeria (see the political map). Cartograms allow for a quick visual comparison of countries in terms of a selected statistic.

⇨ THIS GLOBE is useful for showing Africa's position and size relative to other landmasses, but very little detail is possible at this scale. By using different kinds of maps, mapmakers can show a variety of information in more detail.

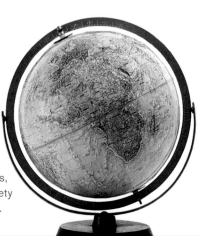

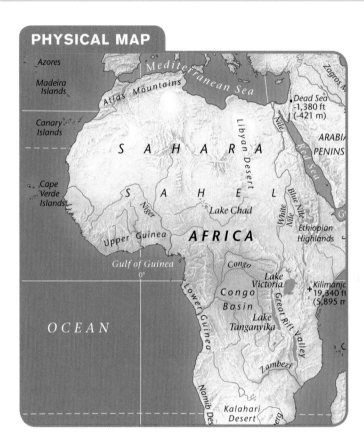

PHYSICAL MAP

Azores
Madeira Islands
Atlas Mountains
Mediterranean Sea
Zagros M.
Canary Islands
Dead Sea -1,380 ft (-421 m)
ARABIA PENINS.
S A H A R A
Libyan Desert
Nile
Red Sea
Cape Verde Islands
S A H E L
Lake Chad
White Nile
Blue Nile
Niger
Upper Guinea
A F R I C A
Ethiopian Highlands
Gulf of Guinea 0°
Congo
Lake Victoria
Kilimanjaro 19,340 ft (5,895 m)
Lower Guinea
Congo Basin
Great Rift Valley
O C E A N
Lake Tanganyika
Zambezi
Namib Des.
Kalahari Desert

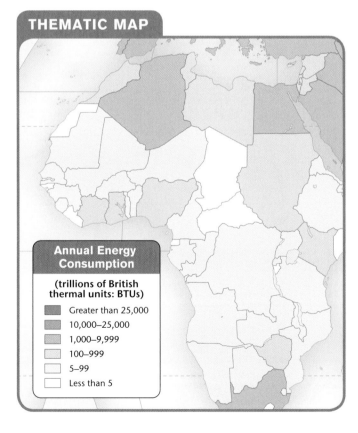

THEMATIC MAP

Annual Energy Consumption

(trillions of British thermal units: BTUs)

	Greater than 25,000
	10,000–25,000
	1,000–9,999
	100–999
	5–99
	Less than 5

POLITICAL MAP

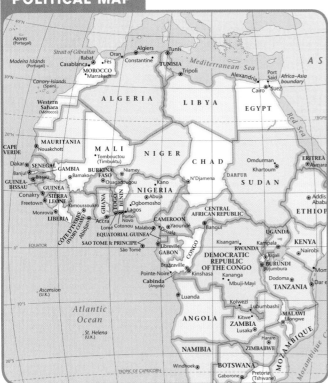

CARTOGRAM

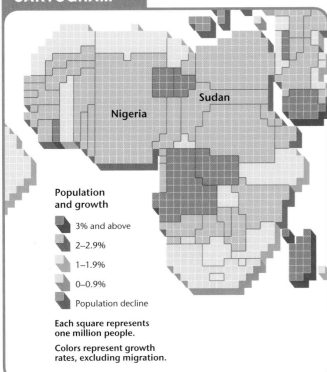

Population and growth

- 3% and above
- 2–2.9%
- 1–1.9%
- 0–0.9%
- Population decline

Each square represents one million people.

Colors represent growth rates, excluding migration.

SATELLITE IMAGE MAPS

Satellites orbiting Earth transmit images of the surface to computers on the ground. These computers translate the information into special maps (below) that use colors to show various characteristics. Such maps are valuable tools for identifying patterns or comparing changes over time.

⇩ **CLOUD COVERAGE**

⇩ **TOPOGRAPHY/BATHYMETRY**

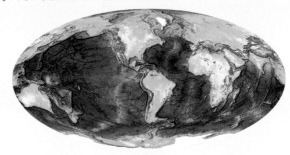

⇩ **SEA LEVEL VARIABILITY**

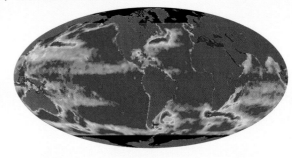

⇩ **SEA SURFACE TEMPERATURE**

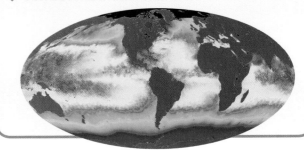

Time Zones

The *Fiji Times*, a newspaper published in Suva, capital of the Fiji Islands, carries the message "The First Newspaper Published in the World Today" on the front page of each edition. How can this newspaper from a small island country make such a claim? Fiji lies west of the date line, an invisible boundary designated to mark the beginning of each new day. The date line is just part of the system we have adopted to keep track of the passage of days.

For most of human history, people determined time by observing the position of the sun in the sky. Slight differences in time did not matter until, in the mid-19th century, the spread of railroads and telegraph lines changed forever the importance of time. High-speed transportation and communications required schedules, and schedules required that everyone agree on the time.

In 1884, an international conference, convened in Washington, D.C., established an international system of 24 time zones based on the fact that Earth turns from west to east 15 degrees of longitude every hour. Each time zone has a central meridian and is 15 degrees wide, 7½ degrees to either side of the named central meridian.

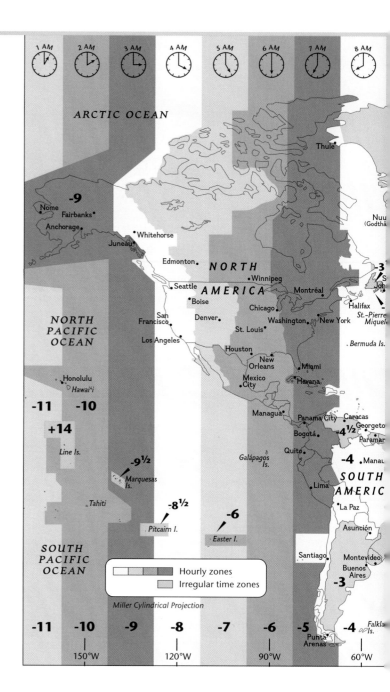

⇐ WORLD TIME CLOCK, in Alexanderplatz in Berlin, Germany, features a large cylinder that is marked with the world's 24 time zones and major cities found in each zone. The cylinder rises almost 33 feet (10 m) above the square and weighs 16 tons.

⇑ A SYSTEM OF STANDARD TIME put trains on schedules, which helped reduce the chance of collisions and the loss of lives and property caused by them.

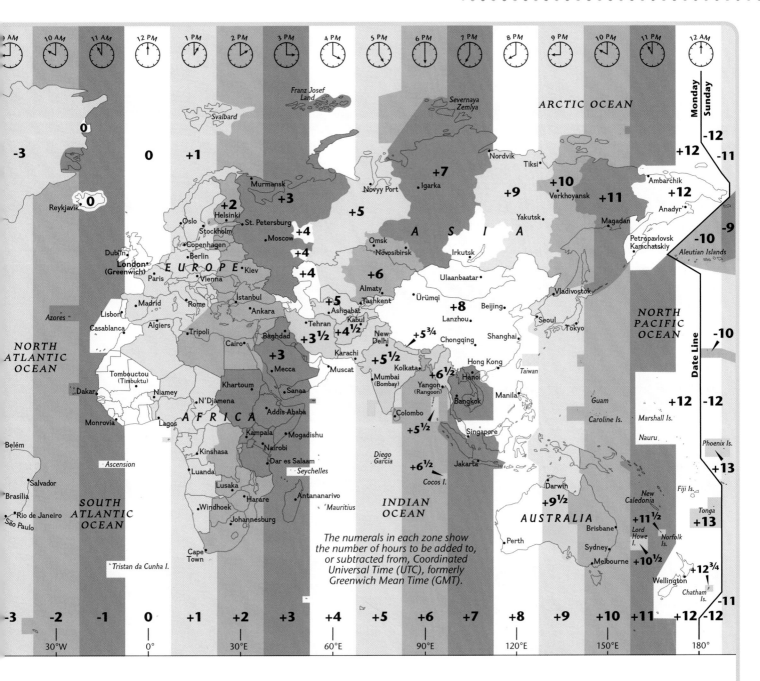

9 AM 10 AM 11 AM 12 PM 1 PM 2 PM 3 PM 4 PM 5 PM 6 PM 7 PM 8 PM 9 PM 10 PM 11 PM 12 AM

ARCTIC OCEAN

Monday / Sunday

-12
+12 **-11**

Franz Josef Land

Svalbard

Severnaya Zemlya

Nordvik

Tiksi

Ambarchik

+10
Verkhoyansk **+12**

0

-3

0

+1

Murmansk

+3

+7
Igarka

+9

Anadyr

-9

Reykjavik **0**

Oslo **+2**
Helsinki
Stockholm St. Petersburg
Copenhagen **+4**
Berlin Moscow

+4

+5

Novyy Port

Novosibirsk

Yakutsk

Magadan

+11

Petropavlovsk
Kamchatskiy
Aleutian Islands

+12

-10

Dublin
London
(Greenwich) Kiev
Paris Vienna

EUROPE

Omsk

A S I A

Vladivostok

NORTH
PACIFIC
OCEAN

Madrid Rome Istanbul
Lisbon Ankara
Azores Casablanca Algiers

+4

+6

Ulaanbaatar

Ürümqi **+8**
Lanzhou

Seoul
Beijing Tokyo

Date Line

-10

+5
Ashgabat
Tripoli Cairo Baghdad Kabul
Tehran **+4½**
+3½ New
Delhi **+5¾**

Tashkent

Almaty
Irkutsk

Shanghai
Chongqing

Hong Kong

NORTH
ATLANTIC
OCEAN

Tombouctou
(Timbuktu)
Dakar

Mecca
+3
Khartoum
Niamey
N'Djamena

Karachi
Muscat
Mumbai **+5½**
(Bombay)

Kolkata **+6½**
Yangon
(Rangoon) Hanoi

Taiwan

+12

-12

Monrovia

A F R I C A

Sanaa

Addis Ababa

Colombo

Bangkok
Manila

Guam

Caroline Is.

Marshall Is.

Lagos
Kampala
Kinshasa Nairobi
Luanda Mogadishu
Dar es Salaam
Seychelles

+5½

Singapore

Nauru

Phoenix Is.

+13

Belém

Salvador
Brasília
Rio de Janeiro
São Paulo

SOUTH
ATLANTIC
OCEAN

Ascension

Lusaka
Harare
Windhoek
Antananarivo
Johannesburg
Mauritius

Diego
Garcia

INDIAN
OCEAN

+6½

Jakarta

Cocos I.

AUSTRALIA

Darwin

+9½

Perth

New
Caledonia

Brisbane

Sydney

Melbourne **+10½**

Fiji Is.

Tonga **+13**

+11½
Lord
Howe
I. Norfolk
Is.

+12¾

Wellington

Chatham
Is.

-11

Cape
Town

Tristan da Cunha I.

The numerals in each zone show the number of hours to be added to, or subtracted from, Coordinated Universal Time (UTC), formerly Greenwich Mean Time (GMT).

-3	-2	-1	0	+1	+2	+3	+4	+5	+6	+7	+8	+9	+10	+11	+12 / -12
			30°W	0°		30°E		60°E		90°E		120°E		150°E	180°

THE DATE LINE (180°) is directly opposite the prime meridian (0°). As Earth rotates, each new day officially begins as the 180° line passes 12 midnight. If you travel west across the date line, you advance one day; if you travel east across the date line, you fall back one day. Notice on the map how the line zigs to the east as it passes through the South Pacific so that the islands of Fiji will not be split between two different days. Also notice that India is 5½ hours ahead of Coordinated Universal Time (formerly Greenwich Mean Time), and China has only one time zone, even though the country spans more than 60 degrees of longitude. These differences are the result of decisions made at the country level.

12 NOON Prime Meridian 10 A.M. 8 A.M.
6 A.M.
2 P.M.
4 A.M.
4 P.M.
2 A.M.
6 P.M.
Monday
Sunday
Date Line
8 P.M. 10 P.M.
ASIA
PACIFIC
OCEAN
INDIAN
OCEAN

The Physical World

Realms of land and water make up the physical world. More than two-thirds of Earth's surface is covered by water: oceans, lakes, and rivers. The rest is land: continents and islands. People inhabit every continent except Antarctica, which lies frozen beneath a vast ice cap at Earth's South Pole. Each continent is unique, but all show evidence of dynamic forces at work. Some forces build up mountains such as the Rockies, the Andes, and the Himalaya; other forces wear down Earth's surface, creating vast sedimentary plains and lowlands. Powerful rivers such as the Mississippi, the Congo, and the Yangtze (Chang) cut through the land and empty billions of gallons of freshwater into the oceans and seas each day.

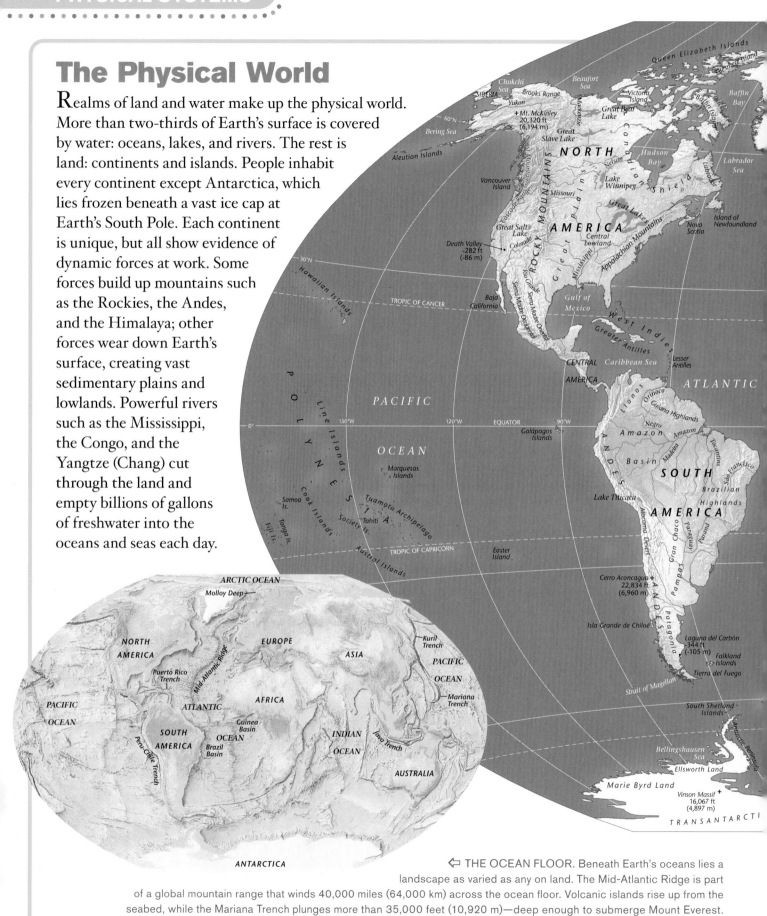

⇐ THE OCEAN FLOOR. Beneath Earth's oceans lies a landscape as varied as any on land. The Mid-Atlantic Ridge is part of a global mountain range that winds 40,000 miles (64,000 km) across the ocean floor. Volcanic islands rise up from the seabed, while the Mariana Trench plunges more than 35,000 feet (10,920 m)—deep enough to submerge Mount Everest.

⇑ THE PHYSICAL WORLD. Great landmasses called continents break Earth's global ocean into four smaller ones. Each continent is unique in terms of the landforms and rivers that etch its surface and the ecosystems that lend colors ranging from the deep greens of the tropical forests of northern South America and southeastern Asia to the browns and yellows of the arid lands of Africa and Australia. Most of Antarctica's features are hidden beneath its ice cap.

ARCTIC OCEAN

GREENLAND

Greenland Sea

ARCTIC CIRCLE

Iceland

Norwegian Sea

Svalbard

Barents Sea

Novaya Zemlya

Kara Sea

Severnaya Zemlya

New Siberian Islands

Laptev Sea

East Siberian Sea

British Isles

Ireland

North Sea

Great Britain

Scandinavia

Baltic

Northern European Plain

Ural Mountains

Ob

West Siberian Plain

Irtysh

Yenisey

S I B E R I A

Central Siberian Plateau

Angara

Lena

Lena

60°N

Bering Sea

Kamchatka Peninsula

Aleutian Is.

Sea of Okhotsk

EUROPE

Alps

Danube

Volga

The Steppes

Elbrus 18,510 ft (5,642 m)

Aral Sea

Caspian Sea

Black Sea

Caucasus Mts.

Altay Mountains

Lake Baikal

Amur

G O B I

A S I A

Kuril Islands

Hokkaido

Sea of Japan (East Sea)

JAPAN

Honshu

Kamchatka

Azores

Madeira Islands

Canary Islands

Cape Verde Islands

Mediterranean Sea

Atlas Mountains

Zagros Mountains

Dead Sea -1,380 ft (-421 m)

ARABIAN PENINSULA

Persian Gulf

Tian Shan

Taklimakan Desert

Kunlun Mountains

Plateau of Tibet

H I M A L A Y A

Mt. Everest 29,035 ft (8,850 m)

Indus

Brahmaputra

Ganges

North China Plain

Yellow (Huang)

Yellow Sea

East China Sea

Taiwan

Korea

Nampo Shoto

30°N

PACIFIC

S A H A R A

Libyan Desert

Nile

SAHEL

Lake Chad

AFRICA

Niger

Upper Guinea

White Nile

Blue Nile

Ethiopian Highlands

Red Sea

Gulf of Aden

Somali Peninsula

Arabian Sea

INDIA

Deccan Plateau

Bay of Bengal

Sri Lanka

Andaman Islands

Nicobar Is.

Andaman Sea

Salween

Mekong

Yangtze (Chang)

Hainan

Indochina Peninsula

South China Sea

Luzon

Philippine Sea

Philippine Islands

Mariana Islands

OCEAN

M I C R O N E S I A

Marshall Islands

Gilbert Islands

EQUATOR

0°

Gulf of Guinea

0°

Congo

Lake Victoria

Congo Basin

Kilimanjaro 19,340 ft (5,895 m)

Lake Tanganyika

Great Rift Valley

Lower Guinea

Maldive Islands

60°E

90°E

Seychelles

INDIAN

Comoros Islands

OCEAN

Madagascar

Mascarene Islands

150°E

Malay Peninsula

Sumatra

Java

I N D O N E S I A

Greater Sunda Islands

Celebes

Borneo

Moluccas

Timor

Arafura Sea

New Guinea

Bismarck Archipelago

Solomon Islands

M E L A N E S I A

New Caledonia

Vanuatu

Fiji Islands

OCEAN

Zambezi

Namib Desert

Kalahari Desert

Drakensberg

Great Sandy Desert

AUSTRALIA

Lake Eyre -52 ft (-16 m)

Great Victoria Desert

Central Lowlands

Darling

Murray

Great Dividing Range

Coral Sea

Tasman Sea

30°S

South Sandwich Islands

Kerguelen Islands

miles 2000

0

kilometers 3000

0

Winkel Tripel Projection

Mt. Kosciuszko 7,310 ft (2,228 m)

Tasmania

NEW ZEALAND

North Island

South Island

Auckland Islands

60°S

ANTARCTIC CIRCLE

Weddell Sea

Queen Maud Land

Transantarctic Mountains

Victoria Land

MOUNTAINS

ANTARCTICA

Earth's Geologic History

Earth is a dynamic planet. Its outer shell, or crust, is broken into huge pieces called plates. These plates ride on the slowly moving molten rock, or magma, that lies beneath the crust. Their movement constantly changes Earth's surface. For instance, along one convergent boundary—a place where two plates meet—the Indian Plate moves northward, colliding with the Eurasian Plate and heaving up the still growing mountains of the Himalaya. Along another convergent boundary, the Nasca Plate dives beneath the South American Plate in a process called subduction. Volcanoes and underwater earthquakes may occur along subduction zones, sometimes triggering giant waves called tsunamis. Along transform zones, such as California's San Andreas Fault, plates grind past each other, resulting in destructive earthquakes. The Mid-Atlantic Ridge is a divergent boundary where plates are pulling apart, allowing rising molten rock to form new ocean floor.

⬇ OUR CHANGING PLANET. The Latin phrase *terra firma* implies planet Earth is solid and unchanging. However, Earth's surface has been anything but unchanging. Geologic evidence suggests that moving plates have collided and moved apart more than once over the course of the planet's long history. As the main map shows, the forces of change show no signs of stopping.

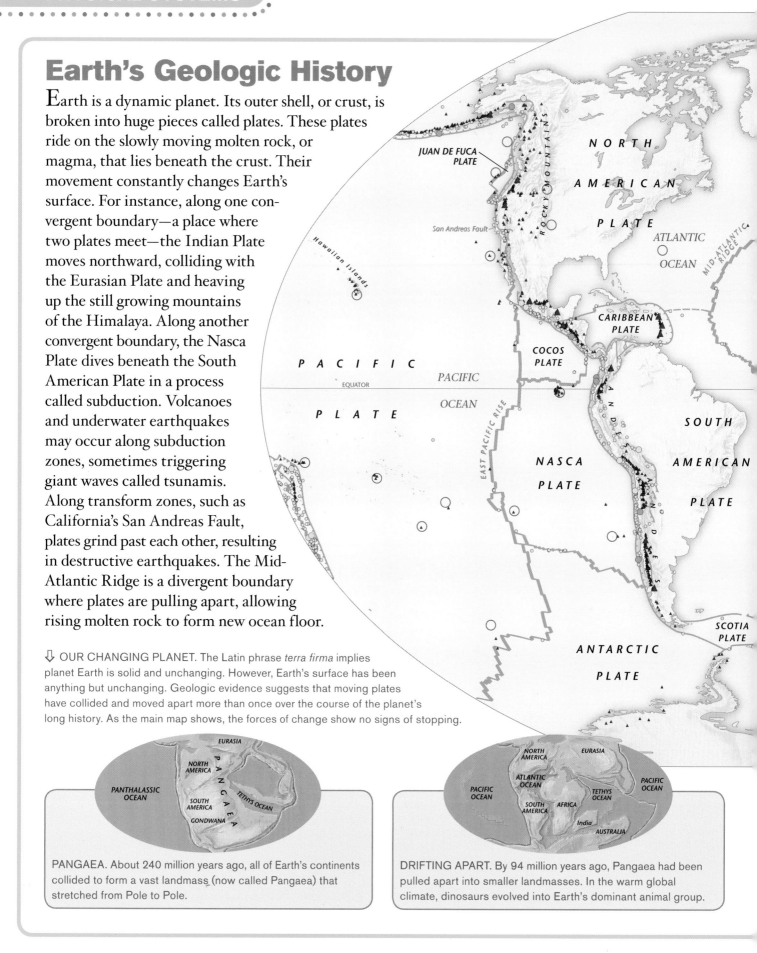

PANGAEA. About 240 million years ago, all of Earth's continents collided to form a vast landmass (now called Pangaea) that stretched from Pole to Pole.

DRIFTING APART. By 94 million years ago, Pangaea had been pulled apart into smaller landmasses. In the warm global climate, dinosaurs evolved into Earth's dominant animal group.

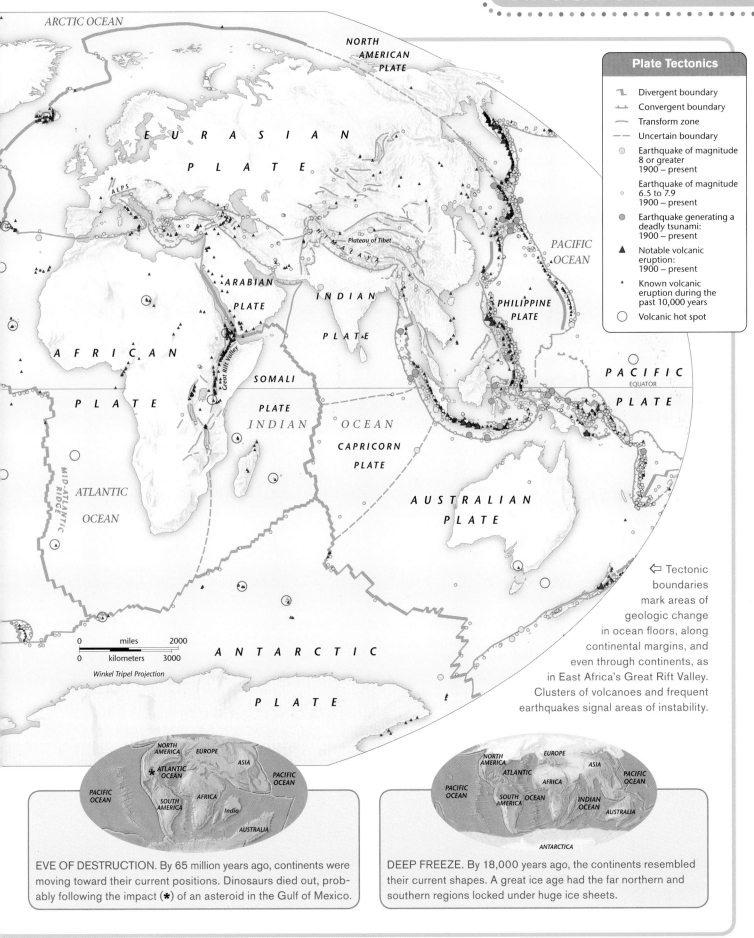

ARCTIC OCEAN

NORTH AMERICAN PLATE

E U R A S I A N   P L A T E

ALPS

ARABIAN PLATE

HIMALAYA

Plateau of Tibet

INDIAN PLATE

PACIFIC OCEAN

PHILIPPINE PLATE

AFRICAN PLATE

Great Rift Valley

SOMALI PLATE

INDIAN OCEAN

CAPRICORN PLATE

PACIFIC PLATE

EQUATOR

MID-ATLANTIC RIDGE

ATLANTIC OCEAN

AUSTRALIAN PLATE

miles 2000
kilometers 3000

Winkel Tripel Projection

ANTARCTIC PLATE

Plate Tectonics

⌐	Divergent boundary
⊥	Convergent boundary
—	Transform zone
– –	Uncertain boundary
○	Earthquake of magnitude 8 or greater 1900 – present
∘	Earthquake of magnitude 6.5 to 7.9 1900 – present
◉	Earthquake generating a deadly tsunami: 1900 – present
▲	Notable volcanic eruption: 1900 – present
▴	Known volcanic eruption during the past 10,000 years
○	Volcanic hot spot

← Tectonic boundaries mark areas of geologic change in ocean floors, along continental margins, and even through continents, as in East Africa's Great Rift Valley. Clusters of volcanoes and frequent earthquakes signal areas of instability.

NORTH AMERICA   EUROPE   ASIA
ATLANTIC OCEAN
PACIFIC OCEAN
SOUTH AMERICA   AFRICA   India
AUSTRALIA

EVE OF DESTRUCTION. By 65 million years ago, continents were moving toward their current positions. Dinosaurs died out, probably following the impact (✶) of an asteroid in the Gulf of Mexico.

NORTH AMERICA   EUROPE   ASIA
ATLANTIC   AFRICA
PACIFIC OCEAN
SOUTH AMERICA   OCEAN   INDIAN OCEAN   PACIFIC OCEAN
AUSTRALIA
ANTARCTICA

DEEP FREEZE. By 18,000 years ago, the continents resembled their current shapes. A great ice age had the far northern and southern regions locked under huge ice sheets.

Earth's Land and Water Features

The largest land and water features on Earth are the continents and the oceans, but many other features—large and small—make each place unique. Mountains, plateaus, and plains give texture to the land. The Rockies and the Andes rise high above the lowlands of North and South America. In Asia, the Himalaya and the Plateau of Tibet form the rugged core of Earth's largest continent. These features are the result of powerful forces within Earth pushing up the land. Other landforms, such as canyons and valleys, are created when weathering and erosion wear down parts of Earth's surface.

Dramatic features are not limited to the land. Submarine mountains, appearing like pale blue threads against the deep blue on the satellite map, rise from the seafloor and trace zones of underwater geologic activity. Deep trenches form where plates collide, causing one to dive beneath the other.

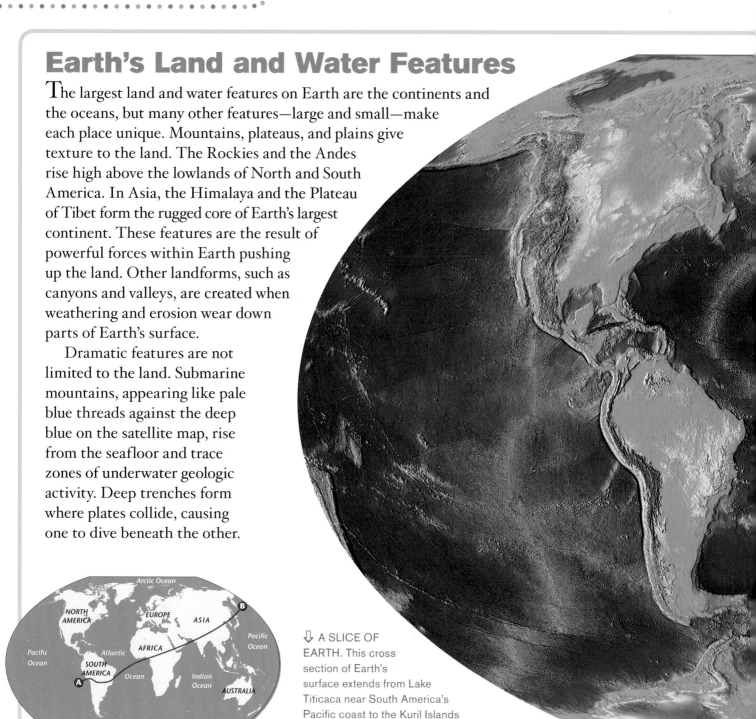

⬇ A SLICE OF EARTH. This cross section of Earth's surface extends from Lake Titicaca near South America's Pacific coast to the Kuril Islands in the northwestern Pacific Ocean. It shows towering mountains, eroded highlands, broad coastal plains, and deep ocean basins.

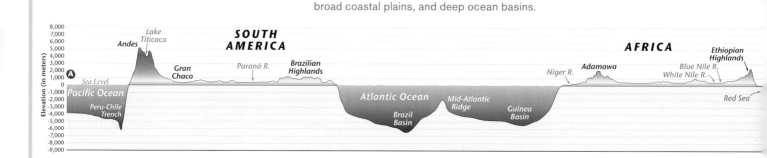

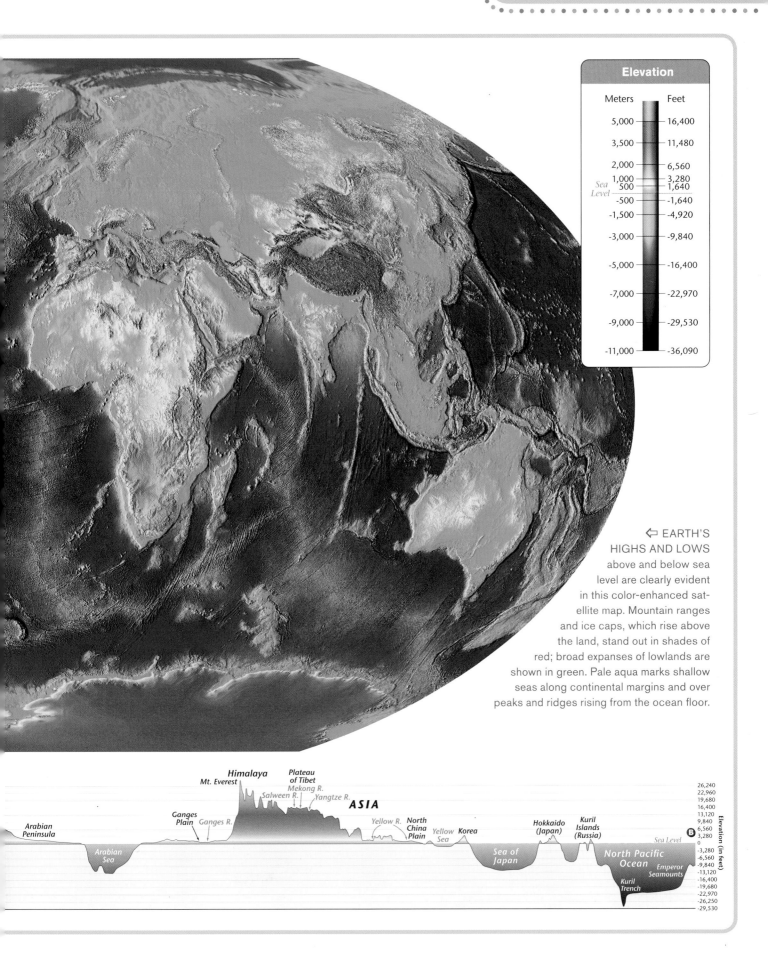

Elevation

Meters	Feet
5,000	16,400
3,500	11,480
2,000	6,560
1,000	3,280
500	1,640
Sea Level	
-500	-1,640
-1,500	-4,920
-3,000	-9,840
-5,000	-16,400
-7,000	-22,970
-9,000	-29,530
-11,000	-36,090

← EARTH'S HIGHS AND LOWS above and below sea level are clearly evident in this color-enhanced satellite map. Mountain ranges and ice caps, which rise above the land, stand out in shades of red; broad expanses of lowlands are shown in green. Pale aqua marks shallow seas along continental margins and over peaks and ridges rising from the ocean floor.

Earth's Climates

Climate is not the same as weather. Climate is the long-term average of conditions in the atmosphere at a particular location on Earth's surface. Weather refers to the momentary conditions of the atmosphere. Climate is important because it influences vegetation and soil development. It also influences people's choices about how and where to live.

There are many different systems for classifying climates. One commonly used system was developed by Russian-born climatologist Wladimir Köppen and later modified by American climatologist Glenn Trewartha. Köppen's system identifies five major climate zones based on average precipitation and temperature, and a sixth zone for highland, or high elevation, areas. Except for continental climate, all climate zones occur in mirror image north and south of the Equator.

⇩ CLIMATE GRAPHS. A climate graph is a combination bar and line graph that shows monthly averages of precipitation and temperature for a particular place. The bar graph shows precipitation in inches and centimeters; the line graph shows temperature in degrees Fahrenheit and Celsius. The graphs below are typical for places in the climate zone represented by their background color. The seeming inversion of the temperature lines for Alice Springs and McMurdo reflects the reversal of seasons south of the Equator, where January is midsummer. The abbreviations for months are across the bottom of each graph.

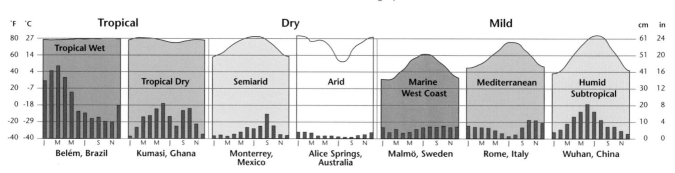

Tropical — Belém, Brazil (Tropical Wet), Kumasi, Ghana (Tropical Dry)
Dry — Monterrey, Mexico (Semiarid), Alice Springs, Australia (Arid)
Mild — Malmö, Sweden (Marine West Coast), Rome, Italy (Mediterranean), Wuhan, China (Humid Subtropical)

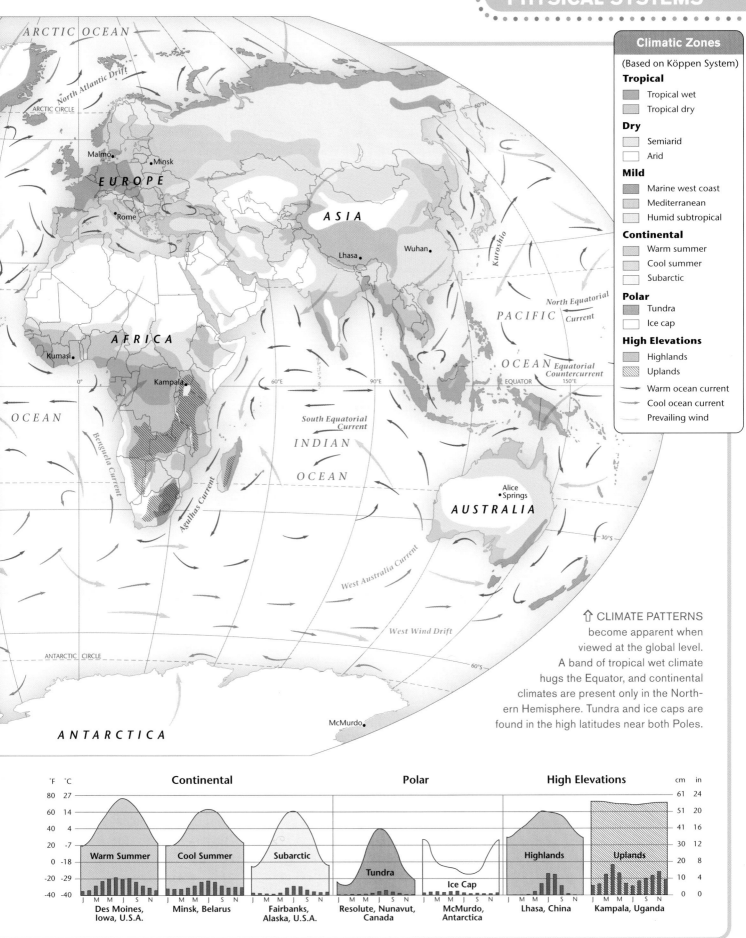

Climatic Zones

(Based on Köppen System)

Tropical
- Tropical wet
- Tropical dry

Dry
- Semiarid
- Arid

Mild
- Marine west coast
- Mediterranean
- Humid subtropical

Continental
- Warm summer
- Cool summer
- Subarctic

Polar
- Tundra
- Ice cap

High Elevations
- Highlands
- Uplands
- → Warm ocean current
- → Cool ocean current
- → Prevailing wind

⇧ CLIMATE PATTERNS become apparent when viewed at the global level. A band of tropical wet climate hugs the Equator, and continental climates are present only in the Northern Hemisphere. Tundra and ice caps are found in the high latitudes near both Poles.

ARCTIC OCEAN

North Atlantic Drift

ARCTIC CIRCLE

Malmö

Minsk

EUROPE

Rome

ASIA

Lhasa

Wuhan

Kuroshio

North Equatorial Current

PACIFIC

OCEAN Equatorial Countercurrent

EQUATOR

AFRICA

Kumasi

Kampala

Benguela Current

Agulhas Current

South Equatorial Current

INDIAN

OCEAN

OCEAN

West Australia Current

AUSTRALIA

Alice Springs

West Wind Drift

ANTARCTIC CIRCLE

McMurdo

ANTARCTICA

Continental

Warm Summer — Des Moines, Iowa, U.S.A.

Cool Summer — Minsk, Belarus

Subarctic — Fairbanks, Alaska, U.S.A.

Polar

Tundra — Resolute, Nunavut, Canada

Ice Cap — McMurdo, Antarctica

High Elevations

Highlands — Lhasa, China

Uplands — Kampala, Uganda

Climate Controls

The patterns of climate vary widely. Some climates, such as those near the Equator and the Poles, are nearly constant year-round. Others experience great seasonal variations, such as the wet and dry patterns of the tropical dry zone and the monthly average temperature extremes of the subarctic.

Climate patterns are not random. They are the result of complex interactions of basic climate controls: **latitude, elevation, prevailing winds, ocean currents, landforms,** and **location.**

These controls combine in various ways to create the bands of climate that can be seen on the world climate map on pages 20–21 and on the climate maps in the individual continent sections of this atlas. At the local level, however, special conditions may create microclimates that differ from those that are more typical of the region.

ELEVATION

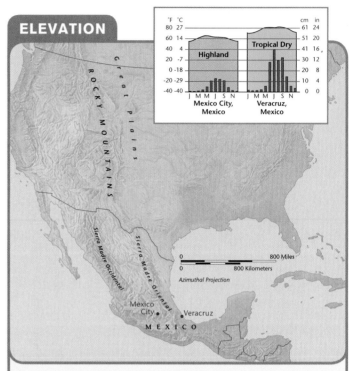

Not all locations at the same latitude experience similar climates. Air at higher elevations is cooler and holds less moisture than air at lower elevations. This explains why the climate at Veracruz, Mexico, which is near sea level, is warm and wet, and the climate at Mexico City, which is more than 7,000 feet (2,100 m) above sea level, is cooler and drier.

LATITUDE

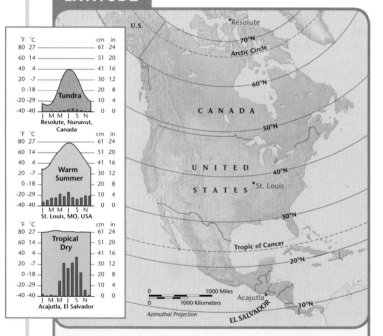

Energy from the sun strikes the Equator at a right angle. As latitude (distance north or south of the Equator) increases, the angle becomes increasingly oblique, or slanted. Less energy is received from the sun, and annual average temperatures fall. Therefore, the annual average temperature decreases as latitude increases from Acajutla, El Salvador, to St. Louis, Missouri, to Resolute, Canada.

LANDFORMS

When air carried by prevailing winds blows across a large body of water, such as the ocean, it picks up moisture. If that air encounters a mountain when it reaches land, it is forced to rise and the air becomes cooler, causing precipitation on the windward side of the mountain (see Portland graph). When air descends on the side away from the wind—the leeward side—the air warms and absorbs available moisture. This creates a dry condition known as rain shadow (see Wallowa graph).

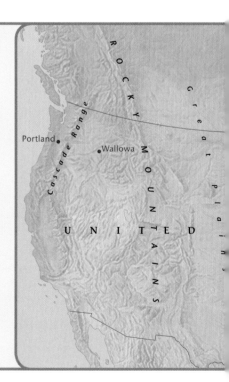

PREVAILING WINDS AND OCEAN CURRENTS

Earth's rotation combined with heat energy from the sun creates patterns of movement in Earth's atmosphere called prevailing winds. In the oceans, similar movements of water are called currents. Prevailing winds and ocean currents bring warm and cold temperatures to land areas. They also bring moisture or take it away. The Gulf Stream and the North Atlantic Drift, for example, are warm-water currents that influence average temperatures in eastern North America and northern Europe. Prevailing winds—trade winds, polar easterlies, and westerlies—also affect temperature and precipitation averages.

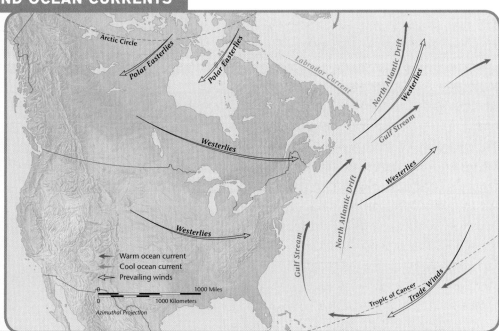

LOCATION

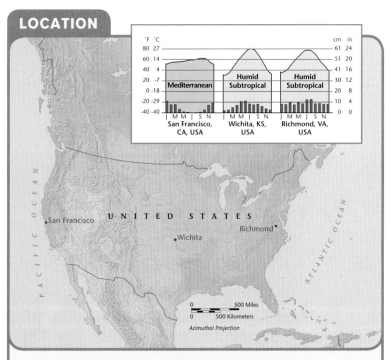

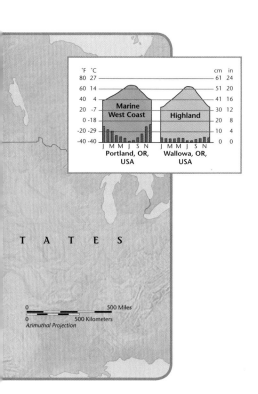

Marine locations—places near large bodies of water—have mild climates with little temperature variation because water gains and loses heat slowly (see San Francisco graph). Interior locations—places far from large water bodies—have much more extreme climates. There are great temperature variations because land gains and loses heat rapidly (see Wichita graph). Richmond, which is relatively near the Atlantic Ocean but which is also influenced by prevailing westerly winds blowing across the land, has moderate characteristics of both conditions.

Earth's Natural Vegetation

Natural vegetation is plant life that would be found in an area if it were undisturbed by human activity. Natural vegetation varies widely depending on climate and soil conditions. In rain forests, trees tower as much as 200 feet (60 m) above the forest floor. In the humid mid-latitudes, deciduous trees shed their leaves during the cold season, while coniferous trees remain green throughout the year. Areas receiving too little rainfall to support trees have grasses. Dry areas have plants such as cacti that tolerate long periods without water. In the tundra, dwarf species of shrubs and flowers are adaptations to harsh conditions at high latitudes and high elevations.

Vegetation is important to human life. It provides oxygen, food, fuel, products with economic value, even lifesaving medicines. Human activities, however, have greatly affected natural vegetation (see pages 28–29). Huge forests have been cut to provide fuel and lumber. Grasslands have yielded to the plow as people extend agricultural lands. As many as one in eight plants may become extinct due to human interference.

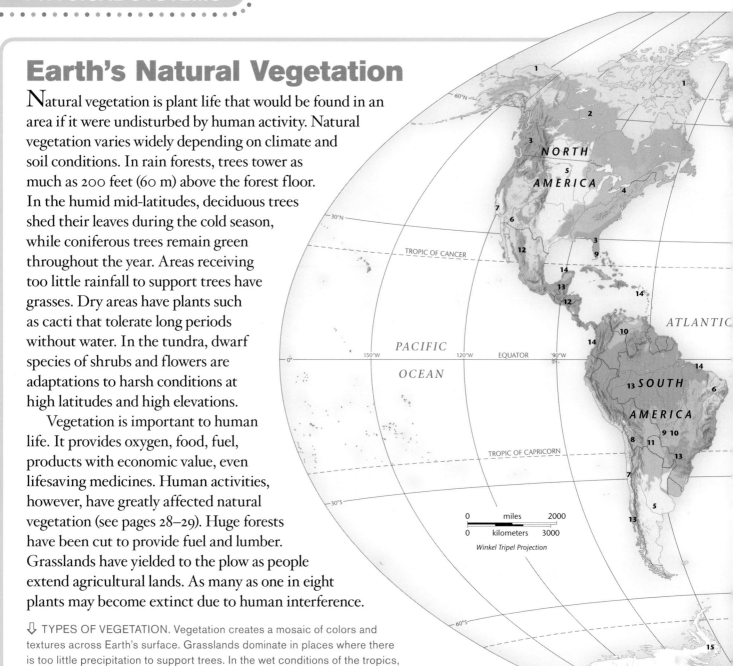

⇩ TYPES OF VEGETATION. Vegetation creates a mosaic of colors and textures across Earth's surface. Grasslands dominate in places where there is too little precipitation to support trees. In the wet conditions of the tropics, rain forests and mangroves flourish. Desert shrubs are adapted to dry climates, and tundra plants survive a short growing season. These photographs show some of the plants found in various vegetation regions. Each is keyed to the map by color and number.

1 TUNDRA

2 NORTHERN CONIFEROUS FOREST

4 TEMPERATE BROADLEAF FOREST

5 TEMPERATE GRASSLAND

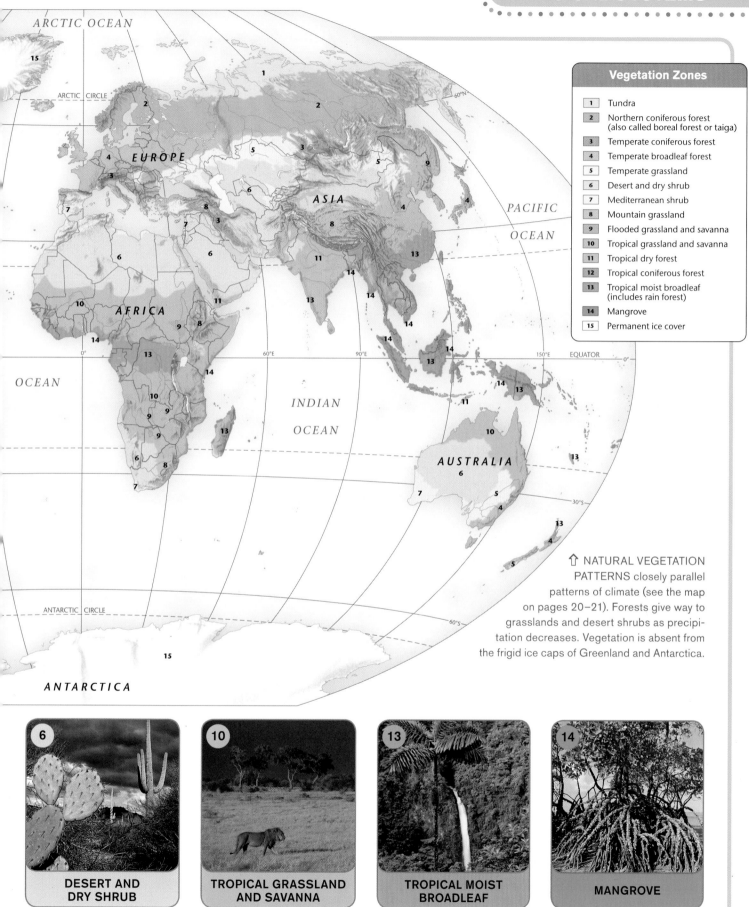

ARCTIC OCEAN

15

ARCTIC CIRCLE

EUROPE

ASIA

PACIFIC

OCEAN

AFRICA

OCEAN

INDIAN

OCEAN

AUSTRALIA

ANTARCTIC CIRCLE

ANTARCTICA

60°N

EQUATOR

30°S

60°S

0°

60°E

90°E

150°E

0°

Vegetation Zones

1	Tundra
2	Northern coniferous forest (also called boreal forest or taiga)
3	Temperate coniferous forest
4	Temperate broadleaf forest
5	Temperate grassland
6	Desert and dry shrub
7	Mediterranean shrub
8	Mountain grassland
9	Flooded grassland and savanna
10	Tropical grassland and savanna
11	Tropical dry forest
12	Tropical coniferous forest
13	Tropical moist broadleaf (includes rain forest)
14	Mangrove
15	Permanent ice cover

⇑ NATURAL VEGETATION PATTERNS closely parallel patterns of climate (see the map on pages 20–21). Forests give way to grasslands and desert shrubs as precipitation decreases. Vegetation is absent from the frigid ice caps of Greenland and Antarctica.

6 DESERT AND DRY SHRUB

10 TROPICAL GRASSLAND AND SAVANNA

13 TROPICAL MOIST BROADLEAF

14 MANGROVE

Earth's Water

Water is essential for life and is one of Earth's most valuable natural resources. It is even more important than food. More than 70 percent of Earth's surface is covered with water in the form of oceans, lakes, rivers, and streams, but most of it—about 97 percent—is salty, and without treatment is unusable for drinking or growing crops. The remaining 3 percent is fresh, but most of this is either trapped in glaciers or ice caps or lies too deep underground to be tapped economically.

Water is a renewable resource. We can use it over and over because the hydrologic, or water, cycle purifies water as it moves through the processes of evaporation, condensation, precipitation, runoff, and infiltration. But like other natural resources, water is unevenly distributed on Earth. Some regions have large drainage areas, called watersheds, that provide ample water for the population living there, while other more densely populated regions have only limited supplies of freshwater (see map at right). In addition, careless use can diminish the supply of usable freshwater. Water may become polluted as a result of dumping from industries, runoff of fertilizers or pesticides from cultivated fields, and sewage released from urban areas.

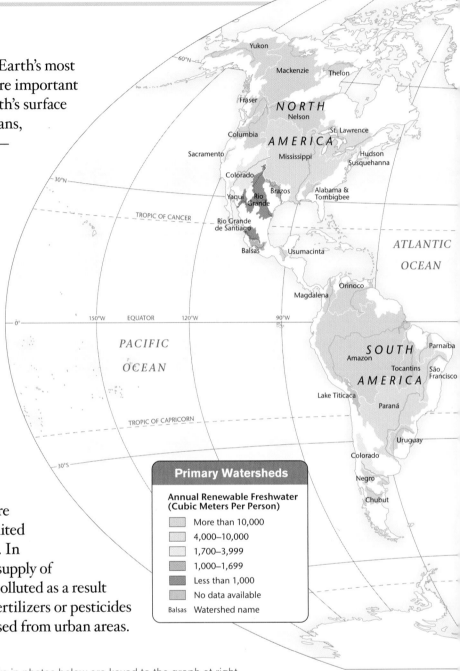

Primary Watersheds

Annual Renewable Freshwater (Cubic Meters Per Person)

- More than 10,000
- 4,000–10,000
- 1,700–3,999
- 1,000–1,699
- Less than 1,000
- No data available

Balsas Watershed name

WATER USES

Note: Color blocks in photos below are keyed to the graph at right.

DOMESTIC. In many less developed regions, women, such as these in Central America, haul water for daily use.

AGRICULTURAL. Irrigation has made agriculture possible in dry areas such as the San Pedro Valley in Arizona, shown here.

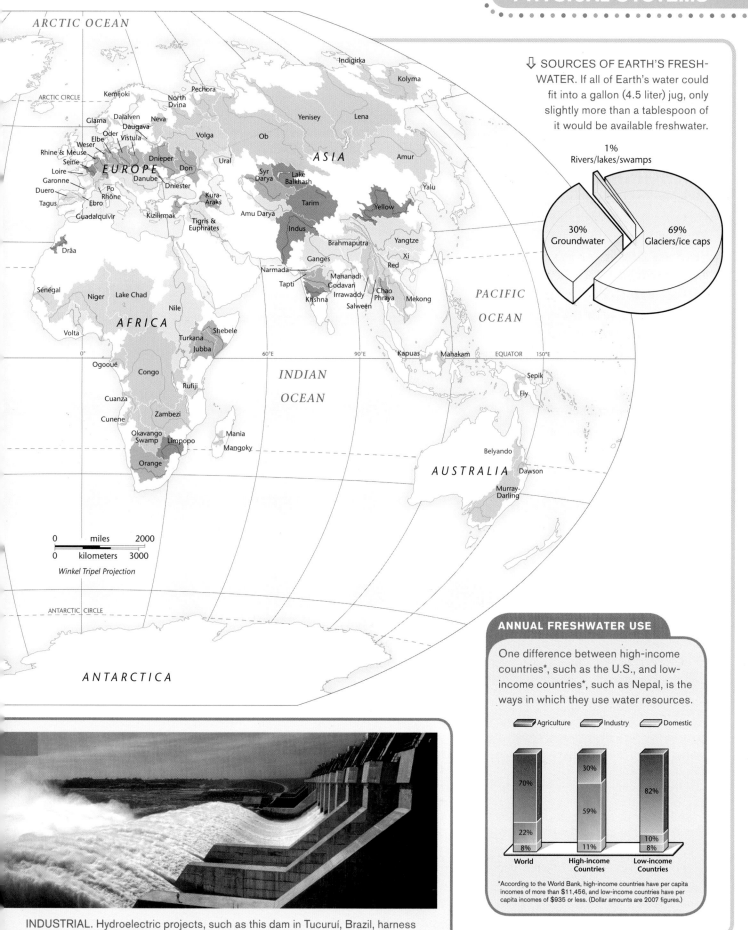

ARCTIC OCEAN

ARCTIC CIRCLE

ASIA

EUROPE

Indigirka
Kolyma
Pechora
Kemijoki
North Dvina
Glama
Dalalven
Daugava
Neva
Oder
Elbe
Weser
Vistula
Volga
Ob
Yenisey
Lena
Amur
Rhine & Meuse
Dnieper
Seine
Loire
Don
Danube
Ural
Yalu
Garonne
Dniester
Duero
Po
Rhône
Syr Darya
Lake Balkhash
Ebro
Tagus
Kizilirmak
Kura-Araks
Tarim
Yellow
Guadalquivir
Tigris & Euphrates
Amu Darya
Indus
Yangtze
Dråa
Brahmaputra
Xi
Red
Narmada
Ganges
Senegal
Tapti
Mahanadi
Godavari
Irrawaddy
Chao Phraya
Mekong
Niger
Lake Chad
Nile
Krishna
Salween
Volta
AFRICA
Turkana
Shebele
Jubba
Ogooué
Congo
Rufiji
Kapuas
Mahakam
EQUATOR
Cuanza
INDIAN OCEAN
Sepik
Cunene
Zambezi
Fly
Okavango Swamp
Limpopo
Mania
Mangoky
Belyando
Orange
AUSTRALIA
Dawson
Murray-Darling
PACIFIC OCEAN

ANTARCTICA

0   miles   2000
0   kilometers   3000
Winkel Tripel Projection

ANTARCTIC CIRCLE

⬇ SOURCES OF EARTH'S FRESH-WATER. If all of Earth's water could fit into a gallon (4.5 liter) jug, only slightly more than a tablespoon of it would be available freshwater.

1%
Rivers/lakes/swamps

30%
Groundwater

69%
Glaciers/ice caps

ANNUAL FRESHWATER USE

One difference between high-income countries*, such as the U.S., and low-income countries*, such as Nepal, is the ways in which they use water resources.

◤ Agriculture   ◪ Industry   ◳ Domestic

	World	High-income Countries	Low-income Countries
Agriculture	70%	30%	82%
Industry	22%	59%	10%
Domestic	8%	11%	8%

*According to the World Bank, high-income countries have per capita incomes of more than $11,456, and low-income countries have per capita incomes of $935 or less. (Dollar amounts are 2007 figures.)

INDUSTRIAL. Hydroelectric projects, such as this dam in Tucuruí, Brazil, harness running water to generate electricity that powers industry.

Environmental Hot Spots

As Earth's human population increases, pressures on the natural environment also increase. In industrialized countries, landfills overflow with the volume of trash produced. Industries generate waste and pollution that foul the air and water. Farmers use chemical fertilizers and pesticides that run off into streams and groundwater. Cars release exhaust fumes that pollute the air and perhaps also contribute to global climate change.

In less developed countries, forests are cut and not replanted, making the land vulnerable to erosion. Fragile grasslands turn to deserts when farmers and herders move onto marginal land as they try to make a living. And cities struggle with issues such as water safety, sanitation, and basic services that accompany the explosive urban growth that characterizes many less developed countries.

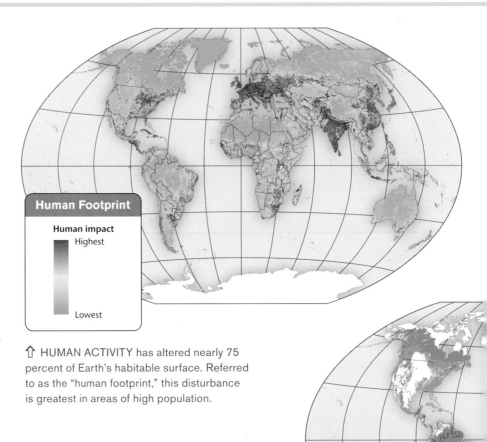

Human Footprint

Human impact

Highest

Lowest

⇧ HUMAN ACTIVITY has altered nearly 75 percent of Earth's habitable surface. Referred to as the "human footprint," this disturbance is greatest in areas of high population.

⇨ FORESTS PLAY a critical role in Earth's natural systems. They regulate water flow, release oxygen and retain carbon, cycle nutrients, and build soils. But humans have cut, burned, altered, and replaced half of all forests that stood 8,000 years ago.

Fragile Forests

Current frontier forest (large, relatively undisturbed forest)

Current non-frontier forest (degraded, regrown, replanted, plantation, or other forest areas)

Estimated extent of frontier forest 8,000 years ago

POLLUTED WATER is a part of life in this New Delhi slum where people bathe and wash clothes in the Yamuna River. More than 25 percent of the city's 16 million residents lack access to piped water, putting them at risk of water-borne diseases.

AN OIL SPILL off the coast of California closed this beach. Clean-up workers are attempting to reduce the amount of damage to the environment.

DEFORESTATION, resulting from logging, slash-and-burn agriculture, and forest fires, threatens Borneo's rain forests, once a rich storehouse of biodiversity.

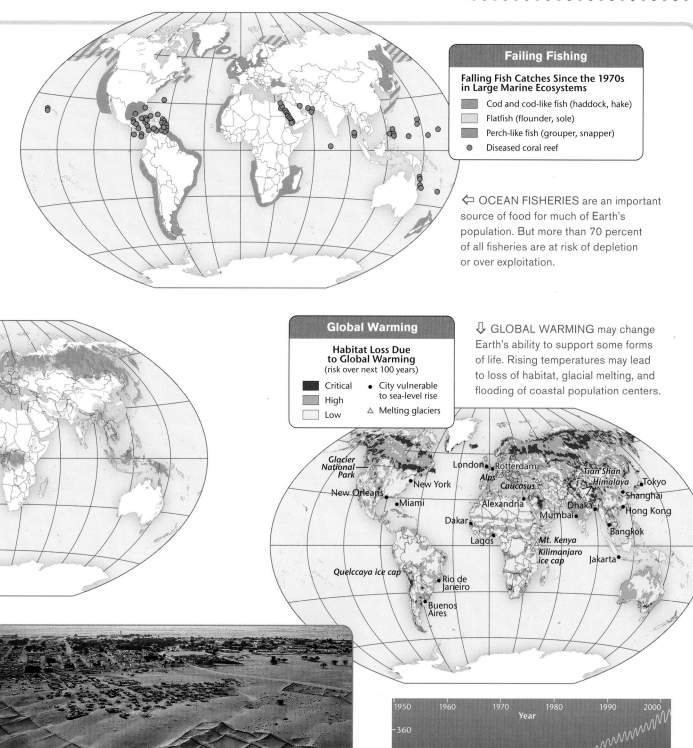

Failing Fishing

Falling Fish Catches Since the 1970s in Large Marine Ecosystems

- Cod and cod-like fish (haddock, hake)
- Flatfish (flounder, sole)
- Perch-like fish (grouper, snapper)
- Diseased coral reef

⇐ OCEAN FISHERIES are an important source of food for much of Earth's population. But more than 70 percent of all fisheries are at risk of depletion or over exploitation.

Global Warming

Habitat Loss Due to Global Warming
(risk over next 100 years)

- Critical
- High
- Low
- City vulnerable to sea-level rise
- △ Melting glaciers

⇩ GLOBAL WARMING may change Earth's ability to support some forms of life. Rising temperatures may lead to loss of habitat, glacial melting, and flooding of coastal population centers.

Glacier National Park · London · Rotterdam · Tian Shan · Tokyo · Alps · Caucasus · Himalaya · Shanghai · New York · New Orleans · Alexandria · Dhaka · Hong Kong · Miami · Mumbai · Dakar · Bangkok · Lagos · Mt. Kenya · Kilimanjaro ice cap · Jakarta · Quelccaya ice cap · Rio de Janeiro · Buenos Aires

DESERT SANDS, moved by high winds, cover large areas of Mauritania. The shifting sands threaten to cover a main road (upper right), which must be cleared daily to prevent loss of an important transportation route. People have laid a grid of branches over the sand to try to slow its advance. The desert has been expanding since the mid-1960s.

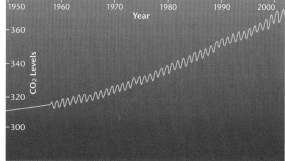

⇧ INCREASING LEVELS of carbon dioxide (CO_2) in Earth's atmosphere contribute to global warming.

The Political World

A map with the names and boundaries of countries shows the political world. Boundaries—some arrived at peacefully, others after years of conflict and war—carve up the land into 194 independent units, or countries, early in the 21st century. Boundaries are dynamic, meaning they change over time as political power shifts. For example, in 1990, West and East Germany became one country, removing a boundary that had separated them since 1949. In 1993 a new boundary divided Czechoslovakia into two separate countries, the Czech Republic and Slovakia.

Countries vary in size. Russia, the largest, stretches across northern Asia into Europe. Other countries are small enough to fit inside another country. For instance, the country of Lesotho lies entirely within the country of South Africa.

⇨ THE SCALE OF THIS MAP makes it impossible to name all 194 independent countries and their capital cities. For a complete listing, refer to pages 126–133 or use the place-name index and the political maps in each continent section.

⇨ VIEW FROM THE NORTH POLE. Ocean, not land, surrounds the area of the North Pole, so there are no political boundaries there. The Arctic Ocean, icebound much of the year, is part of the coastal waters of Earth's northernmost countries.

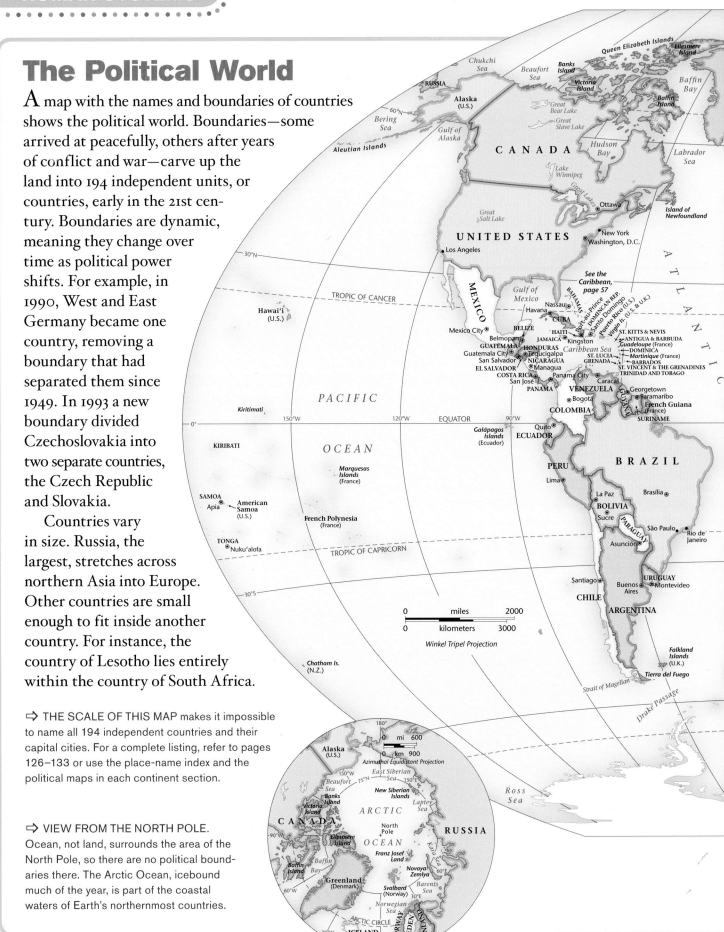

ARCTIC OCEAN

Franz Josef Land

Greenland (Denmark)

Greenland Sea

Svalbard (Norway)

Barents Sea

Kara Sea

Severnaya Zemlya

New Siberian Islands

Laptev Sea

East Siberian Sea

Norwegian Sea

Novaya Zemlya

ARCTIC CIRCLE

● ICELAND
Reykjavík

NORWAY SWEDEN FINLAND

Oslo● Helsinki●
Stockholm

UNITED
KINGDOM
Dublin●
IRELAND

North Sea

DENMARK
Copenhagen●
EST.
LATV.
LITH.

●Minsk

●Moscow

60°N

Sea of Okhotsk

Kamchatka Peninsula

Bering Sea

R U S S I A

Baltic Sea

POLAND BELARUS

●Astana

KAZAKHSTAN

Ulaanbaatar●
MONGOLIA

Sakhalin

Hokkaido

Cities

⊛ Country capital
● Urban area with more than 10 million people

See Europe, pp. 82-83

London●
●Paris
NETH.
BELG.
GERMANY
Berlin●
CZECH
REP.
AUSTRIA
SWITZ.
SLOVAKIA
HUNG.
SLOV.
CRO.

FRANCE

ITALY
Rome●
MONTENEGRO
ALBANIA
MACED.
GREECE
Athens●

ROMANIA
MOLD.

●Kiev
UKRAINE

Black Sea

SERBIA
BULGARIA
●Istanbul

GEORGIA
ARM.
AZERB.

Aral Sea

UZBEKISTAN
Tashkent●

TURKMENISTAN
Ashgabat●

●Bishkek
KYRGYZSTAN
Dushanbe●
TAJIKISTAN

C H I N A

●Beijing

Shanghai●

NORTH
KOREA
Pyongyang●
●Seoul
SOUTH
KOREA

Honshu

JAPAN
●Tokyo
Osaka●

Kyushu

30°N

Azores (Portugal)

PORTUGAL

PORTUGAL

Lisbon●

SPAIN
Madrid●

Tunis●
TUNISIA

Ankara●

TURKEY

CYPRUS
LEBANON
ISRAEL

SYRIA
IRAQ
Baghdad●

IRAN
Tehran●

AFGHANISTAN
Kabul●

Islamabad●

PAKISTAN

NEPAL
Kathmandu●

Thimphu●
BHUTAN

New Delhi●

Taipei

TAIWAN
The People's Republic of China claims Taiwan as its 23rd province. Taiwan's government (Republic of China) maintains that there are two political entities.

Taiwan

P A C I F I C

Madeira Is. (Portugal)

●Rabat

MOROCCO

Mediterranean Sea

Algiers●

Canary Is. (Spain)

Western Sahara (Morocco)

ALGERIA

LIBYA

Tripoli●

EGYPT

Cairo●

JORDAN
KUWAIT
BAHRAIN
QATAR
U.A.E.

Riyadh●

SAUDI ARABIA

Red Sea

OMAN

Muscat●

Karachi●

Mumbai (Bombay)●

I N D I A

Kolkata (Calcutta)●

BANGLADESH
Dhaka●

MYANMAR (BURMA)

Yangon●

Hanoi●

LAOS
Vientiane●

Hainan

South China Sea

Luzon

Philippine Sea

Northern Mariana Islands (U.S.)

Manila●
PHILIPPINES

Guam (U.S.)

O C E A N

MAURITANIA

Nouakchott●

CAPE VERDE

SENEGAL
Dakar●
GAMBIA

Bissau●
GUINEA-BISSAU

Conakry●
GUINEA
Freetown●
SIERRA LEONE
Monrovia●
LIBERIA

MALI

Bamako●

BURKINA FASO
Ouagadougou●

Niamey●
NIGER

N'Djamena●

CHAD

Khartoum●

SUDAN

Asmara●
ERITREA

Addis Ababa●

YEMEN
Sanaa●

DJIBOUTI

Socotra (Yemen)

Arabian Sea

Bay of Bengal

Bangkok●
THAILAND
CAMBODIA
Phnom Penh●

VIETNAM

Mindanao

PALAU

FEDERATED STATES OF MICRONESIA

MARSHALL ISLANDS

KIRIBATI

Yamoussoukro●
CÔTE D'IVOIRE
(IVORY COAST)
Abidjan●

Accra●
GHANA
TOGO
Lomé●

BENIN

NIGERIA
Abuja●

Lagos●

CAMEROON

CENTRAL AFRICAN REPUBLIC
Bangui●

Yaoundé●

ETHIOPIA

SOMALIA

Colombo●
SRI LANKA

Male●

MALDIVES

Mogadishu●

60°E

90°E

Kuala Lumpur●
MALAYSIA

Borneo

Bandar Seri Begawan●
BRUNEI

SINGAPORE●

150°E

EQUATOR

NAURU

0°

EQ. GUINEA
SAO TOME AND PRINCIPE

GABON
Libreville●

CABINDA (Angola)

CONGO
Brazzaville●
Kinshasa●

DEMOCRATIC REPUBLIC OF THE CONGO

UGANDA
Kampala●

Kigali●
RWANDA
Bujumbura●
BURUNDI

Nairobi●
KENYA

Dodoma●

Dar es Salaam●

TANZANIA

SEYCHELLES

COMOROS
Moroni●

I N D I A N

Sumatra

Jakarta●
Java

I N D O N E S I A

Celebes

New Guinea

TIMOR-LESTE (EAST TIMOR)

PAPUA NEW GUINEA

Port Moresby●

SOLOMON ISLANDS

Honiara●

TUVALU

Luanda●

ANGOLA

ZAMBIA
Lusaka●

Lilongwe●
MALAWI

MOZAMBIQUE

Antananarivo●

MAURITIUS
Port Louis●

O C E A N

Réunion (France)

VANUATU

Port-Vila●

New Caledonia (France)

FIJI ISLANDS

Suva●

NAMIBIA
Windhoek●

ZIMBABWE
Harare●

BOTSWANA
Gaborone●

Pretoria (Tshwane)●
Maputo●
SWAZILAND

Coral Sea

A U S T R A L I A

30°S

Bloemfontein●

SOUTH AFRICA

LESOTHO

Cape Town●

Great Australian Bight

●Canberra

Tasman Sea

North Island

Meridian of Greenwich (London)

Kerguelen Islands (France)

Tasmania

NEW ZEALAND

Wellington●

South Island

ANTARCTIC CIRCLE

60°S

Weddell Sea

Ross Sea

A N T A R C T I C A

➡ VIEW FROM THE SOUTH POLE. Covered by ice, the continent of Antarctica has been set aside by treaty for scientific research. It has no permanent population and no political boundaries, although 7 countries claim territory there and 19 operate year-round research stations (see map page 125).

30°W
0°
30°E
ANTARCTIC CIRCLE

ATLANTIC OCEAN

60°W
Weddell Sea
60°E

90°W
Antarctic Peninsula
Ronne Ice Shelf
West Antarctica
+South Pole
East Antarctica

INDIAN OCEAN

90°E

PACIFIC OCEAN
120°W
Ross Ice Shelf
Ross Sea
120°E

0 mi 600
0 km 900
150°W
150°E
180°
Azimuthal Equidistant Projection

A N T A R C T I C A

World Population

Late in 1999 the United Nations announced that Earth's population had surpassed six billion. Although more than 80 million people are added each year, the rate, or annual percent, at which the population is growing is gradually decreasing. Earth's population has very uneven distribution, with huge clusters in Asia and in Europe. Population density, the number of people living in each square mile (or square kilometer) on average, is high in these regions. For example, on average there are more than 2,680 people per square mile (1,035 per sq km) in Bangladesh. Other areas, such as deserts and Arctic tundra, have less than 2 people per square mile (1 person per sq km).

⇩ CROWDED STREETS, like this one in Shanghai, China, may become commonplace as Earth's population continues to increase and as more people move to urban areas.

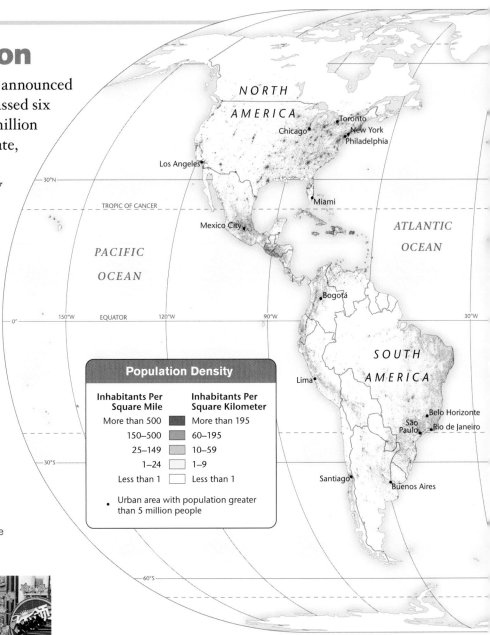

Population Density

Inhabitants Per Square Mile	Inhabitants Per Square Kilometer
More than 500	More than 195
150–500	60–195
25–149	10–59
1–24	1–9
Less than 1	Less than 1

• Urban area with population greater than 5 million people

POPULATION GROWTH OVER TIME

The population's rate of increase—the percent by which it changes each year—was slow until industrial and scientific discoveries in the 1800s brought improved health, a more reliable food supply, and other changes that improved the quality of life. Earth's population began to increase rapidly. Although the rate of increase has begun to slow, the United Nations projects that Earth's population will reach almost 9.2 billion by 2050.

9.2 Billion — 9
7.8 Billion — 8
7.2 Billion — 7
6.1 Billion — 6
Billions of people
5
4
3
2.5 Billion — 2
1.6 Billion
900 Million — 1
425 Million   545 Million   610 Million
0

1500   1600   1700   1800   1900 1950 2000 2025

Year

2015
2050

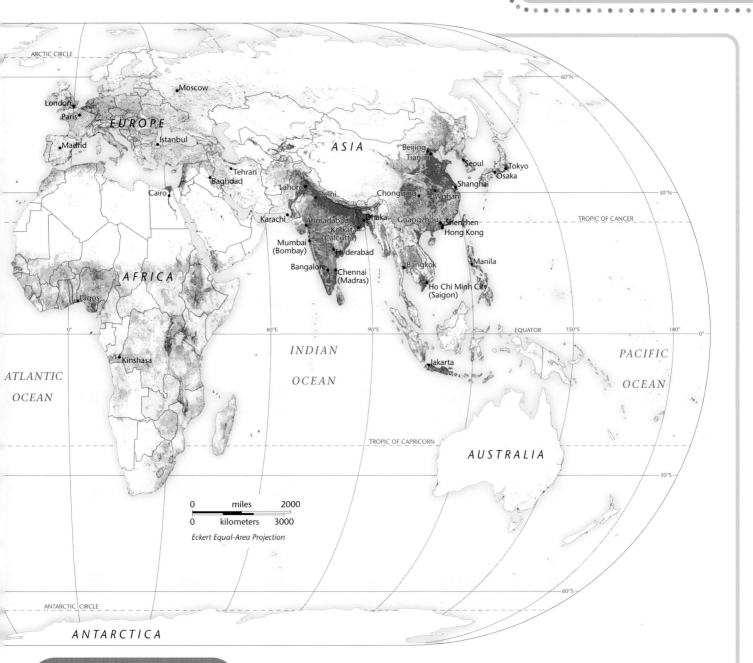

THREE POPULATION PYRAMIDS

A population pyramid is a special type of bar graph that shows the distribution of a country's population by sex and age. Italy has a very narrow pyramid, which shows that most people are in middle age. Its population is said to be aging, meaning the median age is increasing. The United States also has a narrow pyramid, but one that shows some growth due to a median age of about 37 years and a young immigrant population. By contrast, Nigeria's pyramid has a broad base, showing it has a young population. Almost half of its people are younger than 15 years.

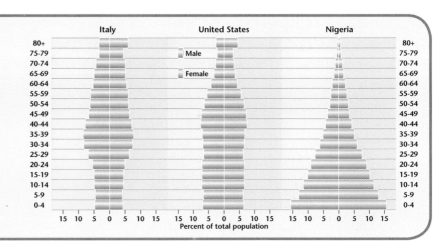

Percent of total population

World Refugees

Every day, people relocate to new cities, new states, even new countries. Most move by choice, but some people, called refugees, move to escape war and persecution that make it impossible to remain where they are. Such forced movement creates severe hardship for families who have to leave behind their possessions. They may find themselves in a new place where they do not speak the local language, where customs are unfamiliar, and where basic necessities, such as food, shelter, and medical care, are in short supply.

An agency of the United Nations, the Office of the High Commissioner for Refugees (UNHCR), is responsible for the safety and well-being of refugees worldwide and for protection of their rights. UNHCR works to find solutions to refugee situations through voluntary return to home countries, integration in a host country, or resettlement to another country.

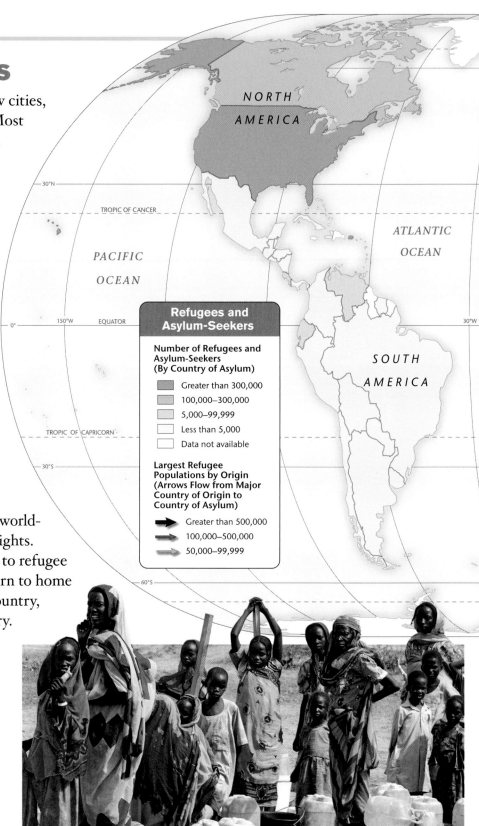

Refugees and Asylum-Seekers

Number of Refugees and Asylum-Seekers (By Country of Asylum)

- Greater than 300,000
- 100,000–300,000
- 5,000–99,999
- Less than 5,000
- Data not available

Largest Refugee Populations by Origin (Arrows Flow from Major Country of Origin to Country of Asylum)

- Greater than 500,000
- 100,000–500,000
- 50,000–99,999

REFUGEE HOSTING COUNTRIES

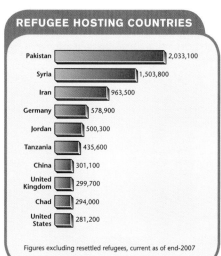

Pakistan	2,033,100
Syria	1,503,800
Iran	963,500
Germany	578,900
Jordan	500,300
Tanzania	435,600
China	301,100
United Kingdom	299,700
Chad	294,000
United States	281,200

Figures excluding resettled refugees, current as of end-2007

⬆ THOUSANDS OF SUDANESE refugees have been forced to leave their homes. Some, called internally displaced persons, or IDPs (above), remain in camps within Sudan. Others are refugees who have crossed into Chad to escape rebel forces attacking their villages.

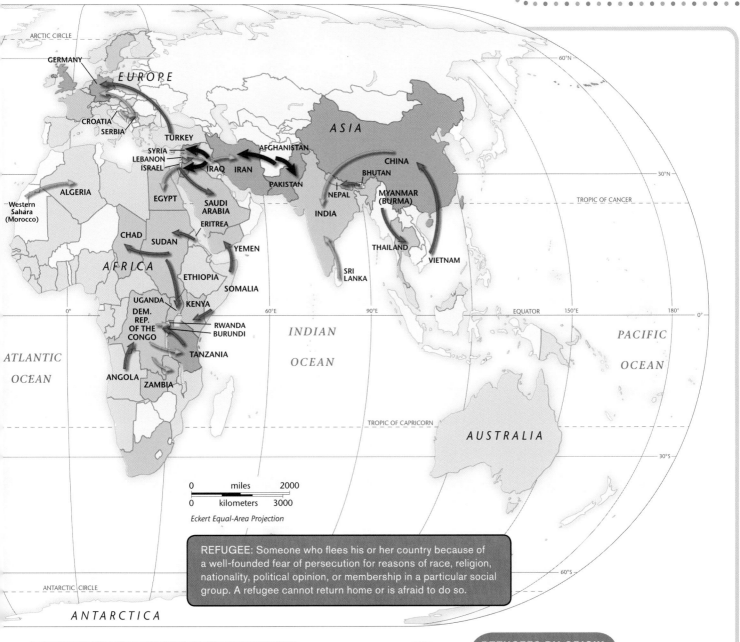

REFUGEE: Someone who flees his or her country because of a well-founded fear of persecution for reasons of race, religion, nationality, political opinion, or membership in a particular social group. A refugee cannot return home or is afraid to do so.

⇧ MANY KURDS, a people who live mainly in Iraq and Turkey, fled to the remote mountains of northern Iraq to escape spreading hostilities. This region, referred to as Kurdistan, is the traditional homeland of these stateless people.

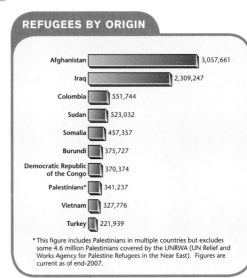

REFUGEES BY ORIGIN

Origin	Refugees
Afghanistan	3,057,661
Iraq	2,309,247
Colombia	551,744
Sudan	523,032
Somalia	457,357
Burundi	375,727
Democratic Republic of the Congo	370,374
Palestinians*	341,237
Vietnam	327,776
Turkey	221,939

* This figure includes Palestinians in multiple countries but excludes some 4.6 million Palestinians covered by the UNRWA (UN Relief and Works Agency for Palestine Refugees in the Near East). Figures are current as of end-2007.

World Cities

Throughout most of history, people have lived spread across the land, first as hunters and gatherers, later as farmers. But urban geographers—people who study cities—have determined that by 2010 the percentage of people living in urban areas will be 50.6 percent. Urban areas include one or more cities and their surrounding suburbs. People living there are employed primarily in industry or in service-related jobs. Large urban areas are sometimes called metropolitan areas. In some countries, such as Belgium, almost all the population lives in cities. But throughout much of Africa and Asia, only about 40 percent of the people live in urban areas. Even so, some of the world's fastest growing urban areas are towns and small cities in Africa and Asia.

MOST POPULOUS URBAN AREAS

In 1950 New York was the larger of just two cities with a population of 10 million or more. By 2007 New York had dropped behind Tokyo, just slightly ahead of Mexico City and Mumbai (Bombay), India, in a list of 19 cities with populations of at least 10 million. By 2025, the list is projected to include 27 cities.

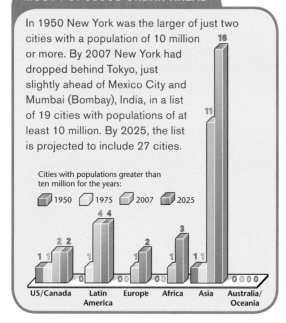

Cities with populations greater than ten million for the years:

🗇 1950   🗇 1975   🗇 2007   🗇 2025

US/Canada   Latin America   Europe   Africa   Asia   Australia/Oceania

⇑ CENTRAL TOKYO, viewed from the special observation deck of Tokyo Tower, 820 feet (250 m) above crowded city streets, contains a mix of modern high-rise and older low-rise buildings. With almost 13 million people, Tokyo is Japan's largest and most densely populated city and one of the world's largest cities.

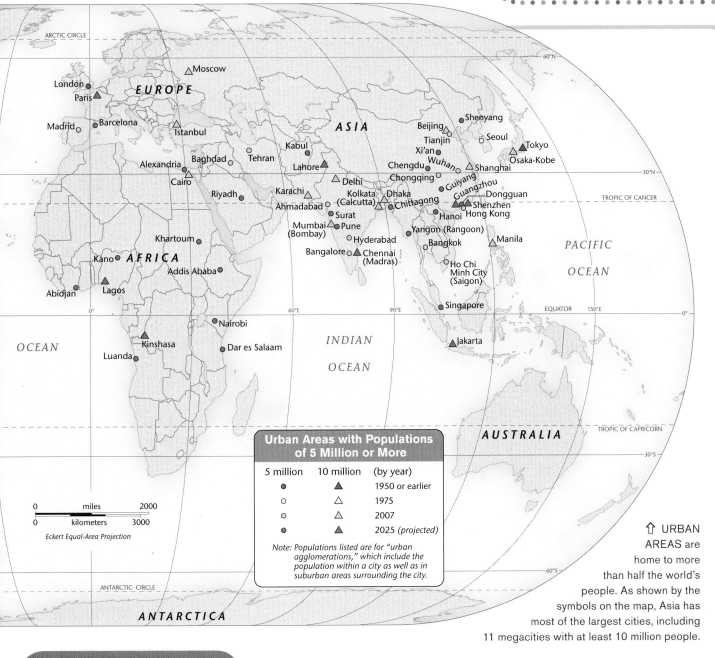

Urban Areas with Populations of 5 Million or More

5 million	10 million	(by year)
●	▲	1950 or earlier
○	△	1975
○	△	2007
●	▲	2025 (projected)

Note: Populations listed are for "urban agglomerations," which include the population within a city as well as in suburban areas surrounding the city.

0 miles 2000
0 kilometers 3000
Eckert Equal-Area Projection

⇧ URBAN AREAS are home to more than half the world's people. As shown by the symbols on the map, Asia has most of the largest cities, including 11 megacities with at least 10 million people.

URBAN AND RURAL POPULATIONS

These graphs show the percentages of people living in urban and rural areas in the world and its various regions. Only Asia and Africa are pre-dominantly rural, although both are experiencing rapid urban growth. Asia, which had just one city of 10 million or more people in 1950, now has 11.

Urban
Rural

Latin America 78% / 22%
Asia 41% / 59%
Australia & Oceania 71% / 29%
United States & Canada 81% / 19%
Europe 72% / 28%
Africa 39% / 61%
World 50% / 50%

World Languages

Culture is all the shared traits that make different groups of people around the world unique. For example, customs, food and clothing preferences, housing styles, and music and art forms are all a part of each group's culture. Language is one of the most defining characteristics of culture.

Language reflects what people value and the way they understand the world. It also reveals how certain groups of people may have had common roots at some point in history. For example, English and German are two very different languages, but both are part of the same Indo-European language family. This means that these two languages share certain characteristics that suggest they have evolved from a common ancestor language.

Patterns on the world language families map (right) offer clues to the diffusion, or movement, of groups of people. For example, the widespread use of English, extending from the United States to India, reflects the far-reaching effects of British colonial empires. Today, English is the main language of the Internet.

About 5,000 languages are spoken in the world today, but experts think many may become extinct as more people become involved in global trade, communications, and travel.

⇨ THE GOLDEN ARCHES icon would help you identify this restaurant in Moscow even if you didn't know how to read the Cyrillic alphabet of the Russian language.

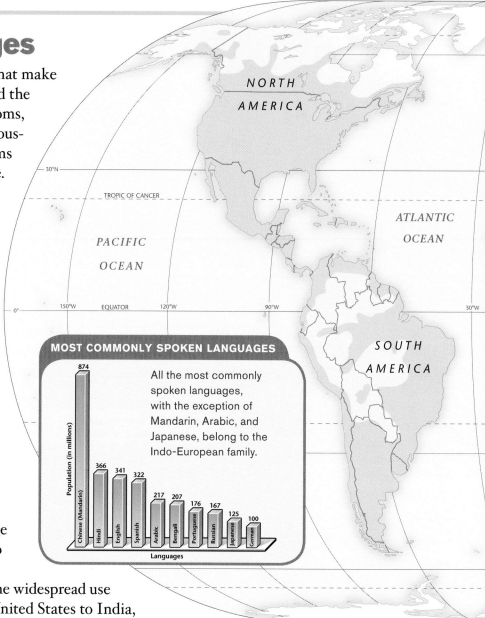

MOST COMMONLY SPOKEN LANGUAGES

All the most commonly spoken languages, with the exception of Mandarin, Arabic, and Japanese, belong to the Indo-European family.

Population (in millions)

- Chinese (Mandarin) — 874
- Hindi — 366
- English — 341
- Spanish — 322
- Arabic — 217
- Bengali — 207
- Portuguese — 176
- Russian — 167
- Japanese — 125
- German — 100

Languages

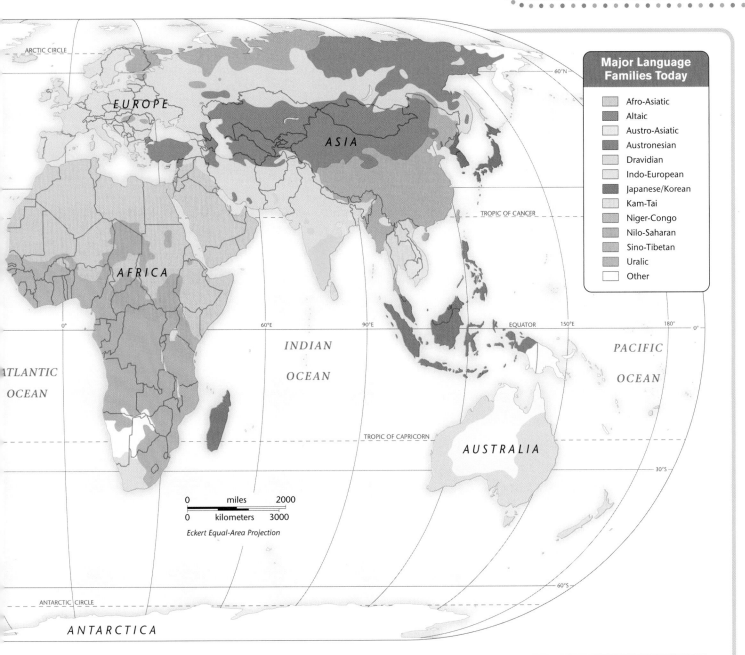

EUROPE

ASIA

AFRICA

INDIAN OCEAN

ATLANTIC OCEAN

PACIFIC OCEAN

AUSTRALIA

ANTARCTICA

ARCTIC CIRCLE

TROPIC OF CANCER

EQUATOR

TROPIC OF CAPRICORN

ANTARCTIC CIRCLE

| 0 | miles | 2000 |
| 0 | kilometers | 3000 |

Eckert Equal-Area Projection

Major Language Families Today

- Afro-Asiatic
- Altaic
- Austro-Asiatic
- Austronesian
- Dravidian
- Indo-European
- Japanese/Korean
- Kam-Tai
- Niger-Congo
- Nilo-Saharan
- Sino-Tibetan
- Uralic
- Other

PENRHOS ARMS GREENALLS

LLANFAIRPWLLGWYNGYLLGOGERYCHWYRNDROBWLLLLANTYSILIOGOGOGOCH

ST MARYS CHURCH IN THE HOLLOW OF THE WHITE HAZEL NEAR TO THE RAPID WHIRLPOOL OF LLANTYSILIO OF THE RED CAVE

⇧ SOME WORDS TELL A STORY, like this place name on the island of Anglesey in Wales. Welsh is an ancient Gaelic language. The alphabet may look familiar, but it has a few more letters than English and different pronunciations.

⇦ BENGALI, a language derived from ancient Sanskrit, appears on the walls of a women's health clinic in Kolkata (Calcutta), India. It is just one of the many languages that make up the Indo-European language family.

World Religions

Religious beliefs are a central element of culture. Religious beliefs and practices help people deal with the unknown. But people in different places have developed a variety of belief systems.

Universalizing religions, such as Christianity, Islam, and Buddhism, seek converts. They have spread throughout the world from their origins in Asia. Other religions, including Judaism, Hinduism, and Shinto—called ethnic religions—tend to be associated with particular groups of people and are concentrated in certain places. Some groups, especially indigenous, or native, people living in the tropical forests of Africa and South America, believe that spirits inhabit all things in the natural world. Such belief systems are known as animistic religions.

Places of worship are often a distinctive part of the cultural landscape. A cathedral, mosque, or temple can reveal much about the people who live in a particular place.

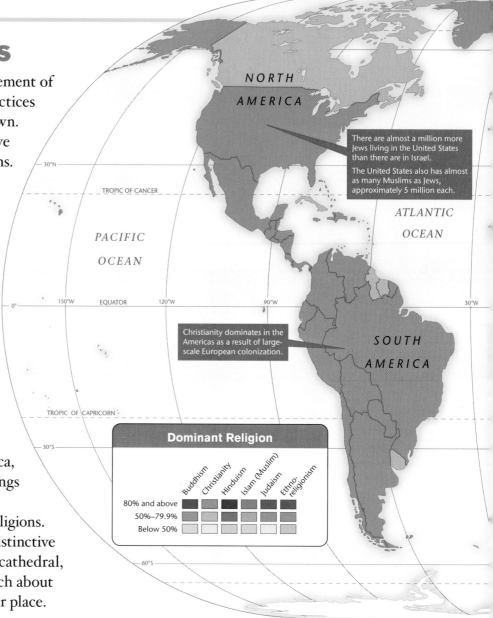

NORTH AMERICA

PACIFIC OCEAN

ATLANTIC OCEAN

SOUTH AMERICA

30°N

TROPIC OF CANCER

EQUATOR

TROPIC OF CAPRICORN

30°S

60°S

150°W   120°W   90°W   30°W

There are almost a million more Jews living in the United States than there are in Israel.

The United States also has almost as many Muslims as Jews, approximately 5 million each.

Christianity dominates in the Americas as a result of large-scale European colonization.

Dominant Religion

	Buddhism	Christianity	Hinduism	Islam (Muslim)	Judaism	Ethno-religionism
80% and above						
50%–79.9%						
Below 50%						

⇧ MOST OF HINDUISM'S 900 million followers live in India and other countries of South Asia. The goddess Durga (above) is regarded as Mother of the Universe and protector of the righteous.

⇩ JERUSALEM IS HOLY to Muslims, Christians, and Jews, a fact that has led to tension and conflict. Below, a Russian orthodox church is silhouetted against the Wailing Wall, while sunlight reflects off the Dome of the Rock mosque.

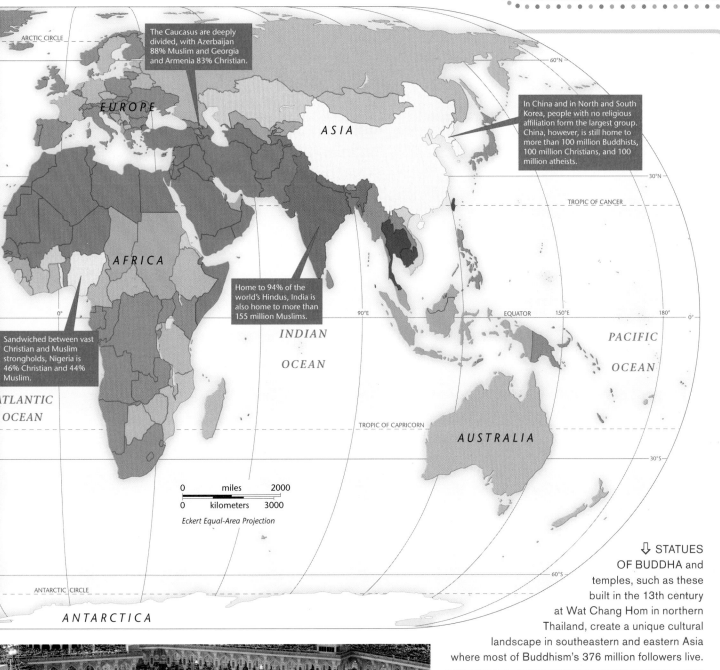

The Caucasus are deeply divided, with Azerbaijan 88% Muslim and Georgia and Armenia 83% Christian.

In China and in North and South Korea, people with no religious affiliation form the largest group. China, however, is still home to more than 100 million Buddhists, 100 million Christians, and 100 million atheists.

Home to 94% of the world's Hindus, India is also home to more than 155 million Muslims.

Sandwiched between vast Christian and Muslim strongholds, Nigeria is 46% Christian and 44% Muslim.

EUROPE

ASIA

AFRICA

ARCTIC CIRCLE

60°N

30°N

TROPIC OF CANCER

INDIAN
OCEAN

90°E

EQUATOR

150°E

180°

0°

PACIFIC
OCEAN

0°

ATLANTIC
OCEAN

TROPIC OF CAPRICORN

AUSTRALIA

30°S

0   miles   2000

0   kilometers   3000

Eckert Equal-Area Projection

60°S

ANTARCTIC CIRCLE

ANTARCTICA

⇩ STATUES OF BUDDHA and temples, such as these built in the 13th century at Wat Chang Hom in northern Thailand, create a unique cultural landscape in southeastern and eastern Asia where most of Buddhism's 376 million followers live.

⇧ MUSLIM WORSHIPPERS surround the sacred Kaaba stone, which lies shrouded in black cloth at the center of the Grand Mosque in Mecca. Each year two million Muslims make a hajj, or pilgrimage, here to Islam's holiest shrine.

Predominant World Economies

Economic activities are the many different ways that people generate income to meet their needs and wants. Long ago most people lived by hunting and gathering. Today most engage in a variety of activities that can be grouped into three categories, or sectors: agriculture, as well as other primary activities such as fishing and forestry; industry, which includes manufacturing and processing activities; and services that range from banking and medicine to information exchange and e-commerce—buying and selling over the Internet. Services and industry, which generate higher incomes, are predominant in more developed countries, while many less developed countries still rely on agriculture.

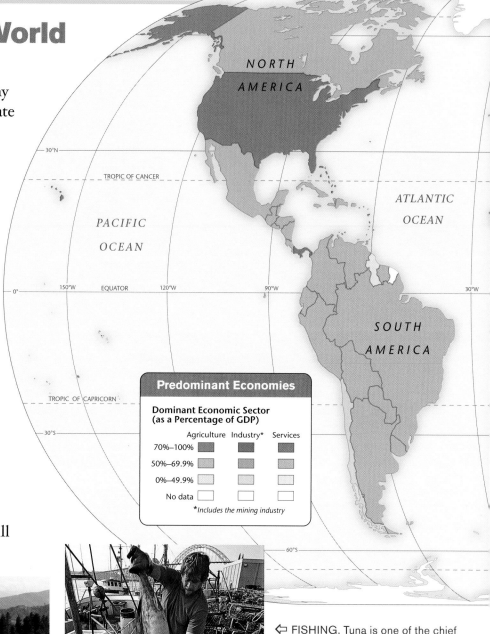

NORTH AMERICA

PACIFIC OCEAN

ATLANTIC OCEAN

SOUTH AMERICA

TROPIC OF CANCER

EQUATOR

TROPIC OF CAPRICORN

30°N
30°S
60°S
150°W
120°W
90°W
30°W
0°

Predominant Economies

Dominant Economic Sector
(as a Percentage of GDP)

	Agriculture	Industry*	Services
70%–100%			
50%–69.9%			
0%–49.9%			
No data			

*Includes the mining industry

⇧ SUBSISTENCE AGRICULTURE. Many people in developing countries, such as these farmers in Bhutan, use traditional methods to grow crops for their daily food requirements rather than for commercial sale.

⇦ FISHING. Tuna is one of the chief commercial fishes as well as a favorite among big game fishermen. Japan is the world's leading harvester of tuna. Albacore, shown here, is one of the top commercial varieties.

⇨ LOGGING. Workers ready logs to float down the Columbia River in Washington State. Processing plants will turn the logs into paper products or cut them into lumber for the construction industry.

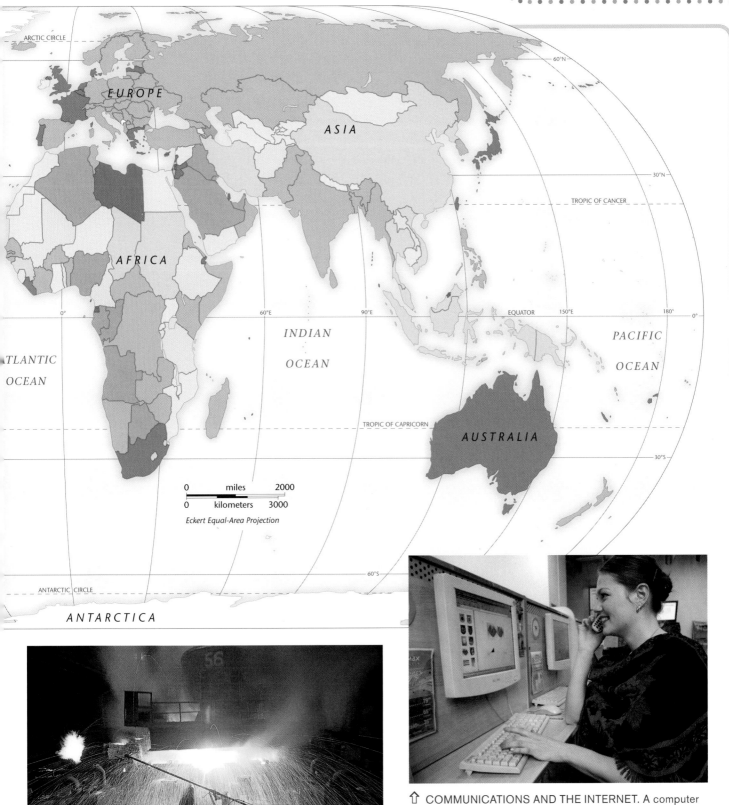

ARCTIC CIRCLE

EUROPE

ASIA

60°N

30°N

TROPIC OF CANCER

AFRICA

0°   60°E   90°E   EQUATOR   150°E   180°   0°

INDIAN
OCEAN

ATLANTIC
OCEAN

PACIFIC
OCEAN

TROPIC OF CAPRICORN

AUSTRALIA

30°S

0   miles   2000
0   kilometers   3000
Eckert Equal-Area Projection

60°S

ANTARCTIC CIRCLE

ANTARCTICA

⇧ MANUFACTURING. This mill in Slovakia processes raw materials—coal and iron ore—to make steel, which in turn is used by other industries to produce cars, machinery, and other kinds of manufactured goods.

⇧ COMMUNICATIONS AND THE INTERNET. A computer and mobile phone link this cybercafé in St. Petersburg, Russia, to the world. The Internet and new technologies have opened a whole new way of exchanging information. E-mail connects people in places near and far, while e-commerce allows them to buy and sell products without ever leaving home.

World Food

In 2008, the world's population surpassed 6.7 billion people—all needing to be fed. However, the productive potential of Earth's surface varies greatly from place to place. Some areas are good for growing crops; some are best used for grazing animals; but large expanses have little or no agricultural potential at all. Grains, such as rice, corn, and wheat, are the main sources of food calories for most of the world's people.

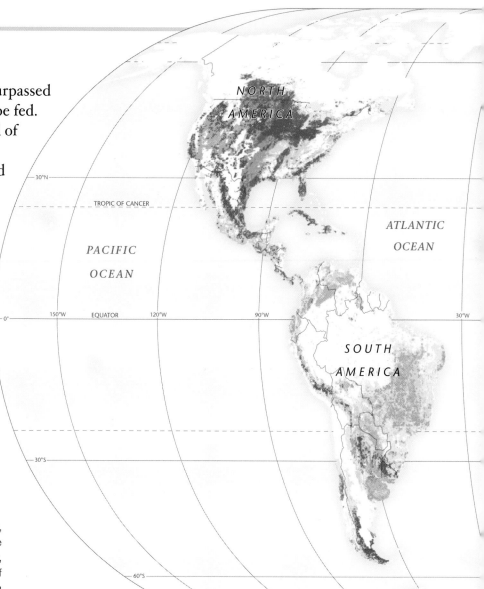

⇐ BREAD, whether made from wheat or corn flour, is a basic part of the diet of people around the world, providing carbohydrates, fiber, vitamins, and minerals.

⇒ THE DEMAND FOR FOOD becomes greater as world population increases. Fertilizer use rose almost 275 percent between 1965 and 1995, as farmers tried to improve crop yields to meet rising demand.

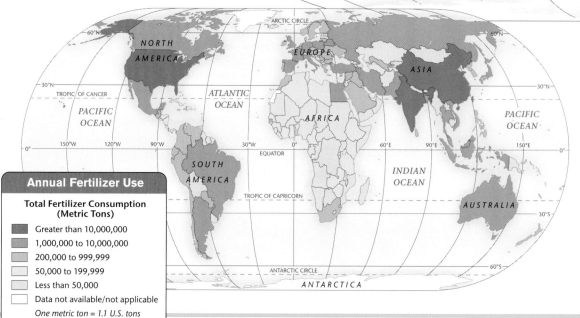

Annual Fertilizer Use

Total Fertilizer Consumption (Metric Tons)

- Greater than 10,000,000
- 1,000,000 to 10,000,000
- 200,000 to 999,999
- 50,000 to 199,999
- Less than 50,000
- Data not available/not applicable

One metric ton = 1.1 U.S. tons

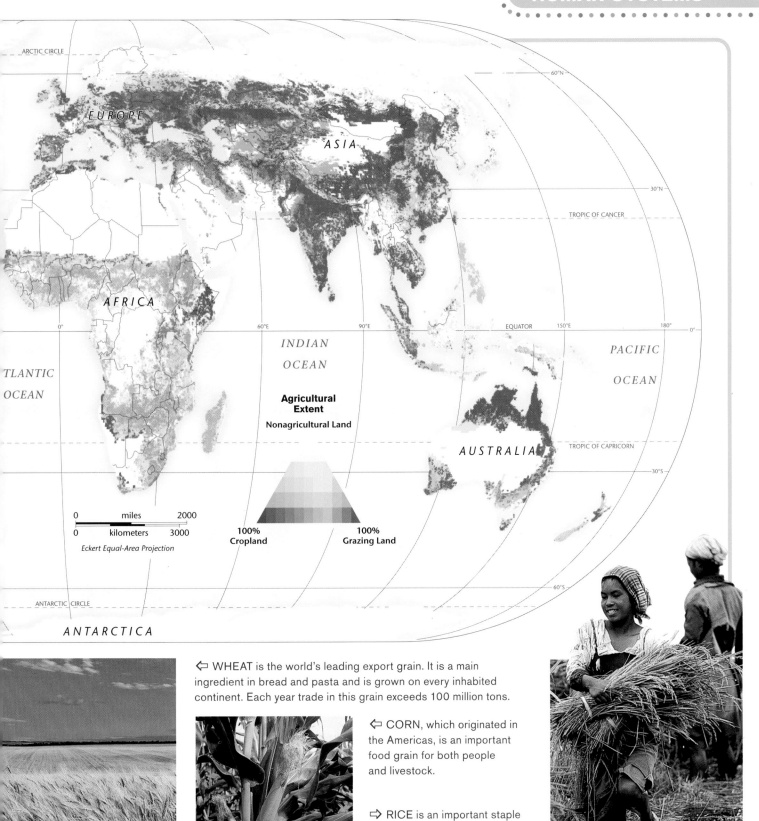

ARCTIC CIRCLE

EUROPE

ASIA

60°N

30°N

TROPIC OF CANCER

AFRICA

0°   60°E   90°E   EQUATOR   150°E   180°   0°

INDIAN
OCEAN

ATLANTIC
OCEAN

PACIFIC

OCEAN

**Agricultural
Extent**

Nonagricultural Land

AUSTRALIA

TROPIC OF CAPRICORN

30°S

0   miles   2000
0   kilometers   3000

Eckert Equal-Area Projection

100%
Cropland

100%
Grazing Land

60°S

ANTARCTIC CIRCLE

ANTARCTICA

⇐ WHEAT is the world's leading export grain. It is a main ingredient in bread and pasta and is grown on every inhabited continent. Each year trade in this grain exceeds 100 million tons.

⇐ CORN, which originated in the Americas, is an important food grain for both people and livestock.

⇒ RICE is an important staple food crop, especially in eastern and southern Asia. Although China produces about one-third of the world's rice, it is also a major importer of rice to feed its population of more than a billion people.

World Energy & Mineral Resources

Beginning in the 19th century, as the Industrial Revolution spread across Europe and around the world, the demand for energy and mineral resources skyrocketed. Fossil fuels—first coal, then oil—provided the energy that kept the wheels of industry turning. Minerals such as iron ore (essential for the production of steel) and copper (used for electrical wiring) became increasingly important.

Energy and minerals, like all nonrenewable resources, are in limited supply and are unevenly distributed. Countries with major deposits play an important role in the global economy. For example, the Organization of Petroleum Exporting Countries (OPEC) influences the world supply of oil and, therefore, fuel prices.

⇩ RENEWABLE ENERGY, including energy from the sun, wind, running water, and heat from within Earth, is an important alternative to fossil fuels, supplies of which are rapidly being depleted.

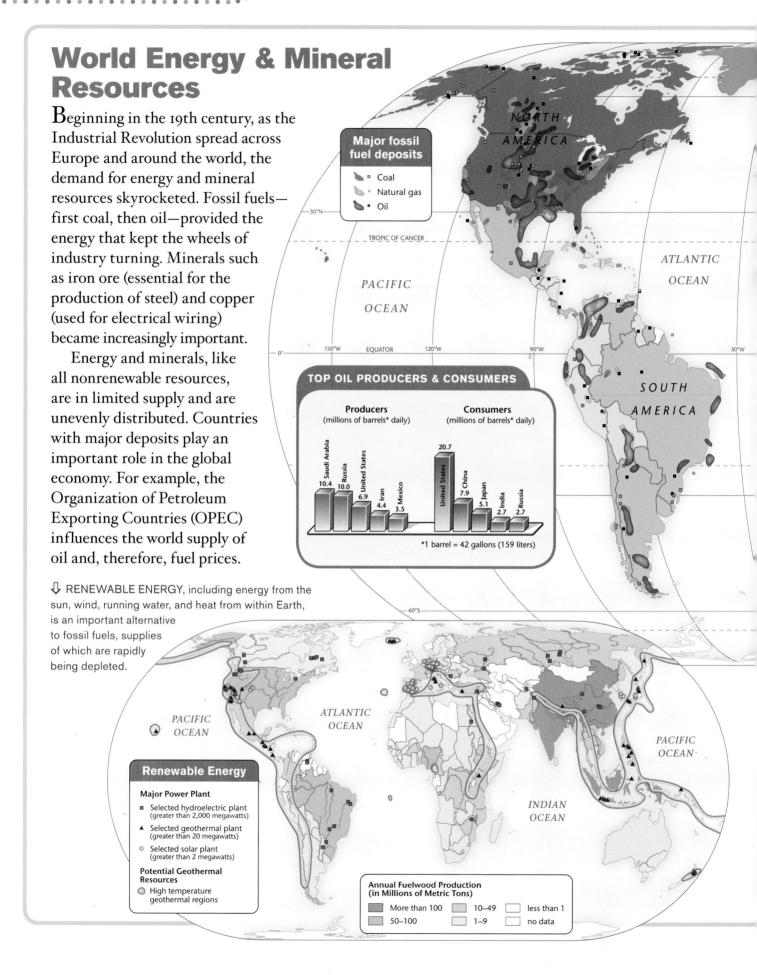

Major fossil fuel deposits
- Coal
- Natural gas
- Oil

TOP OIL PRODUCERS & CONSUMERS

Producers (millions of barrels* daily)

Saudi Arabia	Russia	United States	Iran	Mexico
10.4	10.0	6.9	4.4	3.5

Consumers (millions of barrels* daily)

United States	China	Japan	India	Russia
20.7	7.9	5.1	2.7	2.7

*1 barrel = 42 gallons (159 liters)

Renewable Energy

Major Power Plant
- Selected hydroelectric plant (greater than 2,000 megawatts)
- Selected geothermal plant (greater than 20 megawatts)
- Selected solar plant (greater than 2 megawatts)

Potential Geothermal Resources
- High temperature geothermal regions

Annual Fuelwood Production (in Millions of Metric Tons)
- More than 100
- 50–100
- 10–49
- 1–9
- less than 1
- no data

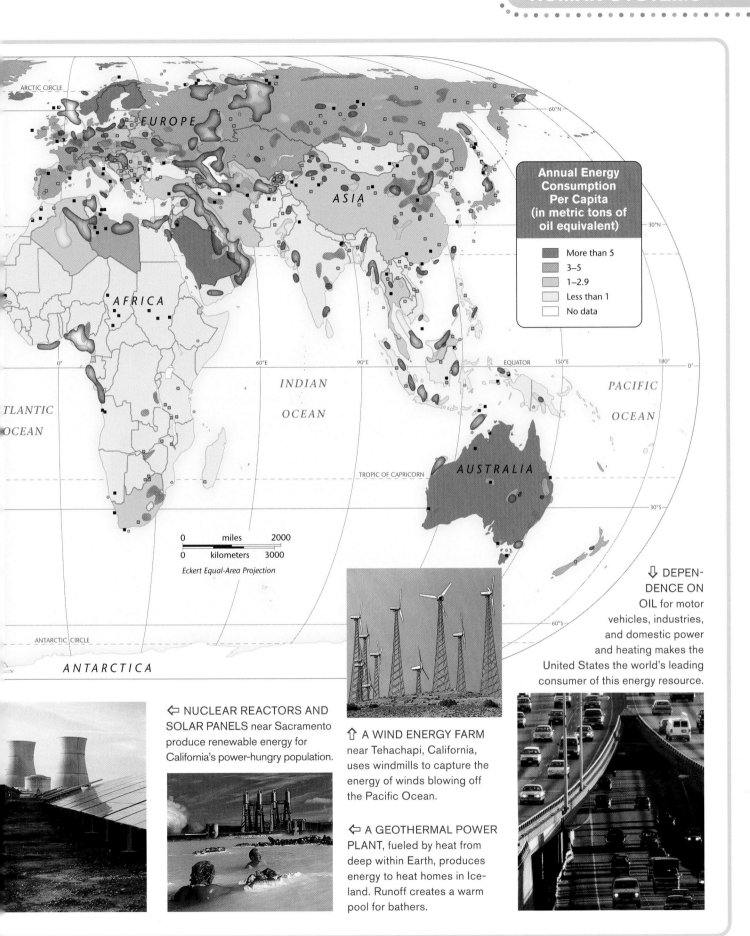

Annual Energy Consumption Per Capita (in metric tons of oil equivalent)

- More than 5
- 3–5
- 1–2.9
- Less than 1
- No data

ARCTIC CIRCLE

EUROPE

ASIA

AFRICA

ATLANTIC OCEAN

INDIAN OCEAN

PACIFIC OCEAN

EQUATOR

TROPIC OF CAPRICORN

AUSTRALIA

ANTARCTIC CIRCLE

ANTARCTICA

0 miles 2000
0 kilometers 3000

Eckert Equal-Area Projection

⇓ DEPENDENCE ON OIL for motor vehicles, industries, and domestic power and heating makes the United States the world's leading consumer of this energy resource.

⇐ NUCLEAR REACTORS AND SOLAR PANELS near Sacramento produce renewable energy for California's power-hungry population.

⇑ A WIND ENERGY FARM near Tehachapi, California, uses windmills to capture the energy of winds blowing off the Pacific Ocean.

⇐ A GEOTHERMAL POWER PLANT, fueled by heat from deep within Earth, produces energy to heat homes in Iceland. Runoff creates a warm pool for bathers.

Globalization

The close of the 20th century saw a technology revolution that changed the way people and countries relate to each other. This revolution in technology is part of a process known as globalization.

Globalization refers to the complex network of interconnections linking people, companies, and places together without regard for national boundaries. Although it began when countries became increasingly active in international trade, the process of globalization has gained momentum in recent years.

Improvements in communications and transportation have enabled companies to employ workers in distant countries. Some workers make clothing; some perform accounting tasks; and others work in call centers answering inquiries about product services. Technology also allows banking transactions to take place faster and over greater distances than ever before. Companies that have offices and conduct business in multiple countries around the world are called transnational companies.

One important aspect of today's global communications system is the Internet, a vast system of computer networks that allows people to access information and to communicate around the world in just seconds. While most Internet users are in North America and Europe, ideas and images travel over the Internet to distant places, introducing change and making places more and more alike.

⇨ MAQUILADORAS, foreign-owned assembly plants located in Mexico, import parts and materials duty-free to produce finished goods for consumers in the U.S. and around the world. Maquiladoras, such as this one in Ciudad Juarez, employ a large work force.

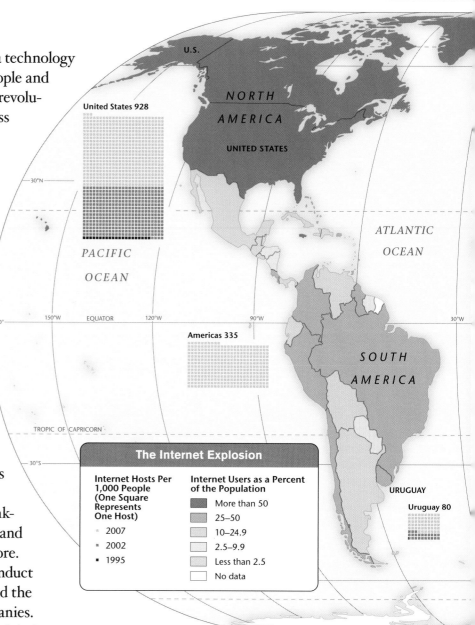

United States 928

NORTH AMERICA

UNITED STATES

U.S.

ATLANTIC OCEAN

PACIFIC OCEAN

SOUTH AMERICA

Americas 335

30°N

150°W   EQUATOR   120°W   90°W   30°W

0°

TROPIC OF CAPRICORN

30°S

URUGUAY

Uruguay 80

The Internet Explosion

Internet Hosts Per 1,000 People (One Square Represents One Host)	Internet Users as a Percent of the Population
▫ 2007	■ More than 50
▪ 2002	25–50
▪ 1995	10–24.9
	2.5–9.9
	Less than 2.5
	No data

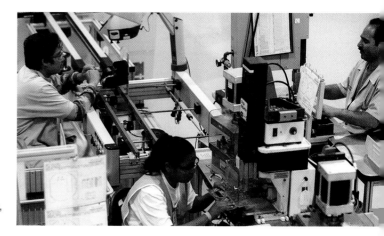

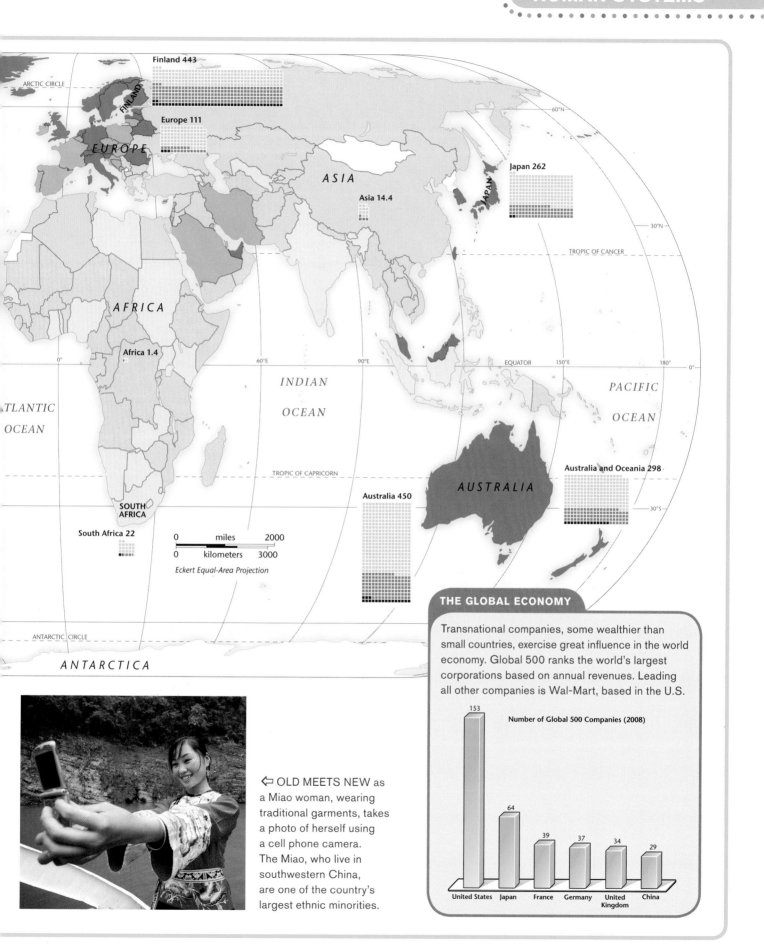

Finland 443

Europe 111

ASIA

Japan 262

Asia 14.4

EUROPE

FINLAND

JAPAN

ARCTIC CIRCLE

60°N

30°N

TROPIC OF CANCER

AFRICA

Africa 1.4

0°   60°E   90°E   EQUATOR   150°E   180°

INDIAN

OCEAN

ATLANTIC

OCEAN

PACIFIC

OCEAN

TROPIC OF CAPRICORN

Australia and Oceania 298

AUSTRALIA

Australia 450

30°S

SOUTH
AFRICA

South Africa 22

0   miles   2000
0   kilometers   3000
Eckert Equal-Area Projection

ANTARCTIC CIRCLE

ANTARCTICA

THE GLOBAL ECONOMY

Transnational companies, some wealthier than small countries, exercise great influence in the world economy. Global 500 ranks the world's largest corporations based on annual revenues. Leading all other companies is Wal-Mart, based in the U.S.

Number of Global 500 Companies (2008)

153 — United States
64 — Japan
39 — France
37 — Germany
34 — United Kingdom
29 — China

⇐ OLD MEETS NEW as a Miao woman, wearing traditional garments, takes a photo of herself using a cell phone camera. The Miao, who live in southwestern China, are one of the country's largest ethnic minorities.

Cultural Diffusion

In the past, when groups of people lived in relative isolation, cultures varied widely from place to place. Customs, styles, and preferences were handed down from one generation to the next.

Today, as a result of high-speed communication, trade, and travel, cultures all around the world are encountering and adopting new ideas. New customs, clothing and music trends, food habits, and lifestyles are being introduced into cultures everywhere at almost the same time. Some people are concerned that this trend in popular culture may result in a loss of cultural distinctiveness that makes places unique. For example, fast food chains once found only in the United States can now be seen in major cities around the world. And denim jeans, once a distinctively American clothing style, are worn by young people everywhere in place of more traditional clothing.

An important key to the spread, or diffusion, of popular culture is the increasing contact between people and places around the world. Cellular telephones, satellite television, and cyber-cafés have opened the world to styles and trends popular in Western countries. And tourists, traveling to places that were once considered remote and isolated, carry with them new ideas and fashions that become catalysts for bringing about cultural change.

⇨ THE INFLUENCE OF IMMIGRANT CULTURES on the American landscape is evident in ethnic communities such as Chinatown in the heart of New York City.

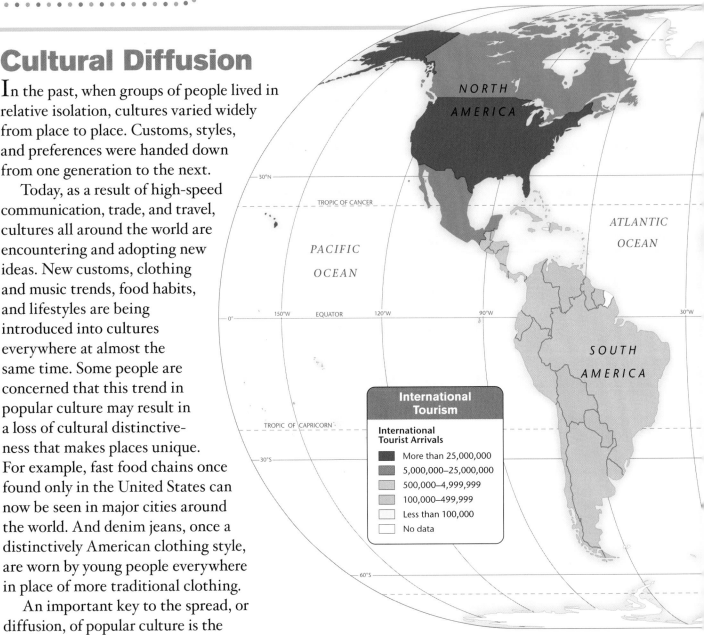

NORTH AMERICA

PACIFIC OCEAN

ATLANTIC OCEAN

SOUTH AMERICA

TROPIC OF CANCER

EQUATOR

TROPIC OF CAPRICORN

30°N

30°S

60°S

150°W

120°W

90°W

30°W

0°

International Tourism

International Tourist Arrivals

More than 25,000,000

5,000,000–25,000,000

500,000–4,999,999

100,000–499,999

Less than 100,000

No data

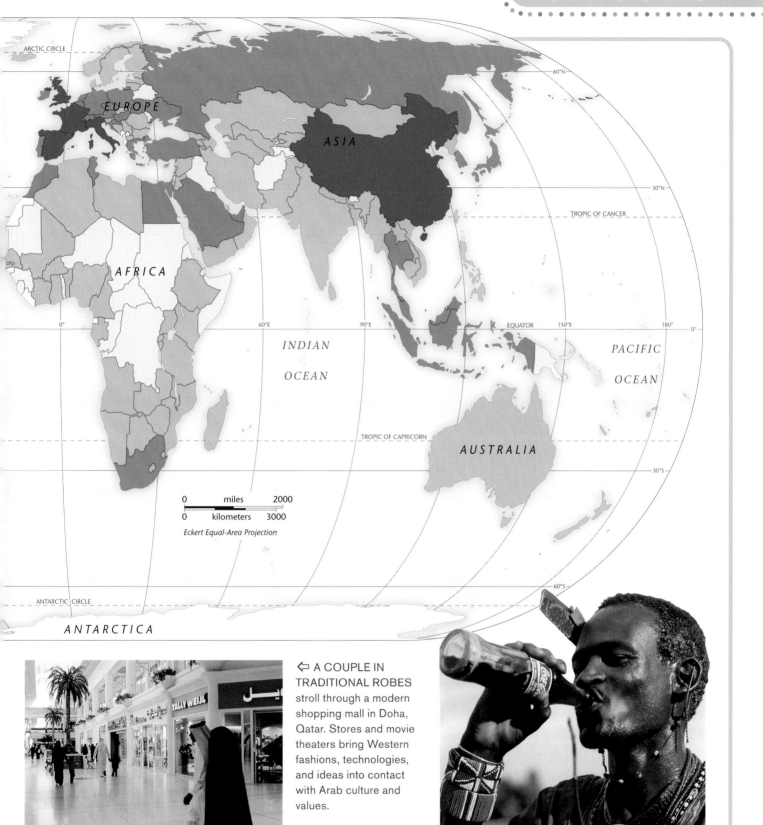

ARCTIC CIRCLE

60°N

EUROPE

ASIA

30°N

TROPIC OF CANCER

AFRICA

0°   60°E   90°E   EQUATOR   150°E   180°   0°

INDIAN

OCEAN

PACIFIC

OCEAN

TROPIC OF CAPRICORN

AUSTRALIA

30°S

```
0        miles      2000
0       kilometers   3000
```
Eckert Equal-Area Projection

60°S

ANTARCTIC CIRCLE

ANTARCTICA

⇐ A COUPLE IN TRADITIONAL ROBES stroll through a modern shopping mall in Doha, Qatar. Stores and movie theaters bring Western fashions, technologies, and ideas into contact with Arab culture and values.

⇒ TAKING A BREAK from a traditional ceremony, a Maasai warrior in Kenya enjoys a soft drink that was once uniquely American.

World Conflicts

The world map reveals a complex mosaic of people and cultures. However, when two groups claim the same territory or when major cultural differences overlap, previously peaceful people may turn to violence. Political differences, opposing value systems, or competition for resources can also create tensions.

Some conflicts are relatively short-lived, while others last years. For example, when the country of Yugoslavia broke into several new countries, conflict in Slovenia, which is culturally homogeneous, did not last very long. But Bosnia and Herzegovina faced years of civil war, as groups with different languages, religions, and traditions struggled for control. In the Middle East, territorial disputes between Muslim Palestinians and Jewish Israelis have been a source of turmoil for more than 50 years. And in eastern Asia, ethnic minorities in Myanmar, Indonesia, and the Philippines frequently protest, sometimes violently, domination by the majority group.

Since the 2001 attack on the United States by the terrorist network known as al Qaeda, American military forces have been engaged in wars in Afghanistan and Iraq. In Africa, a region with a turbulent post-colonial history, long-standing tensions between ethnic groups in Kenya erupted into open conflict following disputed elections in late 2007. And around the world the United Nations maintains 19 multi-national peacekeeping missions in places such as Sudan, Liberia, and Haiti.

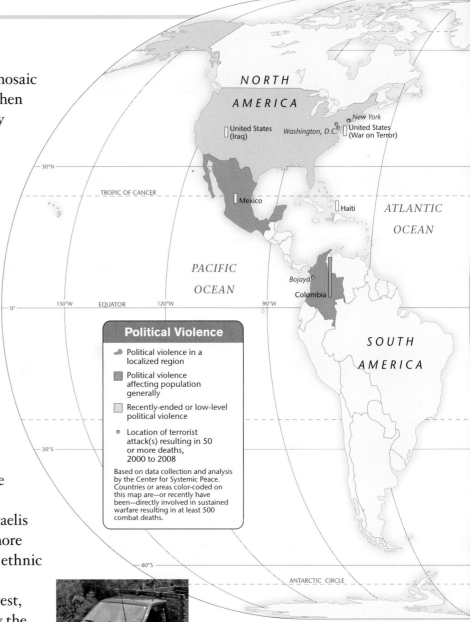

Political Violence

- Political violence in a localized region
- Political violence affecting population generally
- Recently-ended or low-level political violence
- Location of terrorist attack(s) resulting in 50 or more deaths, 2000 to 2008

Based on data collection and analysis by the Center for Systemic Peace. Countries or areas color-coded on this map are—or recently have been—directly involved in sustained warfare resulting in at least 500 combat deaths.

⇧ ARMED GUERRILLAS, members of Colombia's largest rebel group, FARC, maintain a checkpoint southwest of Bogotá. Civil war has plagued the country for decades.

⇩ ETHNIC TENSIONS turned into open conflict following disputed elections in Kenya in late 2007. Smoldering ruins are all that remain of a housing block in the Nairobi slum of Mathare.

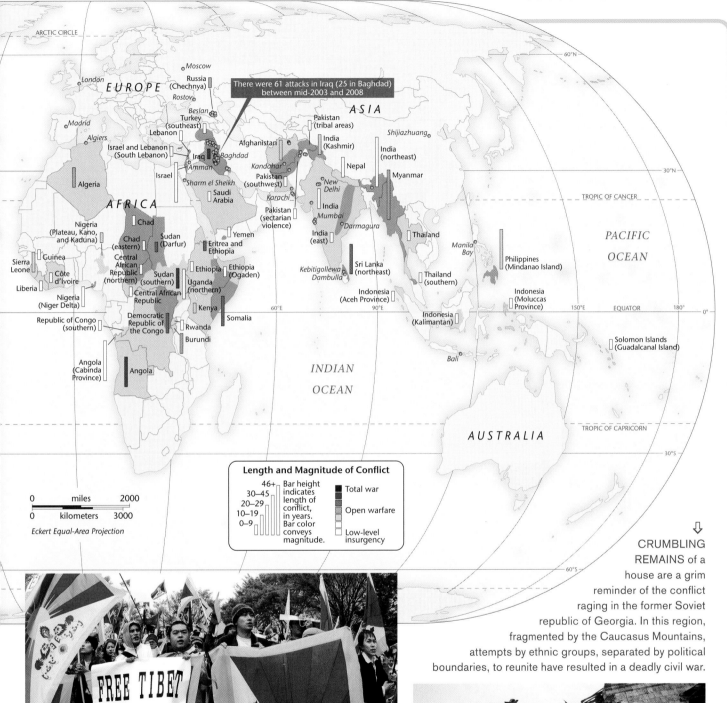

ARCTIC CIRCLE

EUROPE

London

Madrid

Algiers

AFRICA

ASIA

PACIFIC OCEAN

INDIAN OCEAN

AUSTRALIA

Moscow

Russia (Chechnya)

Rostov

There were 61 attacks in Iraq (25 in Baghdad) between mid-2003 and 2008

Beslan

Turkey (southeast)

Lebanon

Israel and Lebanon (South Lebanon)

Iraq · *Baghdad*

Amman

Israel

Sharm el Sheikh

Algeria

Saudi Arabia

Nigeria (Plateau, Kano, and Kaduna)

Chad

Chad (eastern)

Sudan (Darfur)

Central African Republic (northern)

Sudan (southern)

Central African Republic

Sierra Leone

Guinea

Côte d'Ivoire

Liberia

Nigeria (Niger Delta)

Republic of Congo (southern)

Democratic Republic of the Congo

Angola (Cabinda Province)

Angola

Rwanda

Burundi

Yemen

Eritrea and Ethiopia

Ethiopia

Ethiopia (Ogaden)

Uganda (northern)

Kenya

Somalia

Afghanistan

Kandahar

Pakistan (southwest)

Karachi

Pakistan (sectarian violence)

India (east)

Pakistan (tribal areas)

India (Kashmir)

New Delhi

Nepal

India (northeast)

Shijiazhuang

Myanmar

India · *Mumbai*

Darmagura

Kebitigollewa · *Dambulla*

Sri Lanka (northeast)

Thailand

Thailand (southern)

Manila Bay

Philippines (Mindanao Island)

Indonesia (Aceh Province)

Indonesia (Kalimantan)

Indonesia (Moluccas Province)

Bali

Solomon Islands (Guadalcanal Island)

TROPIC OF CANCER

EQUATOR

TROPIC OF CAPRICORN

0 miles 2000
0 kilometers 3000

Eckert Equal-Area Projection

Length and Magnitude of Conflict

46+
30–45
20–29
10–19
0–9

Bar height indicates length of conflict, in years. Bar color conveys magnitude.

■ Total war
▨ Open warfare
□ Low-level insurgency

CRUMBLING REMAINS of a house are a grim reminder of the conflict raging in the former Soviet republic of Georgia. In this region, fragmented by the Caucasus Mountains, attempts by ethnic groups, separated by political boundaries, to reunite have resulted in a deadly civil war.

⇧ POLITICAL PROTESTERS in Nagano, Japan, rally in support of greater autonomy for China's southwestern province of Xizang, better known as Tibet. Located high on the Tibetan Plateau and occupied by China since 1950, the region is led by the Dalai Lama, who lives in exile.

**North America:
A View From Space**

Viewed from high above, North America stretches from the frozen expanses of the Arctic Ocean and Greenland to the lush green of Panama's tropical forests. Hudson Bay and the Great Lakes, fingerprints of long-departed glaciers, dominate the continent's East, while the brown landscapes of the West and Southwest tell of dry lands where water is scarce.

**A view of El Capitan mountain and Bridalveil Falls
at Yosemite National Park, California**

THE CONTINENT: NORTH AMERICA

North America

PHYSICAL			POLITICAL		
Land area 9,449,000 sq mi (24,474,000 sq km)	Lowest point Death Valley, California -282 ft (-86 m)	Largest lake Lake Superior, U.S.-Canada 31,700 sq mi (82,100 sq km)	Population 523,082,000	Largest country Canada 3,855,101 sq mi (9,984,670 sq km)	Most populous country United States Pop. 302,200,000
Highest point Mount McKinley (Denali), Alaska 20,320 ft (6,194 m)	Longest river Mississippi-Missouri, United States 3,710 mi (5,971 km)		Number of independent countries 23	Smallest country St. Kitts and Nevis 104 sq mi (269 sq km)	Least populous country St. Kitts and Nevis Pop. 47,000

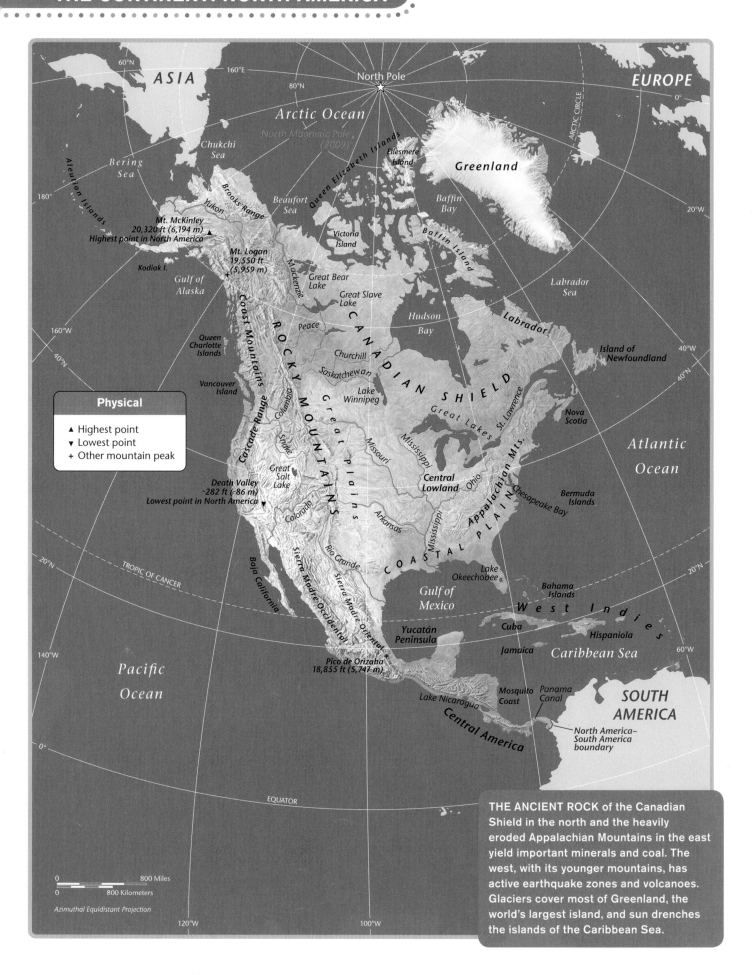

ASIA

EUROPE

North Pole

Arctic Ocean

North Magnetic Pole (2009)

Chukchi Sea

Bering Sea

Aleutian Islands

Brooks Range

Yukon

Mt. McKinley
20,320 ft (6,194 m)
Highest point in North America ▲

Mt. Logan
19,550 ft
(5,959 m)

Kodiak I.

Gulf of Alaska

Beaufort Sea

Queen Elizabeth Islands

Ellesmere Island

Greenland

Baffin Bay

Baffin Island

Victoria Island

Great Bear Lake

Great Slave Lake

Mackenzie

Hudson Bay

Labrador

Labrador Sea

Island of Newfoundland

ARCTIC CIRCLE

Coast Mountains

ROCKY MOUNTAINS

Peace

CANADIAN SHIELD

Queen Charlotte Islands

Churchill

Saskatchewan

Vancouver Island

Physical

▲ Highest point
▼ Lowest point
+ Other mountain peak

Cascade Range

Columbia

Snake

Great Salt Lake

Lake Winnipeg

Great Plains

Missouri

Mississippi

Great Lakes

St. Lawrence

Nova Scotia

Atlantic Ocean

Central Lowland

Ohio

Appalachian Mts.

Chesapeake Bay

Bermuda Islands

Death Valley
-282 ft (-86 m)
Lowest point in North America ▼

Colorado

Arkansas

Mississippi

COASTAL PLAIN

Baja California

Sierra Madre Occidental

Rio Grande

Sierra Madre Oriental

Lake Okeechobee

Gulf of Mexico

Bahama Islands

West Indies

TROPIC OF CANCER

Cuba

Hispaniola

Jamaica

Caribbean Sea

Pacific Ocean

Pico de Orizaba
18,855 ft (5,747 m)

Yucatán Peninsula

Lake Nicaragua

Mosquito Coast

Panama Canal

SOUTH AMERICA

North America–South America boundary

Central America

EQUATOR

0   800 Miles
0   800 Kilometers

Azimuthal Equidistant Projection

THE ANCIENT ROCK of the Canadian Shield in the north and the heavily eroded Appalachian Mountains in the east yield important minerals and coal. The west, with its younger mountains, has active earthquake zones and volcanoes. Glaciers cover most of Greenland, the world's largest island, and sun drenches the islands of the Caribbean Sea.

THE CONTINENT: NORTH AMERICA

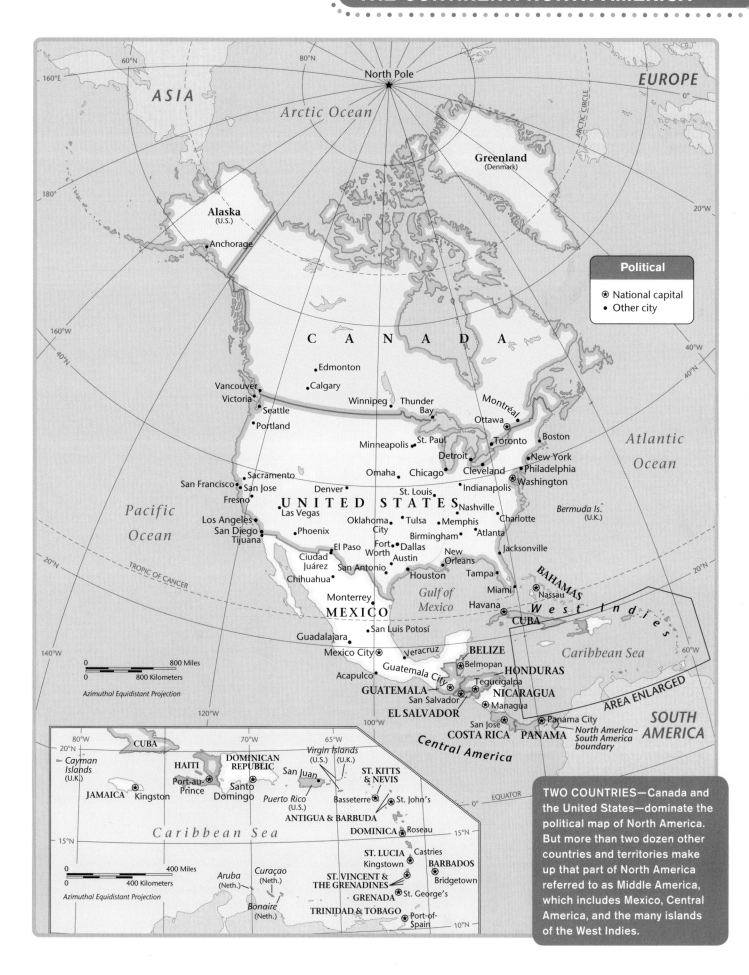

EUROPE

ASIA

Arctic Ocean

North Pole

ARCTIC CIRCLE

0°

160°E

60°N

80°N

20°W

180°

Greenland
(Denmark)

Alaska
(U.S.)

•Anchorage

160°W

40°N

40°W

40°N

C A N A D A

•Edmonton

Vancouver
Victoria
•Seattle
•Portland

•Calgary

Winnipeg •Thunder
Bay

Montréal

Ottawa ⊛

•Boston

Toronto

Atlantic
Ocean

Minneapolis •St. Paul

Detroit

•New York

Sacramento

Omaha •Chicago Cleveland •Philadelphia

San Francisco •San Jose
Fresno

Denver•

•Indianapolis ⊛Washington

St. Louis

Bermuda Is.
(U.K.)

U N I T E D   S T A T E S

Nashville

Pacific

Las Vegas

Oklahoma
City

•Tulsa •Memphis

Charlotte

Ocean

Los Angeles
San Diego
Tijuana

•Phoenix

El Paso
Fort
Worth •Dallas
Austin

Birmingham
•Atlanta

Ciudad
Juárez
San Antonio

New
Orleans

Jacksonville

Chihuahua

Houston

Tampa•

TROPIC OF CANCER

20°N

20°N

Miami

BAHAMAS

W e s t   I n d i e s

Monterrey

Gulf of
Mexico

Havana
⊛

•Nassau

M E X I C O

•San Luis Potosí

CUBA

Caribbean Sea

60°W

Guadalajara

140°W

Mexico City ⊛

Veracruz

BELIZE

120°W

AREA ENLARGED

0   800 Miles
0   800 Kilometers

Acapulco•

Guatemala City

⊛Belmopan
HONDURAS

Azimuthal Equidistant Projection

GUATEMALA

Tegucigalpa ⊛

NICARAGUA

SOUTH
AMERICA

San Salvador

100°W

EL SALVADOR

⊛ Managua

C e n t r a l   A m e r i c a

San José

⊛ Panama City

COSTA RICA   PANAMA

North America–
South America
boundary

EQUATOR

0°

15°N

80°W

70°W

65°W

Virgin Islands
(U.S.) (U.K.)

CUBA

20°N

Cayman
Islands
(U.K.)

DOMINICAN
REPUBLIC

HAITI

San Juan

ST. KITTS
& NEVIS

JAMAICA ⊛Kingston

Port-au-
Prince

Santo
Domingo

Puerto Rico
(U.S.)

Basseterre

⊛St. John's

ANTIGUA & BARBUDA

DOMINICA ⊛Roseau

15°N

C a r i b b e a n   S e a

15°N

ST. LUCIA ⊛Castries

Kingstown

BARBADOS

0   400 Miles
0   400 Kilometers

Aruba
(Neth.)

Curaçao
(Neth.)

ST. VINCENT &
THE GRENADINES

⊛ Bridgetown

⊛St. George's

GRENADA

Azimuthal Equidistant Projection

Bonaire
(Neth.)

TRINIDAD & TOBAGO

⊛Port-of-
Spain

10°N

Political

⊛ National capital
• Other city

TWO COUNTRIES—Canada and
the United States—dominate the
political map of North America.
But more than two dozen other
countries and territories make
up that part of North America
referred to as Middle America,
which includes Mexico, Central
America, and the many islands
of the West Indies.

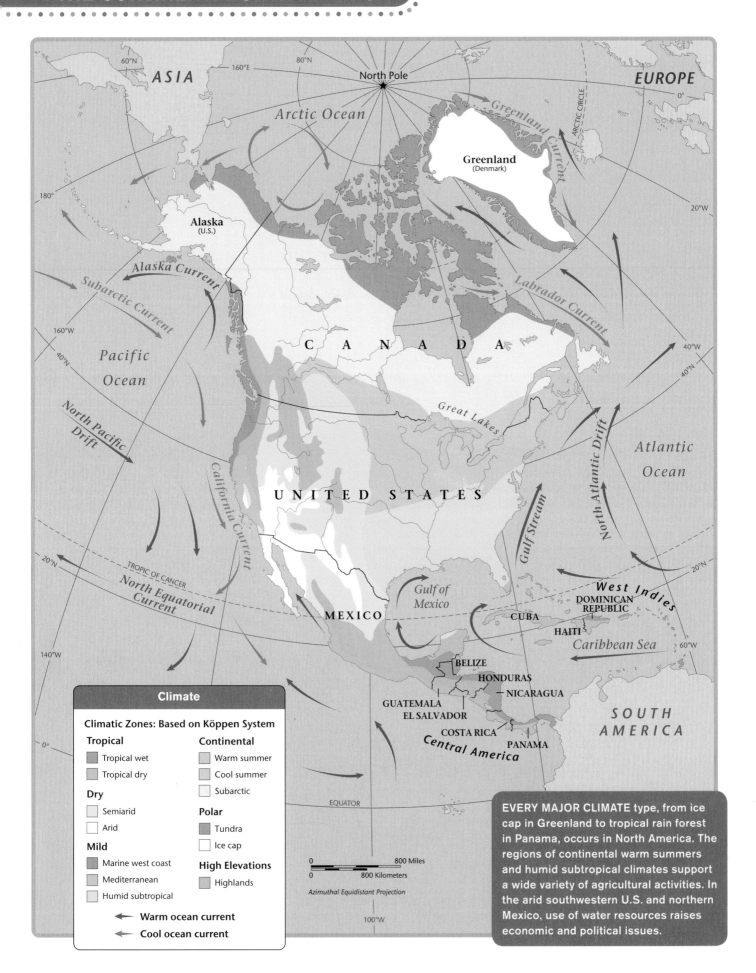

ASIA

80°N

160°E

North Pole

EUROPE

Arctic Ocean

0°

Greenland Current

ARCTIC CIRCLE

20°E

Greenland
(Denmark)

60°N

180°

Alaska
(U.S.)

Alaska Current

Subarctic Current

Labrador Current

20°W

160°W

Pacific
Ocean

40°W

C A N A D A

40°N

40°N

North Pacific
Drift

California Current

Great Lakes

Atlantic
Ocean

North Atlantic Drift

140°W

20°N

TROPIC OF CANCER

North Equatorial
Current

U N I T E D   S T A T E S

20°N

Gulf Stream

West Indies

DOMINICAN
REPUBLIC

60°W

MEXICO

Gulf of
Mexico

CUBA

HAITI

Caribbean Sea

BELIZE

HONDURAS

NICARAGUA

GUATEMALA
EL SALVADOR

COSTA RICA

PANAMA

Central America

SOUTH
AMERICA

0°

EQUATOR

Climate

Climatic Zones: Based on Köppen System

Tropical
- Tropical wet
- Tropical dry

Dry
- Semiarid
- Arid

Mild
- Marine west coast
- Mediterranean
- Humid subtropical

Continental
- Warm summer
- Cool summer
- Subarctic

Polar
- Tundra
- Ice cap

High Elevations
- Highlands

← Warm ocean current

← Cool ocean current

650 Miles

0   800 Miles
0   800 Kilometers

Azimuthal Equidistant Projection

100°W

EVERY MAJOR CLIMATE type, from ice cap in Greenland to tropical rain forest in Panama, occurs in North America. The regions of continental warm summers and humid subtropical climates support a wide variety of agricultural activities. In the arid southwestern U.S. and northern Mexico, use of water resources raises economic and political issues.

THE CONTINENT: NORTH AMERICA

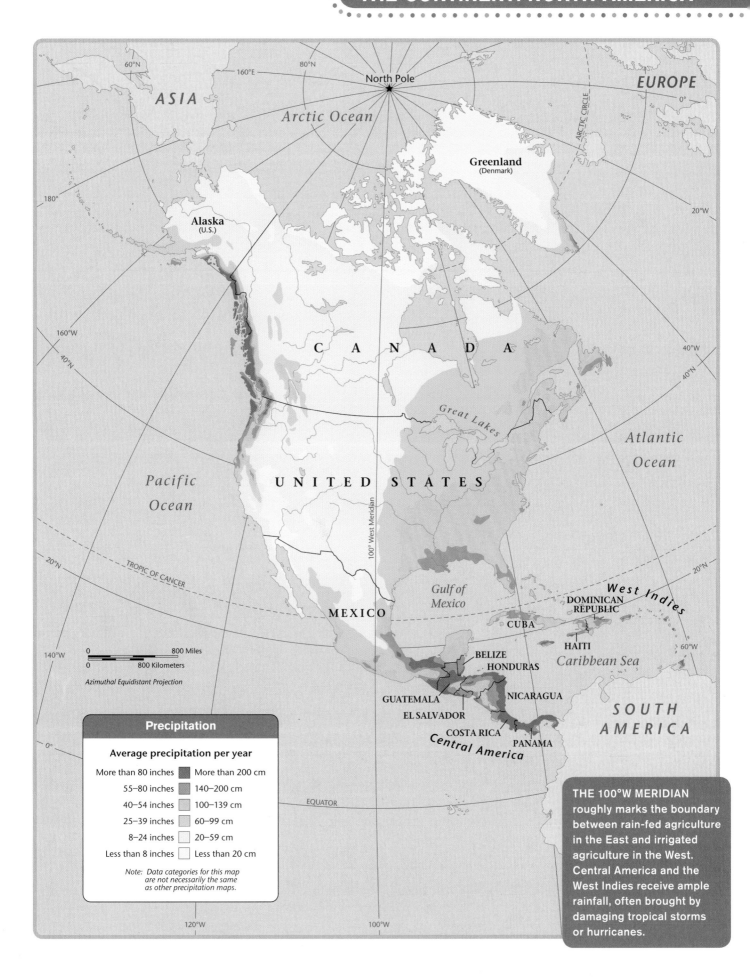

ASIA

Arctic Ocean

North Pole

EUROPE

ARCTIC CIRCLE

Greenland
(Denmark)

Alaska
(U.S.)

C A N A D A

Great Lakes

Atlantic
Ocean

Pacific
Ocean

U N I T E D   S T A T E S

100° West Meridian

TROPIC OF CANCER

Gulf of
Mexico

West Indies

DOMINICAN
REPUBLIC

MEXICO

CUBA

HAITI

Caribbean Sea

BELIZE
HONDURAS

NICARAGUA

SOUTH
AMERICA

GUATEMALA
EL SALVADOR

COSTA RICA

PANAMA

Central America

EQUATOR

0   800 Miles
0   800 Kilometers

Azimuthal Equidistant Projection

Precipitation

Average precipitation per year

More than 80 inches		More than 200 cm
55–80 inches		140–200 cm
40–54 inches		100–139 cm
25–39 inches		60–99 cm
8–24 inches		20–59 cm
Less than 8 inches		Less than 20 cm

Note: Data categories for this map are not necessarily the same as other precipitation maps.

THE 100°W MERIDIAN roughly marks the boundary between rain-fed agriculture in the East and irrigated agriculture in the West. Central America and the West Indies receive ample rainfall, often brought by damaging tropical storms or hurricanes.

THE CONTINENT: NORTH AMERICA

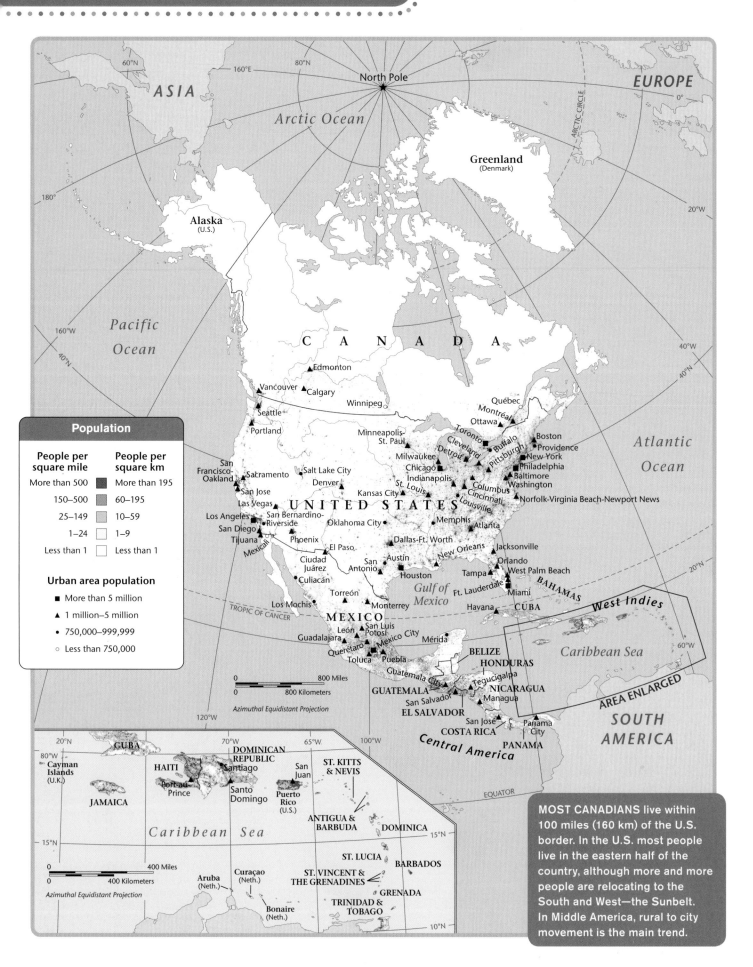

Population

People per square mile	**People per square km**
More than 500	More than 195
150–500	60–195
25–149	10–59
1–24	1–9
Less than 1	Less than 1

Urban area population

- ■ More than 5 million
- ▲ 1 million–5 million
- • 750,000–999,999
- ○ Less than 750,000

0 ——— 800 Miles
0 ——— 800 Kilometers

Azimuthal Equidistant Projection

0 ——— 400 Miles
0 ——— 400 Kilometers

Azimuthal Equidistant Projection

MOST CANADIANS live within 100 miles (160 km) of the U.S. border. In the U.S. most people live in the eastern half of the country, although more and more people are relocating to the South and West—the Sunbelt. In Middle America, rural to city movement is the main trend.

THE CONTINENT: NORTH AMERICA

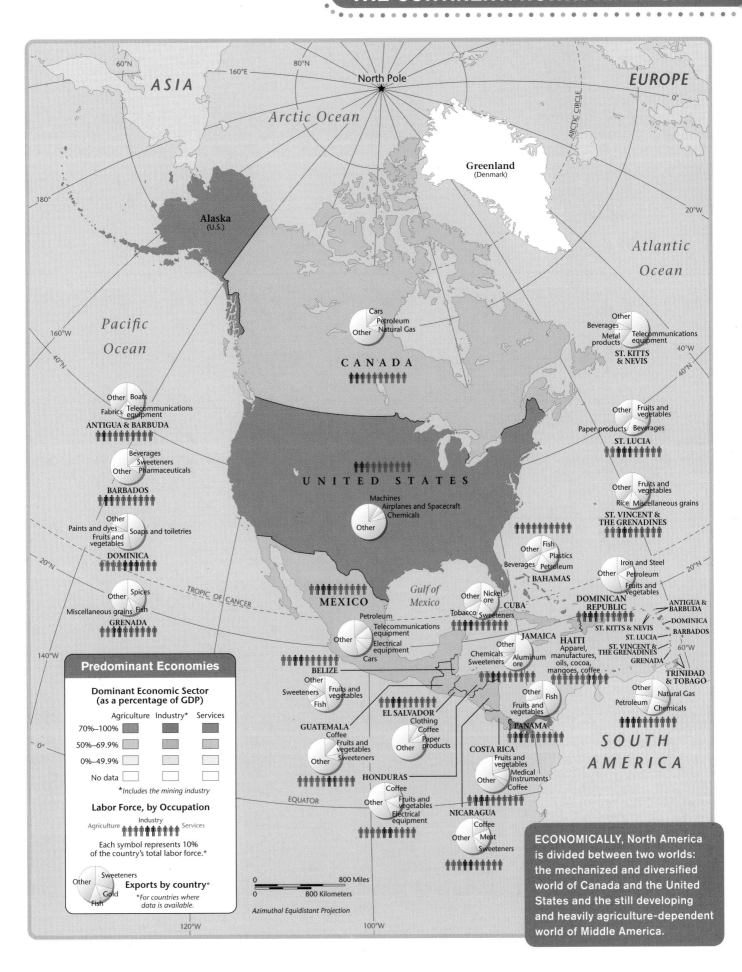

ASIA

Arctic Ocean

North Pole

EUROPE

Greenland
(Denmark)

Alaska
(U.S.)

Atlantic
Ocean

Pacific
Ocean

Cars
Petroleum
Other   Natural Gas

CANADA

Other
Beverages
Metal   Telecommunications
products   equipment
ST. KITTS
& NEVIS

Other   Boats
Fabrics   Telecommunications
         equipment
ANTIGUA & BARBUDA

Other   Fruits and
        vegetables
Paper products   Beverages
ST. LUCIA

Beverages
Sweeteners
Other   Pharmaceuticals
BARBADOS

U N I T E D   S T A T E S

Other   Fruits and
        vegetables
Rice   Miscellaneous grains
ST. VINCENT &
THE GRENADINES

Other
Paints and dyes   Soaps and toiletries
Fruits and
vegetables
DOMINICA

Machines
Airplanes and Spacecraft
Chemicals
Other

Other   Fish
Plastics
Beverages   Petroleum
BAHAMAS

Other   Spices
Miscellaneous grains   Fish
GRENADA

Gulf of
Mexico

Other   Nickel
        ore
Tobacco   Sweeteners
CUBA

Other   Iron and Steel
        Petroleum
Fruits and
vegetables
DOMINICAN
REPUBLIC

ANTIGUA &
BARBUDA

DOMINICA

TROPIC OF CANCER

MEXICO

Petroleum
Telecommunications
equipment
Other   Electrical
        equipment
Cars

ST. KITTS & NEVIS
ST. LUCIA

BARBADOS

JAMAICA
Other
Chemicals   Aluminum
Sweeteners   ore

HAITI
Apparel,
manufactures,
oils, cocoa,
mangoes, coffee

ST. VINCENT &
THE GRENADINES

GRENADA

TRINIDAD
& TOBAGO

Other   Natural Gas
Petroleum   Chemicals

BELIZE
Other
Sweeteners   Fruits and
            vegetables
Fish

EL SALVADOR
Clothing
Coffee
Other   Paper
        products

PANAMA

Other   Fish
Fruits and
vegetables

SOUTH

AMERICA

GUATEMALA
Coffee
Fruits and
vegetables
Other   Sweeteners

COSTA RICA
Fruits and
vegetables
Other   Medical
        instruments
        Coffee

HONDURAS
Coffee
Other   Fruits and
        vegetables
        Electrical
        equipment

NICARAGUA
Coffee
Other   Meat
        Sweeteners

EQUATOR

ANTIGUA & BARBUDA
DOMINICA
BARBADOS
ST. VINCENT &
THE GRENADINES
GRENADA

Predominant Economies

Dominant Economic Sector
(as a percentage of GDP)

	Agriculture	Industry*	Services
70%–100%			
50%–69.9%			
0%–49.9%			
No data			

*Includes the mining industry

Labor Force, by Occupation

Agriculture   Industry   Services

Each symbol represents 10%
of the country's total labor force.*

Other   Sweeteners
        Gold
Fish

Exports by country*

*For countries where
data is available.

0   800 Miles
0   800 Kilometers

Azimuthal Equidistant Projection

ECONOMICALLY, North America
is divided between two worlds:
the mechanized and diversified
world of Canada and the United
States and the still developing
and heavily agriculture-dependent
world of Middle America.

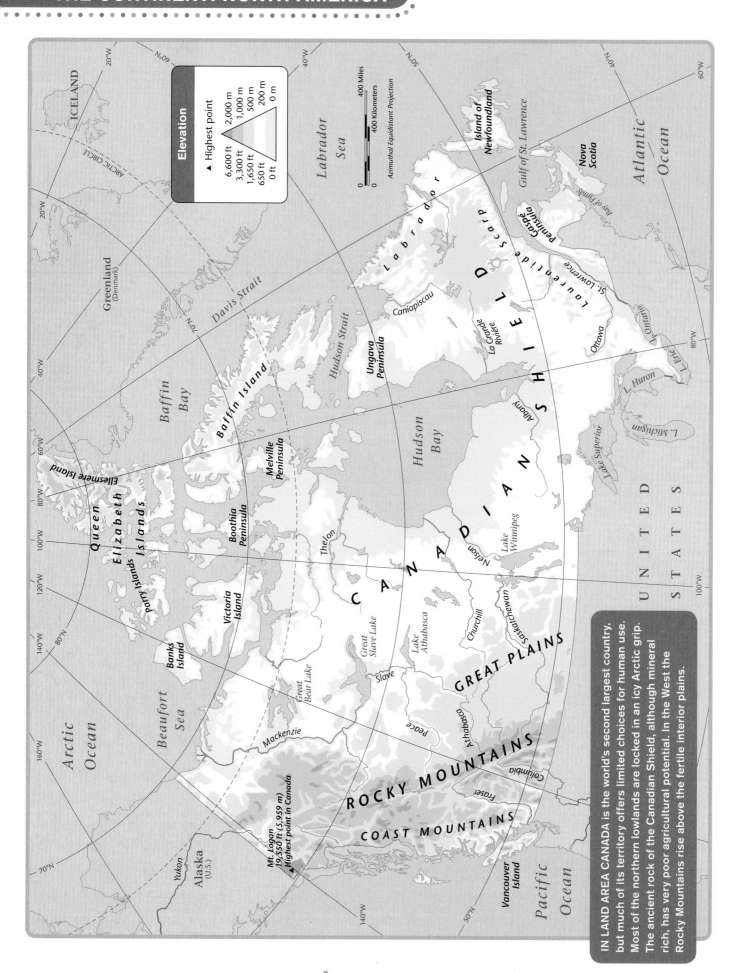

Elevation

▲ Highest point

6,600 ft	2,000 m
3,300 ft	1,000 m
1,650 ft	500 m
650 ft	200 m
0 ft	0 m

400 Miles
400 Kilometers
Azimuthal Equidistant Projection

ICELAND

Greenland
(Denmark)

ARCTIC CIRCLE

Davis Strait

Labrador
Sea

Island of
Newfoundland

Gulf of St. Lawrence

Nova
Scotia

Bay of Fundy

Atlantic
Ocean

Baffin
Bay

Baffin Island

Hudson Strait

Ungava
Peninsula

Labrador

Gaspé
Peninsula

St. Lawrence

Caniapiscau

Laurentide Scarp

Ellesmere Island

Queen
Elizabeth
Islands

Parry Islands

Melville
Peninsula

Boothia
Peninsula

La Grande
Rivière

Ottawa

L. Erie

L. Ontario

C   A   N   A   D   I   A   N   S   H   I   E   L   D

Banks
Island

Victoria
Island

Great
Bear Lake

Thelon

Hudson
Bay

Albany

Nelson

Lake
Winnipeg

Lake Superior

L. Michigan

L. Huron

Beaufort
Sea

Arctic
Ocean

Mackenzie

Great
Slave Lake

Slave

Lake
Athabasca

Churchill

Saskatchewan

GREAT PLAINS

U   N   I   T   E   D
S   T   A   T   E   S

Peace

Athabasca

Mt. Logan
(9,550 ft (5,959 m)
▲ Highest point in Canada

Columbia

R O C K Y   M O U N T A I N S

Fraser

Yukon

Alaska
(U.S.)

COAST MOUNTAINS

Vancouver
Island

Pacific
Ocean

IN LAND AREA CANADA is the world's second largest country,
but much of its territory offers limited choices for human use.
Most of the northern lowlands are locked in an icy Arctic grip.
The ancient rock of the Canadian Shield, although mineral
rich, has very poor agricultural potential. In the West the
Rocky Mountains rise above the fertile interior plains.

THE CONTINENT: NORTH AMERICA

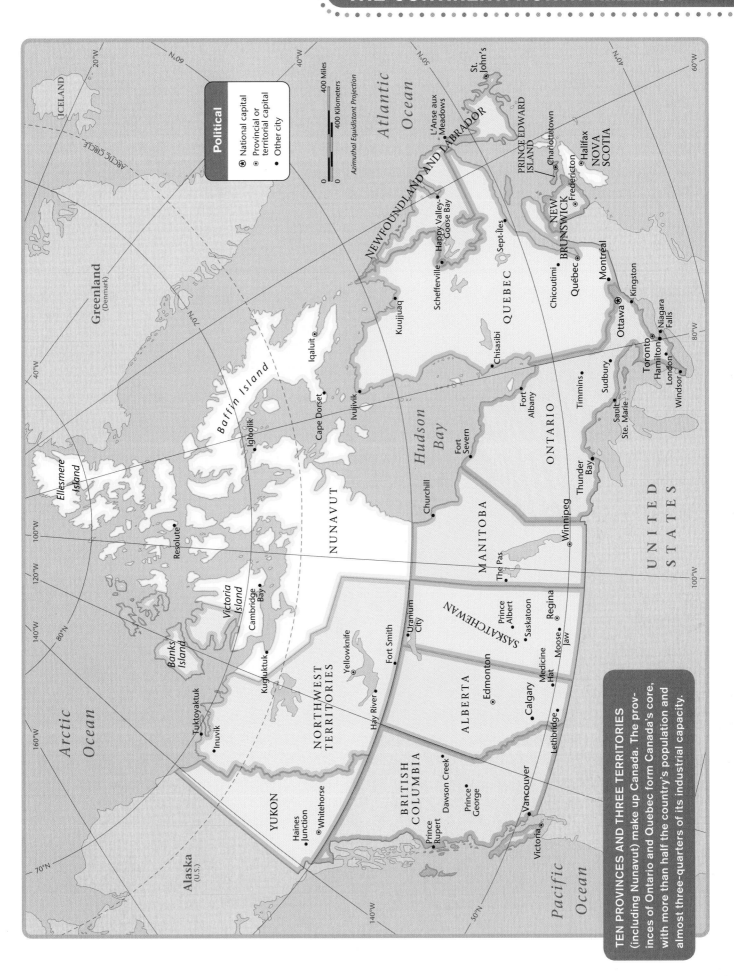

Political

⊛ National capital
⊚ Provincial or territorial capital
• Other city

400 Miles
400 Kilometers

Azimuthal Equidistant Projection

ICELAND

ARCTIC CIRCLE

Greenland
(Denmark)

Ellesmere
Island

Baffin Island

Atlantic
Ocean

St. John's

L'Anse aux Meadows

NEWFOUNDLAND AND LABRADOR

PRINCE EDWARD ISLAND

Charlottetown

Fredericton

Halifax
NOVA SCOTIA

NEW BRUNSWICK

Scefferville

Happy Valley-
Goose Bay

Sept-Îles

QUÉBEC

Chicoutimi

Québec

Montréal

Kingston

Kuujjuaq

Chisasibi

Ottawa

Niagara Falls

Iqaluit

Toronto
Hamilton
London
Windsor

Cape Dorset

Igloolik

Ivujivik

Fort Albany

ONTARIO

Timmins

Sudbury

Sault Ste. Marie

Resolute

Hudson
Bay

Fort Severn

Thunder Bay

NUNAVUT

Churchill

UNITED STATES

Victoria Island

Cambridge Bay

MANITOBA

The Pas

Winnipeg

Banks
Island

Arctic
Ocean

Tuktoyaktuk

Inuvik

Kugluktuk

NORTHWEST
TERRITORIES

Yellowknife

Fort Smith

Uranium City

SASKATCHEWAN

Prince Albert

Saskatoon

Regina

Moose Jaw

Medicine Hat

ALBERTA

Edmonton

Calgary

Lethbridge

Hay River

Haines Junction

Whitehorse

YUKON

BRITISH COLUMBIA

Dawson Creek

Prince George

Prince Rupert

Vancouver

Victoria

Alaska
(U.S.)

Pacific
Ocean

TEN PROVINCES AND THREE TERRITORIES (including Nunavut) make up Canada. The provinces of Ontario and Quebec form Canada's core, with more than half the country's population and almost three-quarters of its industrial capacity.

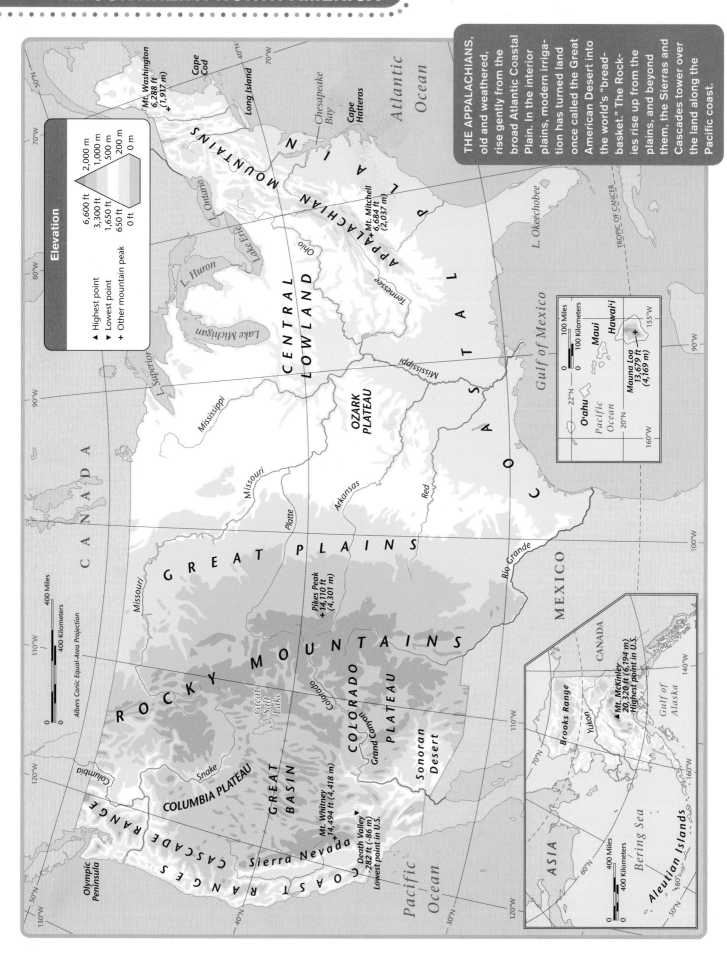

Elevation

	2,000 m	1,000 m	500 m	200 m	0 m
	6,600 ft	3,300 ft	1,650 ft	650 ft	0 ft

▲ Highest point
▼ Lowest point
+ Other mountain peak

THE APPALACHIANS, old and weathered, rise gently from the broad Atlantic Coastal Plain. In the interior plains, modern irrigation has turned land once called the Great American Desert into the world's "breadbasket." The Rockies rise up from the plains, and beyond them, the Sierras and Cascades tower over the land along the Pacific coast.

CANADA

Mt. Washington
6,288 ft
(1,917 m) +

Cape Cod

Long Island

Chesapeake Bay

Cape Hatteras

Atlantic Ocean

APPALACHIAN MOUNTAINS

+ Mt. Mitchell
6,684 ft
(2,037 m)

L. Ontario

Lake Erie

L. Huron

Lake Michigan

L. Superior

Ohio

Tennessee

CENTRAL LOWLAND

COASTAL PLAIN

OZARK PLATEAU

Mississippi

Missouri

Arkansas

Red

L. Okeechobee

Gulf of Mexico

TROPIC OF CANCER

Platte

GREAT PLAINS

Pikes Peak
+ 14,110 ft
(4,301 m)

Rio Grande

MEXICO

Colorado

ROCKY MOUNTAINS

COLORADO PLATEAU

Great Salt Lake

Grand Canyon

Sonoran Desert

Snake

COLUMBIA PLATEAU

GREAT BASIN

Mt. Whitney
+ 14,494 ft (4,418 m)

Death Valley ▼
282 ft (-86 m)
Lowest point in U.S.

Sierra Nevada

COAST RANGES

CASCADE RANGE

Olympic Peninsula

Columbia

Pacific Ocean

Missouri

400 Miles
0
400 Kilometers
0

Albers Conic Equal-Area Projection

Hawai'i inset:

100 Miles
0
100 Kilometers
0

Maui

O'ahu

Hawai'i

22°N

20°N

Pacific Ocean

Mauna Loa
13,679 ft
(4,169 m) +

Alaska inset:

CANADA

Brooks Range

Yukon

▲ Mt. McKinley
20,320 ft (6,194 m)
Highest point in U.S.

Gulf of Alaska

ASIA

Bering Sea

Aleutian Islands

400 Miles
0
400 Kilometers
0

THE CONTINENT: NORTH AMERICA

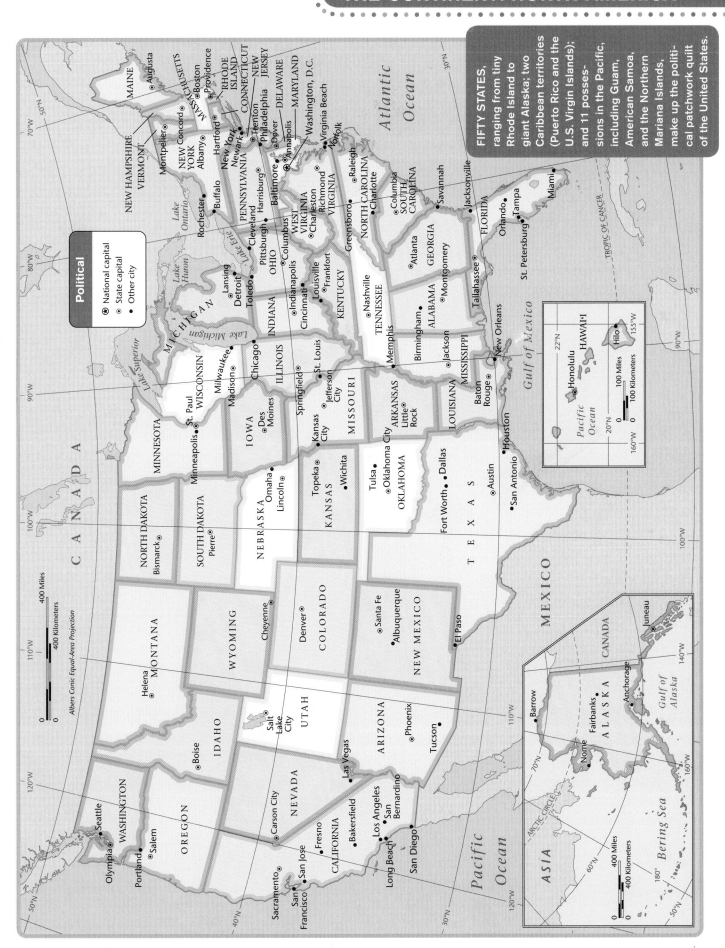

FIFTY STATES, ranging from tiny Rhode Island to giant Alaska; two Caribbean territories (Puerto Rico and the U.S. Virgin Islands); and 11 possessions in the Pacific, including Guam, American Samoa, and the Northern Mariana Islands, make up the political patchwork quilt of the United States.

Political

⊛ National capital
◉ State capital
• Other city

MAINE
Augusta
NEW HAMPSHIRE
VERMONT
Montpelier
Concord
MASSACHUSETTS
Boston
Providence
RHODE ISLAND
CONNECTICUT
NEW JERSEY
New Concord
NEW YORK
Albany
Hartford
New York
Newark
Trenton
Philadelphia
Dover
DELAWARE
MARYLAND
Baltimore
Washington, D.C.
Annapolis
Virginia Beach
Norfolk

Atlantic Ocean

30°N
50°N
70°W
80°W

Lake Ontario
Rochester
Buffalo
PENNSYLVANIA
Harrisburg
Pittsburgh
Cleveland
WEST VIRGINIA
Richmond
Charleston
VIRGINIA
Greensboro
Raleigh
NORTH CAROLINA
Charlotte
Columbia
SOUTH CAROLINA
Savannah
Jacksonville

Lake Erie
Lake Huron
Lansing
Detroit
Toledo
OHIO
Columbus
Cincinnati
Indianapolis
INDIANA
Louisville
Frankfort
KENTUCKY
Nashville
TENNESSEE
Atlanta
GEORGIA
Montgomery
ALABAMA
Birmingham
Tallahassee
FLORIDA
Orlando
Tampa
St. Petersburg
Miami

TROPIC OF CANCER

MICHIGAN
Lake Michigan
Lake Superior
WISCONSIN
Milwaukee
Madison
Chicago
ILLINOIS
Springfield
St. Louis
MISSOURI
Jefferson City
Memphis
ARKANSAS
Little Rock
MISSISSIPPI
Jackson
LOUISIANA
Baton Rouge
New Orleans
Gulf of Mexico

St. Paul
MINNESOTA
Minneapolis
IOWA
Des Moines

Omaha
Lincoln
NEBRASKA
Topeka
Kansas City
Wichita
KANSAS
Tulsa
Oklahoma City
OKLAHOMA

Fort Worth
Dallas
Austin
San Antonio
Houston
T E X A S

90°W
MEXICO
100°W

22°N
HAWAI'I
Hilo
Honolulu
Pacific Ocean
20°N
155°W
160°W
90°W
100 Miles
100 Kilometers

NORTH DAKOTA
Bismarck
SOUTH DAKOTA
Pierre

Santa Fe
Albuquerque
NEW MEXICO
El Paso

C A N A D A
100°W
110°W
120°W

WYOMING
Cheyenne
COLORADO
Denver

MONTANA
Helena

IDAHO
Boise

Salt Lake City
UTAH

ARIZONA
Phoenix
Tucson

NEVADA
Carson City
Las Vegas

CALIFORNIA
Sacramento
San Francisco
San Jose
Fresno
Bakersfield
Los Angeles
San Bernardino
Long Beach
San Diego

WASHINGTON
Seattle
Olympia
Portland
Salem
OREGON

Pacific Ocean

400 Miles
400 Kilometers
Albers Conic Equal-Area Projection

50°N
40°N
30°N
120°W

M E X I C O

CANADA
Juneau
ALASKA
Barrow
Nome
Fairbanks
Anchorage
Gulf of Alaska
ASIA
Bering Sea
ARCTIC CIRCLE
70°N
60°N
50°N
140°W
160°W
180°
400 Miles
400 Kilometers
110°W

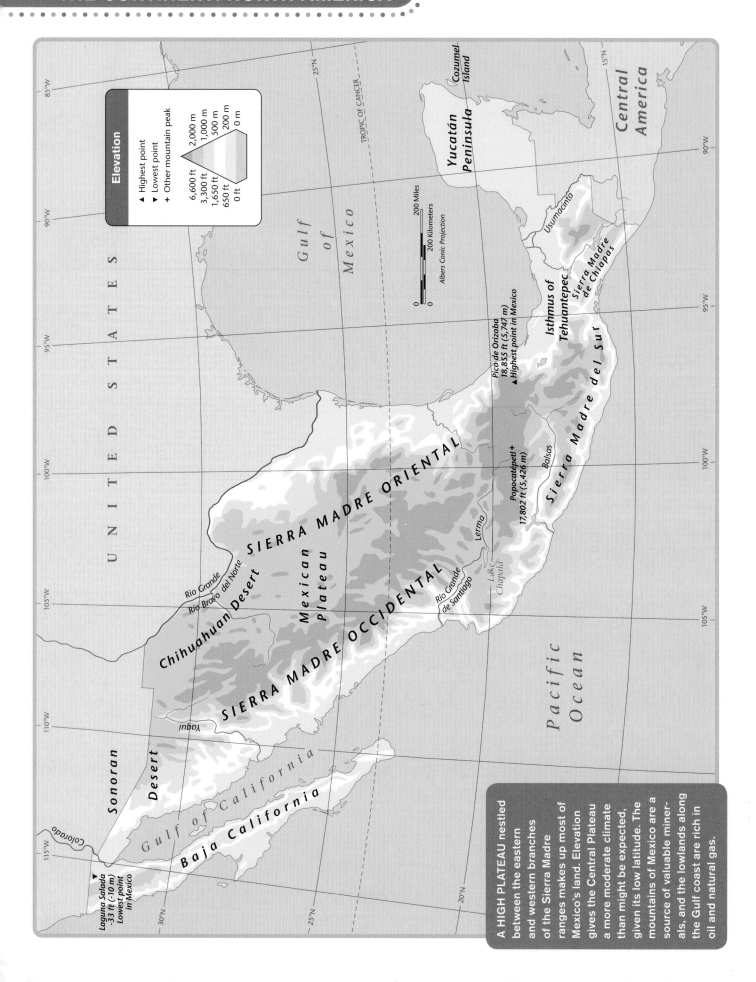

Elevation

▲ Highest point
▼ Lowest point
+ Other mountain peak

2,000 m
1,000 m
500 m
200 m
0 m

6,600 ft
3,300 ft
1,650 ft
650 ft
0 ft

85°W
90°W
95°W
100°W
105°W
110°W
115°W

25°N
20°N
25°N
30°N
15°N

TROPIC OF CANCER

UNITED STATES

Gulf of Mexico

Cozumel Island

Yucatán Peninsula

Central America

200 Miles
200 Kilometers
Albers Conic Projection

Usumacinta

Sierra Madre de Chiapas

Isthmus of Tehuantepec

Pico de Orizaba
18,855 ft (5,747 m)
▲ Highest point in Mexico

Popocatépetl +
17,802 ft (5,426 m)

Bolsas

Sierra Madre del Sur

SIERRA MADRE ORIENTAL

Mexican Plateau

Lerma

Lake Chapala

Rio Grande de Santiago

Chihuahuan Desert

SIERRA MADRE OCCIDENTAL

Rio Grande
Río Bravo del Norte

Yaqui

Sonoran

Desert

Gulf of California

Baja California

Pacific Ocean

Colorado

Laguna Salada
-33 ft (-10 m)
Lowest point in Mexico

A HIGH PLATEAU nestled between the eastern and western branches of the Sierra Madre ranges makes up most of Mexico's land. Elevation gives the Central Plateau a more moderate climate than might be expected, given its low latitude. The mountains of Mexico are a source of valuable minerals, and the lowlands along the Gulf coast are rich in oil and natural gas.

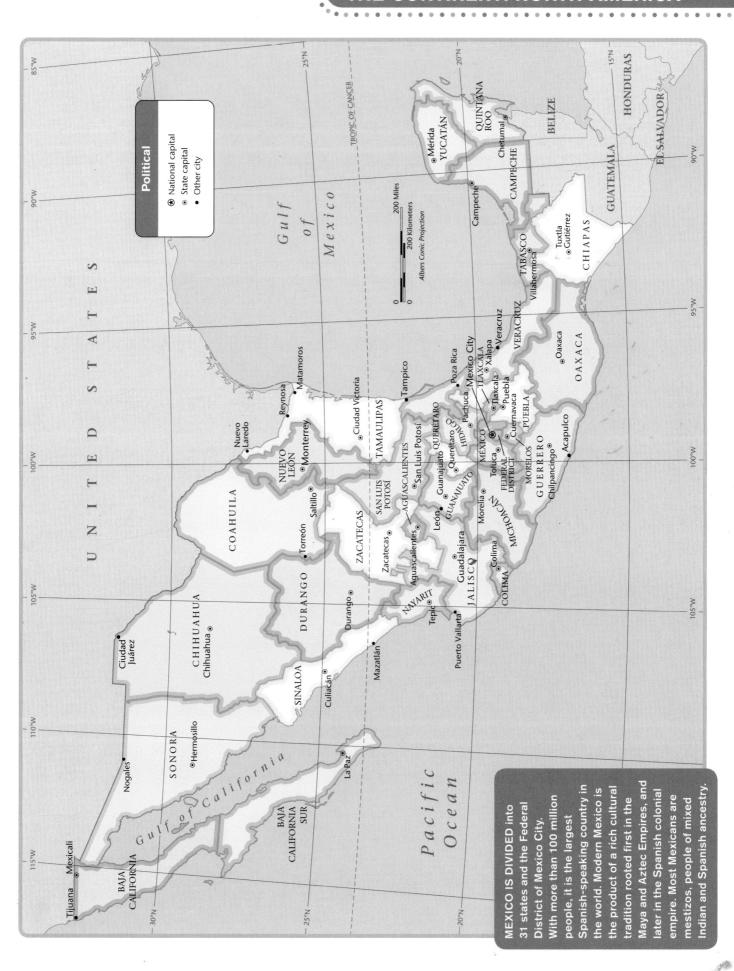

Political
⊕ National capital
◉ State capital
• Other city

85°W
80°W
90°W
95°W
100°W
105°W
110°W
115°W

25°N
20°N
15°N

TROPIC OF CANCER

Gulf of Mexico

200 Miles
200 Kilometers
Albers Conic Projection

UNITED STATES

HONDURAS
EL SALVADOR
GUATEMALA
BELIZE

QUINTANA ROO
YUCATAN
Mérida
Chetumal
CAMPECHE
Campeche
TABASCO
Villahermosa
CHIAPAS
Tuxtla Gutiérrez

VERACRUZ
Veracruz
Xalapa
Poza Rica
Mexico City
TLAXCALA
Tlaxcala
Puebla
PUEBLA
Cuernavaca
MORELOS
FEDERAL DISTRICT
MEXICO
Toluca
GUERRERO
Chilpancingo
Acapulco
OAXACA
Oaxaca

Tampico
Ciudad Victoria
TAMAULIPAS
Matamoros
Reynosa
Monterrey
NUEVO LEÓN
Nuevo Laredo
HIDALGO
Pachuca
QUERÉTARO
Querétaro
San Luis Potosí
SAN LUIS POTOSÍ
GUANAJUATO
Guanajuato
AGUASCALIENTES
Aguascalientes
ZACATECAS
Zacatecas
León
Morelia
MICHOACÁN
Guadalajara
JALISCO
Colima
COLIMA
NAYARIT
Tepic
Puerto Vallarta

COAHUILA
Saltillo
Torreón
DURANGO
Durango
Mazatlán
SINALOA
Culiacán

CHIHUAHUA
Chihuahua
Ciudad Juárez

SONORA
Hermosillo
Nogales

BAJA CALIFORNIA
Mexicali
Tijuana

Gulf of California

BAJA CALIFORNIA SUR
La Paz

Pacific Ocean

30°N
25°N
20°N

MEXICO IS DIVIDED into 31 states and the Federal District of Mexico City. With more than 100 million people, it is the largest Spanish-speaking country in the world. Modern Mexico is the product of a rich cultural tradition rooted first in the Maya and Aztec Empires, and later in the Spanish colonial empire. Most Mexicans are mestizos, people of mixed Indian and Spanish ancestry.

NATURAL HAZARDS: SELECTED STATISTICS

Hurricanes
This list names North America's eight most intense hurricanes (based on barometric pressure) since 1950. Average sea-level pressure is 1,013.25 millibars or 29.92 inches.

1968	Camille	909 mbr/26.84 in
2005	Katrina	920 mbr/27.17 in
1992	Andrew	922 mbr/27.23 in
1960	Donna	930 mbr/27.46 in
1961	Carla	931 mbr/27.49 in
1989	Hugo	934 mbr/27.58 in
2005	Rita	937 mbr/27.67 in
1954	Hazel	938 mbr/27.70 in

Tornadoes
The following states had the highest average annual number of tornadoes from 1953 to 2004.

Texas: 139

Oklahoma: 57

Florida: 55

Kansas: 55

Nebraska: 45

Iowa: 37

Earthquakes
This list shows the number of earthquakes in North America since 1900 that had a magnitude of 8.0 or greater on the Richter scale.

Alaska (U.S.): 6

Mexico: 4

British Columbia (Canada): 1

Dominican Republic: 1

Volcanoes
This list shows major volcanic eruptions in the U.S. since 1980.

Mount St. Helens (WA): 1980–1986

Kilauea (HI): 1983–ongoing

Mauna Loa (HI): 1984

Augustine (AK): 1986

Redoubt (AK): 1989–1990

Natural Hazards

The forces of nature inspire awe. They can also bring damage and destruction, especially when people locate homes and businesses in places that are at risk of experiencing violent storms, earthquakes, volcanoes, floods, wildfires, or other natural hazards. Tornadoes—violent, swirling storms with winds that can exceed 200 miles (300 km) per hour—strike the U.S. more than 800 times each year. Hurricanes, massive low-pressure storms that form over warm ocean waters, bring destructive winds and rain primarily to the Gulf of Mexico and the southeastern mainland. Melting spring snows and heavy rains trigger flooding; periods of drought make other regions vulnerable to wildfires. These and other hazards of nature are not limited to this continent. Natural hazards pose serious threats to lives and property wherever people live.

⇧ VOLCANOES. From deep inside Earth, molten rock, called magma, rises and breaks through the surface, sometimes quietly, but more often violently, shooting billowing ash clouds as shown here at Mount St. Helens, in Washington State.

⇩ WILDFIRES. Putting lives and property at great risk, wildfires destroy millions of acres of forest each year. At the same time, fires help renew ecosystems by removing debris and encouraging seedling growth.

⇨ FLOODS. Towns located along rivers are always at risk of floods. In 2008 residents of Clarksville, Missouri, had to resort to boats as rising waters of the Mississippi River flooded the town.

THE CONTINENT: NORTH AMERICA

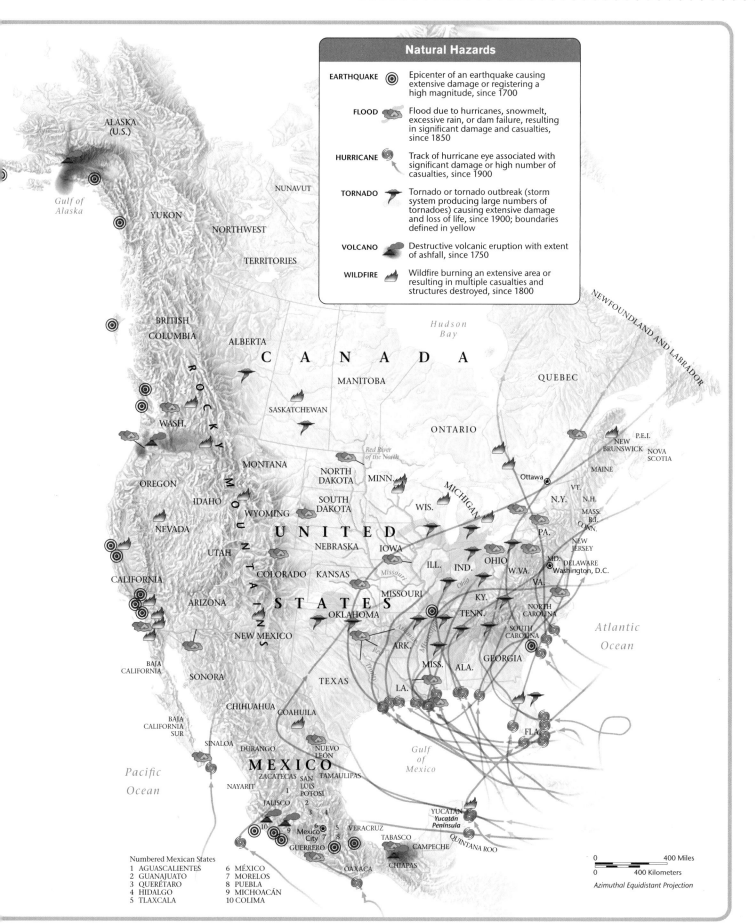

Natural Hazards

EARTHQUAKE — Epicenter of an earthquake causing extensive damage or registering a high magnitude, since 1700

FLOOD — Flood due to hurricanes, snowmelt, excessive rain, or dam failure, resulting in significant damage and casualties, since 1850

HURRICANE — Track of hurricane eye associated with significant damage or high number of casualties, since 1900

TORNADO — Tornado or tornado outbreak (storm system producing large numbers of tornadoes) causing extensive damage and loss of life, since 1900; boundaries defined in yellow

VOLCANO — Destructive volcanic eruption with extent of ashfall, since 1750

WILDFIRE — Wildfire burning an extensive area or resulting in multiple casualties and structures destroyed, since 1800

Numbered Mexican States
1 AGUASCALIENTES
2 GUANAJUATO
3 QUERÉTARO
4 HIDALGO
5 TLAXCALA
6 MÉXICO
7 MORELOS
8 PUEBLA
9 MICHOACÁN
10 COLIMA

0 — 400 Miles
0 — 400 Kilometers

Azimuthal Equidistant Projection

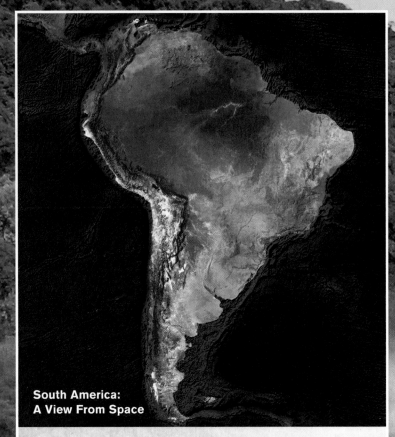

**South America:
A View From Space**

From the towering, snow-capped Andes in the west to the steamy rain forest of the Amazon Basin in the north, and from the fertile grasslands of the Pampas to the arid Atacama Desert along the Pacific coast, South America is a continent of extremes. North to south the continent extends from the tropical waters of the Caribbean Sea to the wind-blown islands of Tierra del Fuego. Its longest river, the Amazon, carries more water than any other river in the world.

A rainbow arches over Iguazu Falls, Argentina.

South America

PHYSICAL			POLITICAL		
Land area 6,880,000 sq mi (17,819,000 sq km)	**Lowest point** Laguna del Carbón, Argentina -344 ft (-105 m)	**Largest lake** Lake Titicaca, Bolivia-Peru 3,200 sq mi (8,290 sq km)	**Population** 381,045,000	**Largest country** Brazil 3,300,169 sq mi (8,547,403 sq km)	**Most populous country** Brazil Pop. 189,335,000
Highest point Cerro Aconcagua, Argentina 22,834 ft (6,960 m)	**Longest river** Amazon 4,000 mi (6,437 km)		**Number of independent countries** 12	**Smallest country** Suriname 63,037 sq mi (163,265 sq km)	**Least populous country** Suriname Pop. 503,000

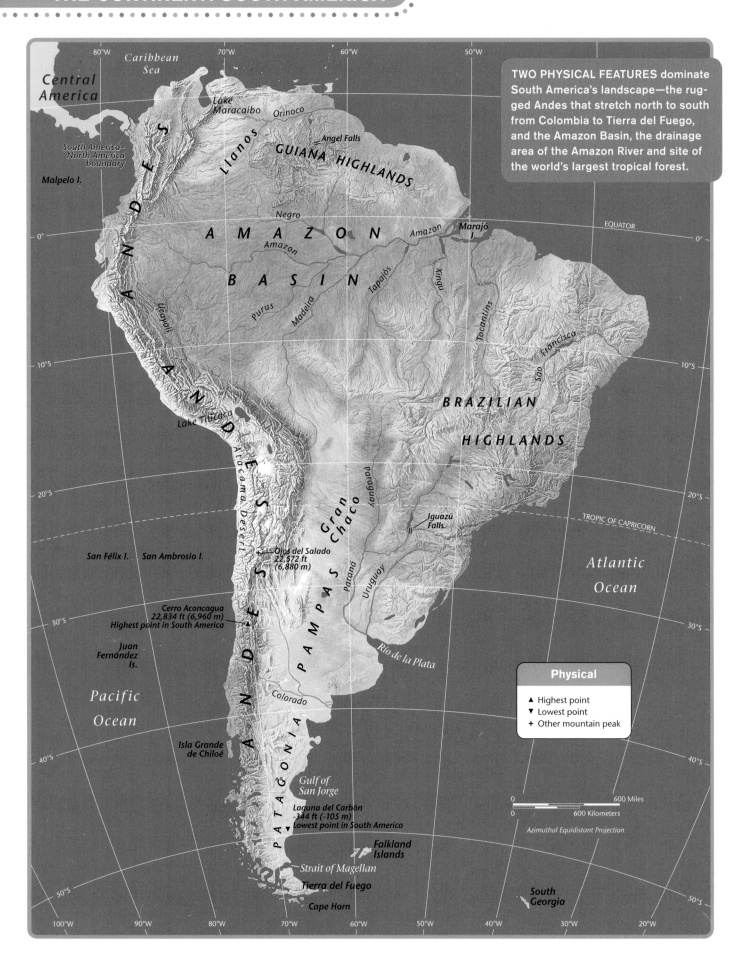

TWO PHYSICAL FEATURES dominate South America's landscape—the rugged Andes that stretch north to south from Colombia to Tierra del Fuego, and the Amazon Basin, the drainage area of the Amazon River and site of the world's largest tropical forest.

Central America

Caribbean Sea

South America–North America boundary

Malpelo I.

Lake Maracaibo

Orinoco

Angel Falls

Llanos

GUIANA HIGHLANDS

EQUATOR

Negro

A M A Z O N

Amazon

Amazon

Marajó I.

B A S I N

Purus

Madeira

Tapajós

Xingu

Tocantins

São Francisco

BRAZILIAN

HIGHLANDS

Ucayali

A N D E S

Lake Titicaca

Atacama Desert

San Félix I.   San Ambrosio I.

+ Ojos del Salado
22,572 ft
(6,880 m)

Gran Chaco

Pilcomayo

Paraguay

Iguazú Falls

TROPIC OF CAPRICORN

Cerro Aconcagua
22,834 ft (6,960 m)
Highest point in South America

PAMPAS

Paraná

Uruguay

Atlantic Ocean

Juan Fernández Is.

Pacific Ocean

Colorado

Río de la Plata

Isla Grande de Chiloé

PATAGONIA

A N D E S

Gulf of San Jorge

Laguna del Carbón
-344 ft (-105 m)
Lowest point in South America

Falkland Islands

Strait of Magellan

Tierra del Fuego

Cape Horn

South Georgia

Physical

▲ Highest point
▼ Lowest point
+ Other mountain peak

0   600 Miles
0   600 Kilometers

Azimuthal Equidistant Projection

THE CONTINENT: SOUTH AMERICA

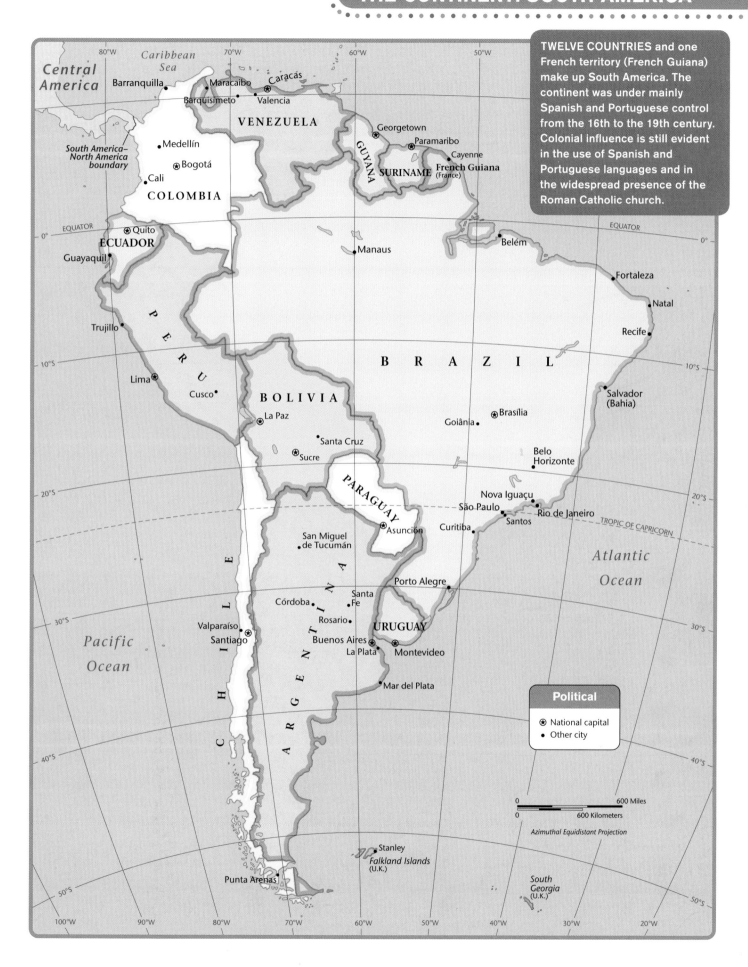

TWELVE COUNTRIES and one French territory (French Guiana) make up South America. The continent was under mainly Spanish and Portuguese control from the 16th to the 19th century. Colonial influence is still evident in the use of Spanish and Portuguese languages and in the widespread presence of the Roman Catholic church.

Central America

Caribbean Sea

Barranquilla
Maracaibo
Caracás
Barquisimeto
Valencia

VENEZUELA

Georgetown
Paramaribo
Cayenne
French Guiana (France)

GUYANA
SURINAME

Medellín
Bogotá
Cali

South America–North America boundary

COLOMBIA

EQUATOR

Quito
ECUADOR
Guayaquil

Manaus

Belém

Fortaleza

Natal

Recife

P E R U

Trujillo

Lima
Cusco

BOLIVIA
La Paz
Santa Cruz
Sucre

B R A Z I L

Salvador (Bahia)

Goiânia
Brasília

Belo Horizonte

PARAGUAY

Asunción

Nova Iguaçu
São Paulo
Rio de Janeiro
Santos
Curitiba

TROPIC OF CAPRICORN

San Miguel de Tucumán

Porto Alegre

Atlantic Ocean

Córdoba
Santa Fe
Rosario

A R G E N T I N A

C H I L E

Valparaíso
Santiago

Buenos Aires
La Plata
URUGUAY
Montevideo

Mar del Plata

Pacific Ocean

Political

⊛ National capital
• Other city

0   600 Miles
0   600 Kilometers

Azimuthal Equidistant Projection

Stanley
Falkland Islands (U.K.)

Punta Arenas

South Georgia (U.K.)

EQUATOR

0°

10°S

20°S

30°S

40°S

50°S

80°W   70°W   60°W   50°W   100°W   90°W   80°W   70°W   60°W   50°W   40°W   30°W   20°W

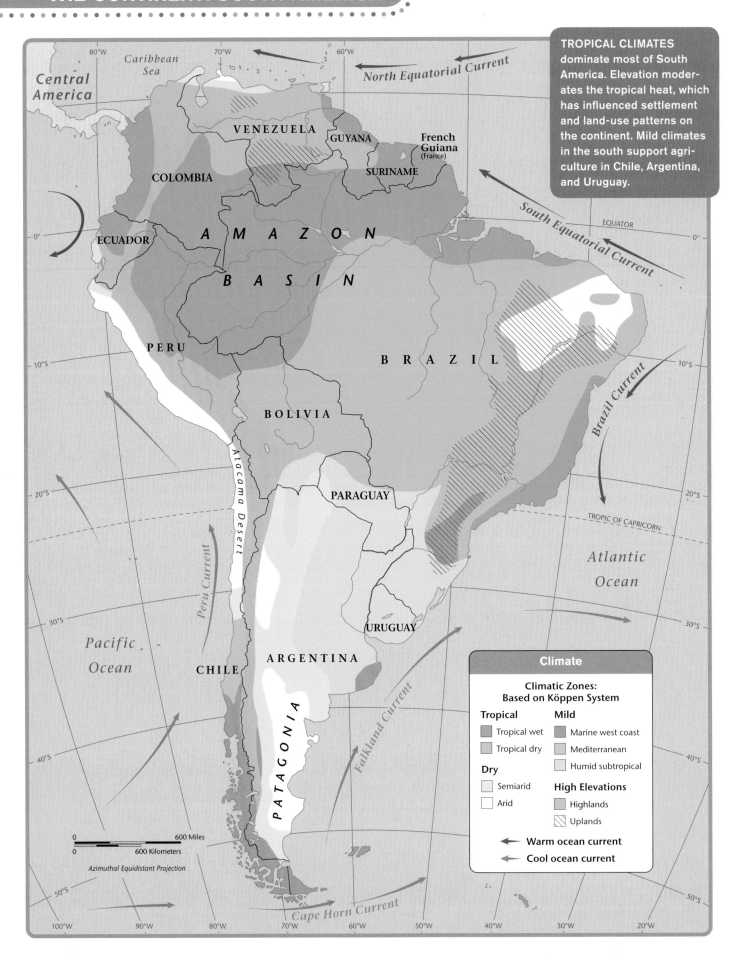

TROPICAL CLIMATES dominate most of South America. Elevation moderates the tropical heat, which has influenced settlement and land-use patterns on the continent. Mild climates in the south support agriculture in Chile, Argentina, and Uruguay.

Caribbean Sea

Central America

North Equatorial Current

VENEZUELA

GUYANA

French Guiana (France)

SURINAME

COLOMBIA

South Equatorial Current

EQUATOR

A M A Z O N

ECUADOR

B A S I N

PERU

BRAZIL

Brazil Current

BOLIVIA

Atacama Desert

Peru Current

PARAGUAY

TROPIC OF CAPRICORN

Atlantic Ocean

URUGUAY

Pacific Ocean

CHILE

ARGENTINA

P A T A G O N I A

Falkland Current

0   600 Miles
0   600 Kilometers

Azimuthal Equidistant Projection

Cape Horn Current

Climate

Climatic Zones: Based on Köppen System

Tropical
- Tropical wet
- Tropical dry

Dry
- Semiarid
- Arid

Mild
- Marine west coast
- Mediterranean
- Humid subtropical

High Elevations
- Highlands
- Uplands

← Warm ocean current
← Cool ocean current

THE CONTINENT: SOUTH AMERICA

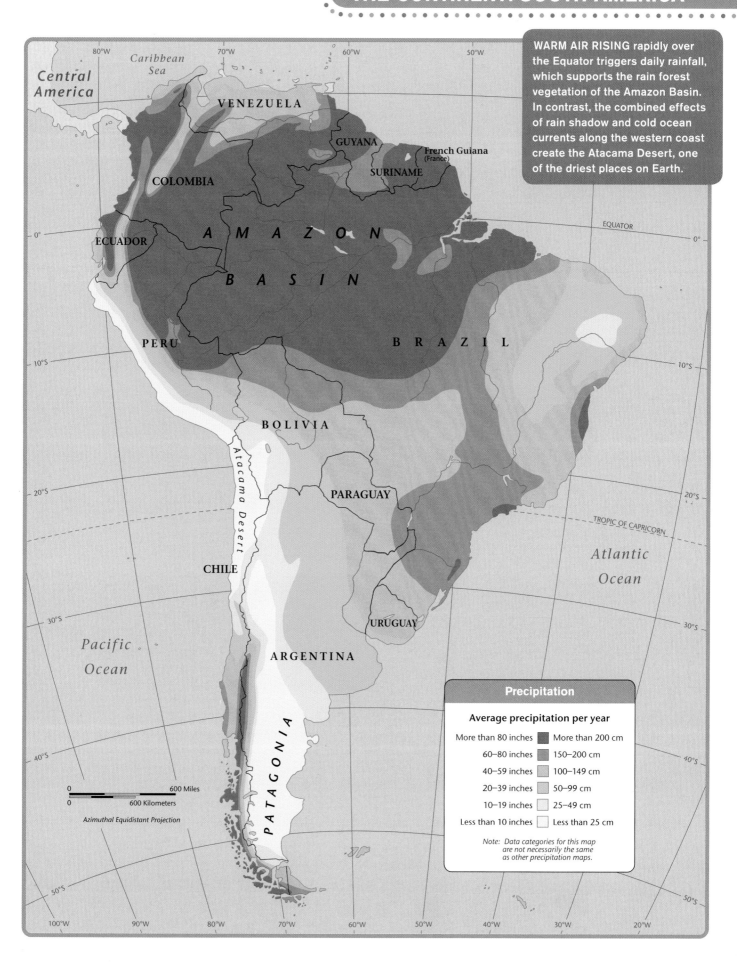

WARM AIR RISING rapidly over the Equator triggers daily rainfall, which supports the rain forest vegetation of the Amazon Basin. In contrast, the combined effects of rain shadow and cold ocean currents along the western coast create the Atacama Desert, one of the driest places on Earth.

Central America

Caribbean Sea

VENEZUELA

COLOMBIA

GUYANA

French Guiana (France)

SURINAME

ECUADOR

EQUATOR

A M A Z O N

B A S I N

PERU

B R A Z I L

BOLIVIA

PARAGUAY

TROPIC OF CAPRICORN

Atacama Desert

CHILE

Atlantic Ocean

URUGUAY

Pacific Ocean

ARGENTINA

P A T A G O N I A

0   600 Miles
0   600 Kilometers

Azimuthal Equidistant Projection

Precipitation

Average precipitation per year

More than 80 inches	■	More than 200 cm
60–80 inches	■	150–200 cm
40–59 inches	■	100–149 cm
20–39 inches	■	50–99 cm
10–19 inches	□	25–49 cm
Less than 10 inches	□	Less than 25 cm

Note: Data categories for this map are not necessarily the same as other precipitation maps.

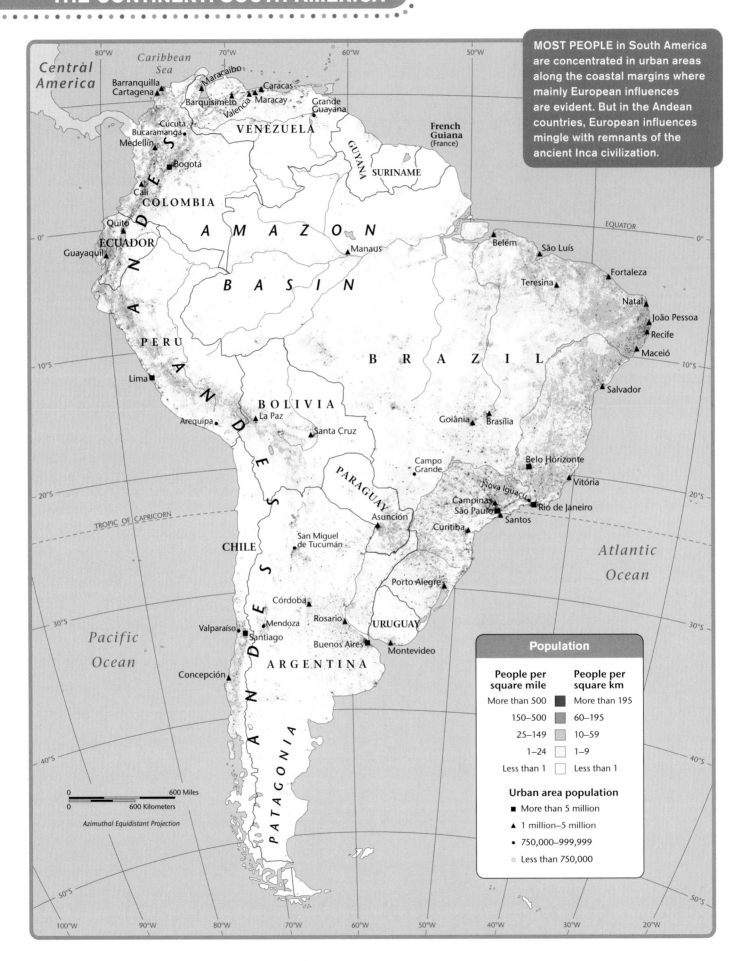

MOST PEOPLE in South America are concentrated in urban areas along the coastal margins where mainly European influences are evident. But in the Andean countries, European influences mingle with remnants of the ancient Inca civilization.

Population

People per square mile	People per square km
More than 500	More than 195
150–500	60–195
25–149	10–59
1–24	1–9
Less than 1	Less than 1

Urban area population

- More than 5 million
- 1 million–5 million
- 750,000–999,999
- Less than 750,000

Azimuthal Equidistant Projection

600 Miles
600 Kilometers

THE CONTINENT: SOUTH AMERICA

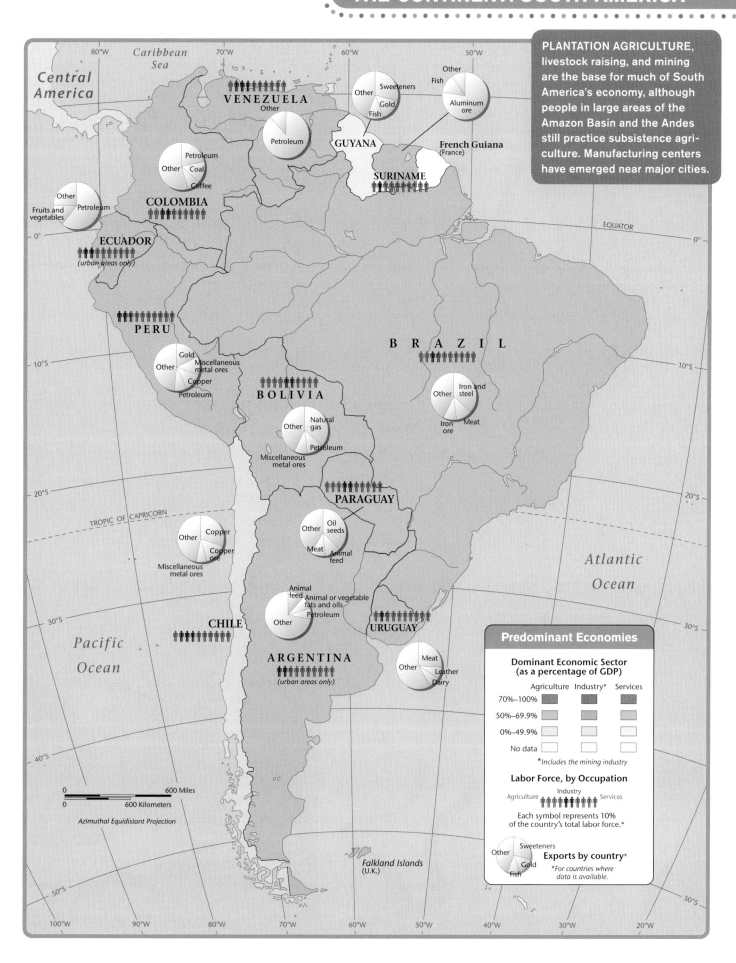

PLANTATION AGRICULTURE, livestock raising, and mining are the base for much of South America's economy, although people in large areas of the Amazon Basin and the Andes still practice subsistence agriculture. Manufacturing centers have emerged near major cities.

Caribbean Sea

Central America

VENEZUELA
Other
Petroleum

GUYANA
Other
Sweeteners
Gold
Fish

French Guiana (France)

SURINAME
Other
Fish
Aluminum ore

COLOMBIA
Petroleum
Other
Coal
Coffee

ECUADOR
(urban areas only)
Other
Fruits and vegetables
Petroleum

EQUATOR

0°

PERU
Gold
Other
Miscellaneous metal ores
Copper
Petroleum

BOLIVIA
Other
Natural gas
Petroleum
Miscellaneous metal ores

BRAZIL
Other
Iron and steel
Iron ore
Meat

10°S

PARAGUAY
Other
Oil seeds
Meat
Animal feed

CHILE
Other
Copper
Copper ore
Miscellaneous metal ores

TROPIC OF CAPRICORN

20°S

URUGUAY
Other
Meat
Leather
Dairy

Atlantic Ocean

ARGENTINA
(urban areas only)
Animal feed
Animal or vegetable fats and oils
Petroleum
Other

30°S

Pacific Ocean

0 — 600 Miles
0 — 600 Kilometers

Azimuthal Equidistant Projection

40°S

Falkland Islands (U.K.)

50°S

Predominant Economies

Dominant Economic Sector
(as a percentage of GDP)

	Agriculture	Industry*	Services
70%–100%			
50%–69.9%			
0%–49.9%			
No data			

*Includes the mining industry

Labor Force, by Occupation

Agriculture — Industry — Services

Each symbol represents 10% of the country's total labor force.*

Exports by country*
Other
Sweeteners
Gold
Fish

*For countries where data is available.

Amazon Rain Forest

The Amazon rain forest, which covers approximately 2.7 million square miles (7 million sq km), is the world's largest tropical forest. Located mainly in Brazil, the Amazon rain forest accounts for more than 20 percent of all the world's tropical forests. Known in Brazil as the selva, the rain forest is a vast storehouse of biological diversity, filled with plants and animals both familiar and exotic. According to estimates, at least half of all species are found in tropical forests, but many of these species have not yet been identified.

Tropical forests contain many valuable resources, including cacao (chocolate), nuts, spices, rare hardwoods, and plant extracts used to make medicines. Some drugs used in treating cancer and heart disease come from plants found only in tropical forests. But human intervention—logging, mining, and clearing land for crops and grazing—has put tropical forests at great risk. In Brazil, roads cut into the rain forest have opened the way for settlers, who clear away the forest only to discover soil too poor in nutrients to sustain agriculture for more than a few years. Land usually is cleared by a method called slash-and-burn, which contributes to global warming by releasing great amounts of carbon dioxide into the atmosphere.

TROPICAL RAIN FORESTS: FACTS & FIGURES

- Tropical rain forests cover 6 percent of Earth's surface, but are home to half of Earth's species.
- Average monthly temperature is 68° to 82°F (20° to 28°C).
- Total annual rainfall averages 5 to 33 feet (1.5 to 10 m).
- Trees in tropical rain forests can grow up to 200 feet (60 m) in height.
- Most nutrients in tropical rain forests are stored in the vegetation rather than in the soil, which is very poor.
- Some of Earth's most valuable woods, such as teak, mahogany, rosewood, and sandalwood, grow in tropical rain forests.
- Up to 25 percent of all medicines include products originating in tropical rain forests.
- Tropical rain forests absorb carbon dioxide and release oxygen.
- Deforestation of tropical rain forests contributes to climate change.
- An estimated 100 acres (40 ha) of rain forest are lost every minute.
- Brazil loses 10.6 million acres (4.3 million ha) of tropical forests annually, but Nigeria, in Africa, has the highest rate of deforestation—more than 11 percent annually.

⇧ SLOW-MOVING, this three-toed sloth spends most of its life in the treetops. It is one of the many unusual species of animals that make their homes in the forests of the Amazon Basin.

⇩ DENSE CANOPY OF THE RAIN FOREST stands in sharp contrast to the silt-laden waters of one of the Amazon's many tributaries. Although seemingly endless, the forest in Brazil is decreasing in size at the rate of almost 15,000 acres (6,070 ha) per day.

⇩ SLASH-AND-BURN is a method used in the tropics for clearing land for farms. But the soil is poor in nutrients, and good yields are short-lived.

THE CONTINENT: SOUTH AMERICA

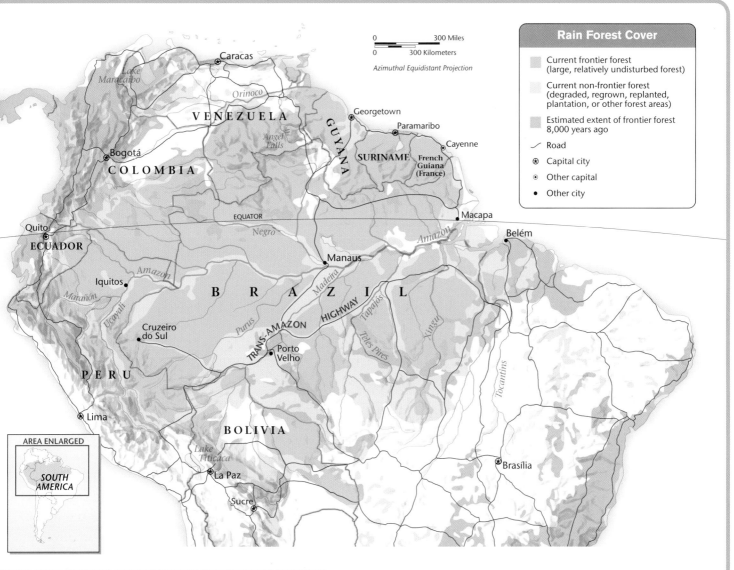

0 — 300 Miles
0 — 300 Kilometers
Azimuthal Equidistant Projection

Rain Forest Cover

- Current frontier forest (large, relatively undisturbed forest)
- Current non-frontier forest (degraded, regrown, replanted, plantation, or other forest areas)
- Estimated extent of frontier forest 8,000 years ago
- ╱ Road
- ⊛ Capital city
- ⊙ Other capital
- • Other city

Caracas

Lake Maracaibo

Orinoco

VENEZUELA

Angel Falls

GUYANA

Georgetown

Paramaribo

Cayenne

SURINAME

French Guiana (France)

Bogotá

COLOMBIA

EQUATOR

Macapa

Quito

Negro

Amazon

Belém

ECUADOR

Manaus

Amazon

Iquitos

B R A Z I L

Madeira

Marañón

Purus

TRANS-AMAZON HIGHWAY

Tapajós

Teles Pires

Xingu

Tocantins

Ucayali

Cruzeiro do Sul

Porto Velho

P E R U

Lima

AREA ENLARGED

SOUTH AMERICA

BOLIVIA

Lake Titicaca

Brasília

La Paz

Sucre

⇐ MINING OPERATIONS, such as this tin mine, remove forests to gain access to mineral deposits.

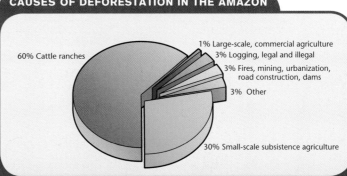

CAUSES OF DEFORESTATION IN THE AMAZON

60% Cattle ranches

1% Large-scale, commercial agriculture
3% Logging, legal and illegal
3% Fires, mining, urbanization, road construction, dams
3% Other

30% Small-scale subsistence agriculture

Human activity, especially clearing forests to open up land for cattle ranches and subsistence farms, has resulted in serious loss of this valuable ecosystem.

Europe:
A View From Space

Smaller than every other continent except Australia, Europe is a mosaic of islands and peninsulas. In fact, Europe itself is one big peninsula, jutting westward from the huge landmass of Asia and nearly touching Africa to the south. Europe's ragged coastline measures more than one and a half times the length of the Equator—38,279 miles (61,603 km) to be exact—giving 32 of its 46 countries direct access to the sea.

Hallstatt, Austria in the morning light

THE CONTINENT: EUROPE

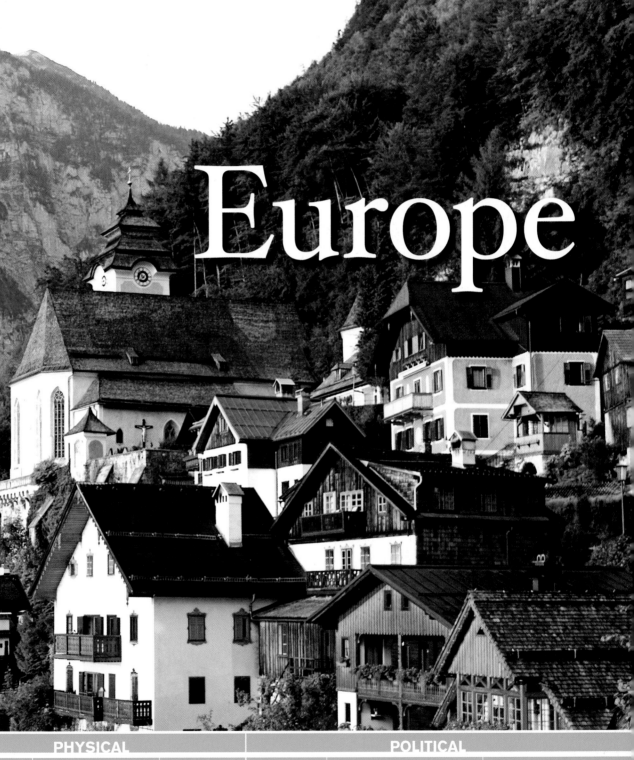

Europe

PHYSICAL			POLITICAL		
Land area 3,841,000 sq mi (9,947,000 sq km)	Lowest point Caspian Sea -92 ft (-28 m)	Largest lake entirely in Europe Ladoga, Russia 6,853 sq mi (17,703 sq km)	Population 732,552,000	Largest country entirely in Europe Ukraine 233,090 sq mi (603,700 sq km)	Most populous country entirely in Europe Germany Pop. 82,254,000
Highest point El'brus, Russia 18,510 ft (5,642 m)	Longest river Volga, Russia 2,290 mi (3,685 km)		Number of independent countries 46	Smallest country Vatican City 0.2 sq mi (0.4 sq km)	Least populous country Vatican City Pop. 798

THE CONTINENT: EUROPE

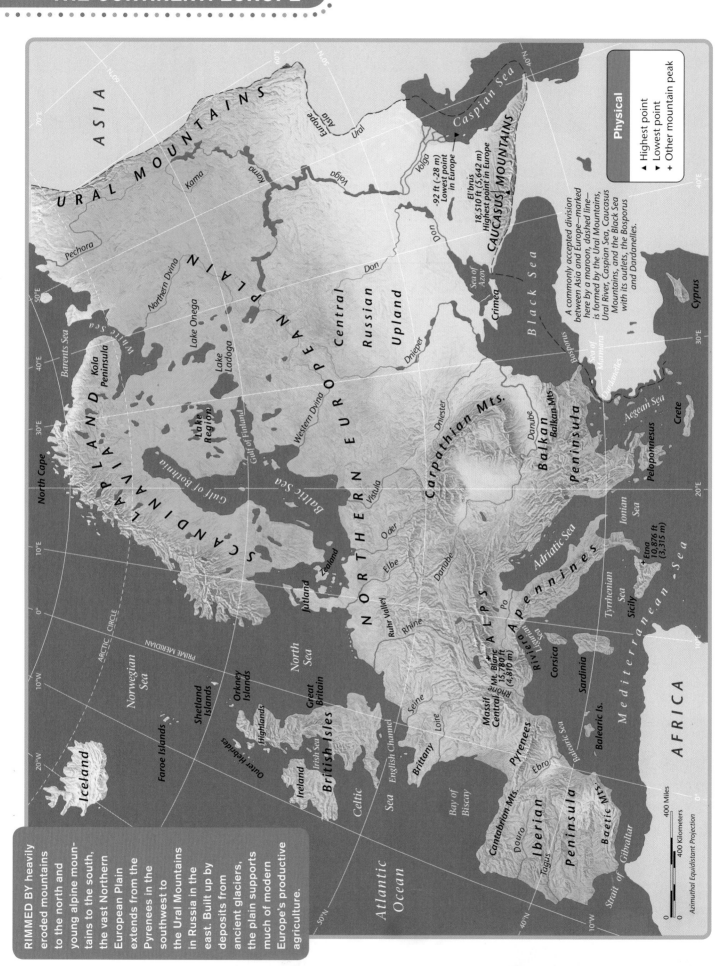

A S I A

U R A L   M O U N T A I N S

Europe
Asia

Ural

Kama

Kama

Pechora

Northern Dvina

Barents Sea

White Sea

North Cape

Kola Peninsula

L A P L A N D

Lake Onega

Lake Ladoga

Lake Region

Gulf of Bothnia

Gulf of Finland

Western Dvina

S C A N D I N A V I A N

N O R T H E R N   E U R O P E A N   P L A I N

Central Russian Upland

Dnieper

Don

Don

Volga

Volga

-92 ft (-28 m)
Lowest point in Europe

El'brus
18,510 ft (5,642 m)
Highest point in Europe

CAUCASUS MOUNTAINS

Caspian Sea

Sea of Azov

Crimea

Black Sea

Bosporus

Sea of Marmara

Dardanelles

A commonly accepted division between Asia and Europe—marked here by a maroon, dashed line—is formed by the Ural Mountains, Ural River, Caspian Sea, Caucasus Mountains, and the Black Sea with its outlets, the Bosporus and Dardanelles.

Cyprus

Aegean Sea

Crete

Peloponnesus

Ionian Sea

Balkan Peninsula

Balkan Mts.

Carpathian Mts.

Dniester

Danube

Danube

Vistula

Oder

Elbe

Rhine

Ruhr Valley

Zealand

Jutland

Baltic Sea

North Sea

Great Britain

British Isles

Highlands

Outer Hebrides

Ireland

Irish Sea

Celtic Sea

English Channel

Brittany

Seine

Loire

Bay of Biscay

Orkney Islands

Shetland Islands

Faroe Islands

Iceland

Norwegian Sea

Atlantic Ocean

ARCTIC CIRCLE

PRIME MERIDIAN

A L P S

Mt. Blanc
15,780 ft
(4,810 m)

Massif Central

Rhône

Riviera

Po

Apennines

+ Etna
10,876 ft
(3,315 m)

Adriatic Sea

Tyrrhenian Sea

Corsica

Sardinia

Sicily

Ionian

M e d i t e r r a n e a n   S e a

Balearic Is.

Balearic Sea

Pyrenees

Cantabrian Mts.

Douro

Tagus

Ebro

Iberian Peninsula

Baetic Mts.

Strait of Gibraltar

A F R I C A

Physical
▲ Highest point
▼ Lowest point
+ Other mountain peak

400 Miles
400 Kilometers
Azimuthal Equidistant Projection

RIMMED BY heavily eroded mountains to the north and young alpine mountains to the south, the vast Northern European Plain extends from the Pyrenees in the southwest to the Ural Mountains in Russia in the east. Built up by deposits from ancient glaciers, the plain supports much of modern Europe's productive agriculture.

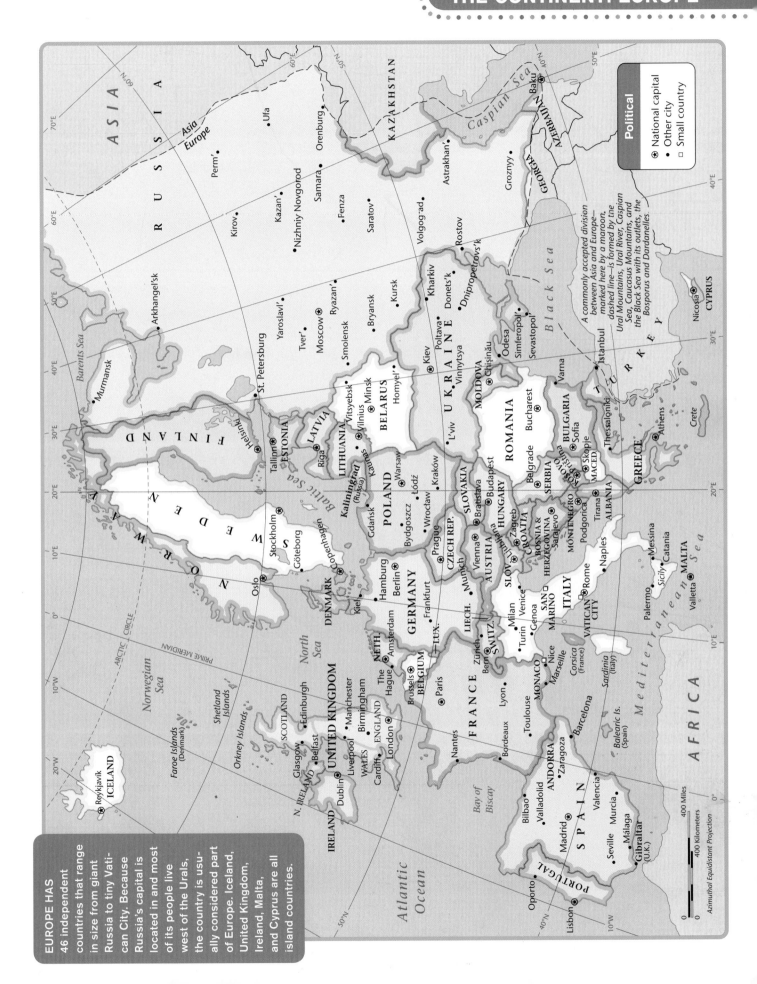

THE CONTINENT: EUROPE

Political
- ⊛ National capital
- • Other city
- □ Small country

A commonly accepted division between Asia and Europe—marked here by a maroon, dashed line—is formed by the Ural Mountains, Ural River, Caspian Sea, Caucasus Mountains, and the Black Sea with its outlets, the Bosporus and Dardanelles.

EUROPE HAS 46 independent countries that range in size from giant Russia to tiny Vatican City. Because Russia's capital is located in and most of its people live west of the Urals, the country is usually considered part of Europe. Iceland, United Kingdom, Ireland, Malta, and Cyprus are all island countries.

Azimuthal Equidistant Projection

400 Miles
400 Kilometers

THE CONTINENT: EUROPE

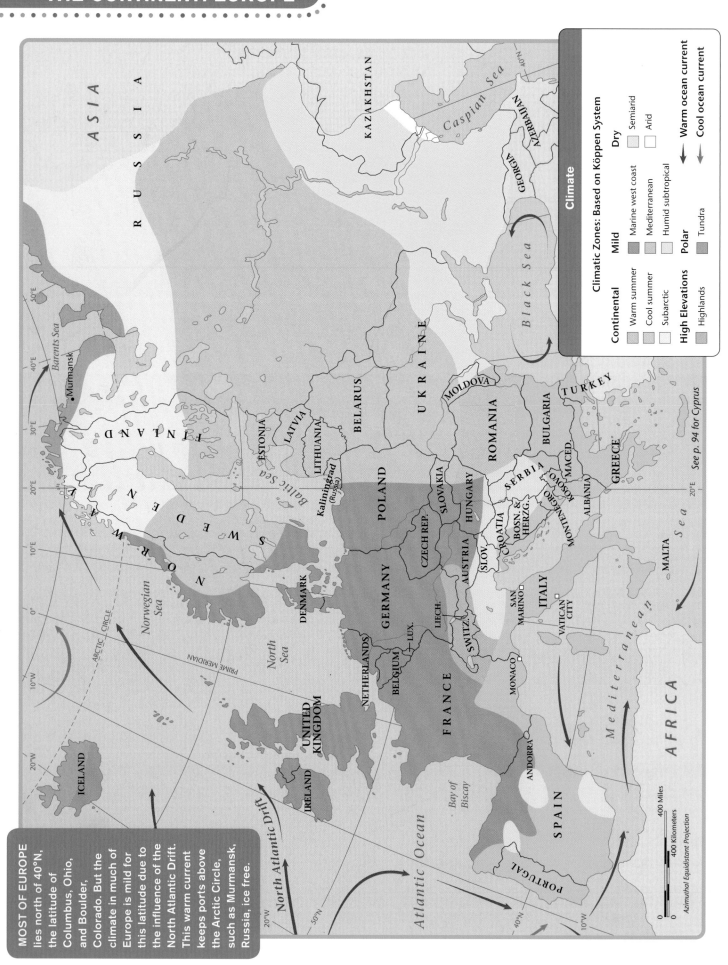

MOST OF EUROPE lies north of 40°N, the latitude of Columbus, Ohio, and Boulder, Colorado. But the climate in much of Europe is mild for this latitude due to the influence of the North Atlantic Drift. This warm current keeps ports above the Arctic Circle, such as Murmansk, Russia, ice free.

Climate

Climatic Zones: Based on Köppen System

Continental
- Warm summer
- Cool summer
- Subarctic

Mild
- Marine west coast
- Mediterranean
- Humid subtropical

Dry
- Semiarid
- Arid

Polar
- Tundra

High Elevations
- Highlands

→ Warm ocean current
→ Cool ocean current

See p. 94 for Cyprus

400 Miles
400 Kilometers

Azimuthal Equidistant Projection

THE CONTINENT: EUROPE

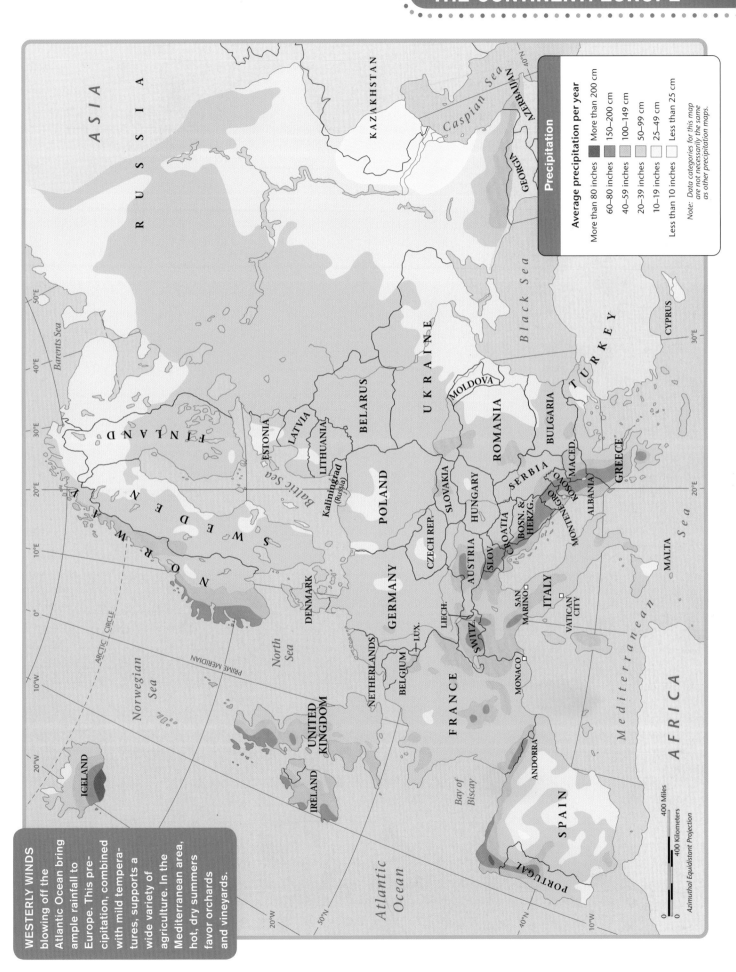

Precipitation

Average precipitation per year

More than 80 inches	More than 200 cm
60–80 inches	150–200 cm
40–59 inches	100–149 cm
20–39 inches	50–99 cm
10–19 inches	25–49 cm
Less than 10 inches	Less than 25 cm

Note: Data categories for this map are not necessarily the same as other precipitation maps.

WESTERLY WINDS blowing off the Atlantic Ocean bring ample rainfall to Europe. This precipitation, combined with mild temperatures, supports a wide variety of agriculture. In the Mediterranean area, hot, dry summers favor orchards and vineyards.

ASIA

RUSSIA

KAZAKHSTAN

Caspian Sea

AZERBAIJAN

GEORGIA

Barents Sea

Black Sea

TURKEY

CYPRUS

FINLAND

UKRAINE

MOLDOVA

ROMANIA

BULGARIA

MACED.

GREECE

ESTONIA

LATVIA

LITHUANIA

BELARUS

Baltic Sea

Kaliningrad (Russia)

POLAND

SLOVAKIA

HUNGARY

SERBIA

KOSOVO

ALBANIA

NORWAY

SWEDEN

CZECH REP.

AUSTRIA

SLOV.

CROATIA

BOSN. & HERZ.

MONTENEGRO

DENMARK

GERMANY

LIECH.

SWITZ.

SAN MARINO

ITALY

VATICAN CITY

MALTA

Mediterranean Sea

North Sea

Norwegian Sea

NETHERLANDS

BELGIUM

LUX.

FRANCE

MONACO

AFRICA

ARCTIC CIRCLE

PRIME MERIDIAN

ICELAND

UNITED KINGDOM

IRELAND

Bay of Biscay

ANDORRA

SPAIN

PORTUGAL

Atlantic Ocean

400 Miles

400 Kilometers

Azimuthal Equidistant Projection

40°E 30°E 20°E 10°E 0° 10°W 20°W

70°N 50°N 40°N

30°E 20°E 10°E

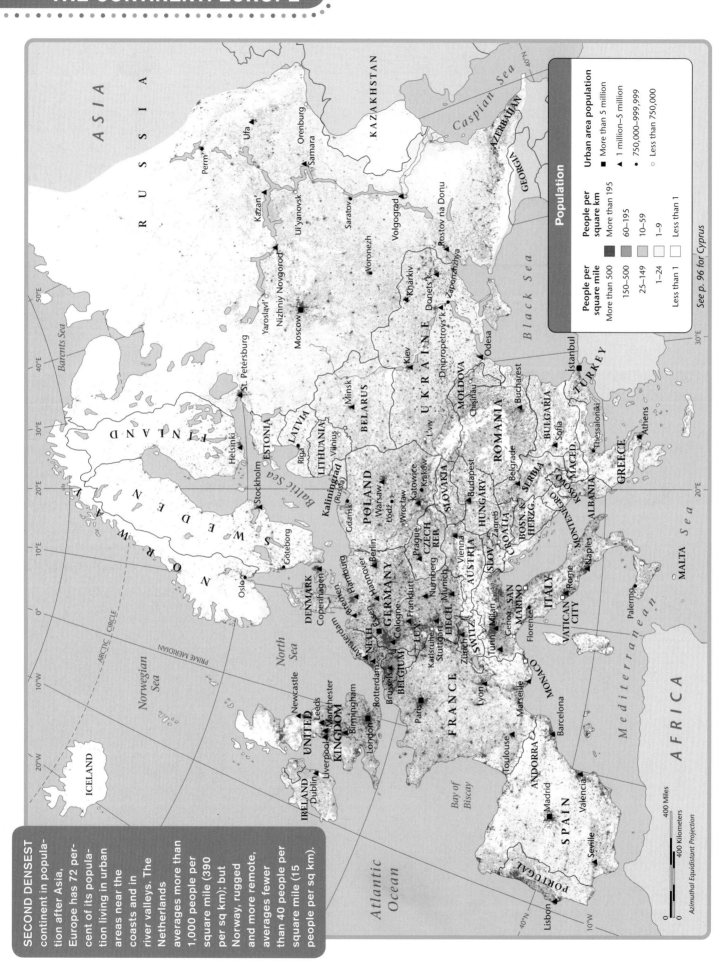

SECOND DENSEST continent in population after Asia, Europe has 72 percent of its population living in urban areas near the coasts and in river valleys. The Netherlands averages more than 1,000 people per square mile (390 per sq km); but Norway, rugged and more remote, averages fewer than 40 people per square mile (15 people per sq km).

Population

People per square mile
- More than 500
- 150–500
- 25–149
- 1–24
- Less than 1

People per square km
- More than 195
- 60–195
- 10–59
- 1–9
- Less than 1

Urban area population
- ■ More than 5 million
- ▲ 1 million–5 million
- • 750,000–999,999
- ○ Less than 750,000

See p. 96 for Cyprus

Azimuthal Equidistant Projection

0 400 Miles
0 400 Kilometers

THE CONTINENT: EUROPE

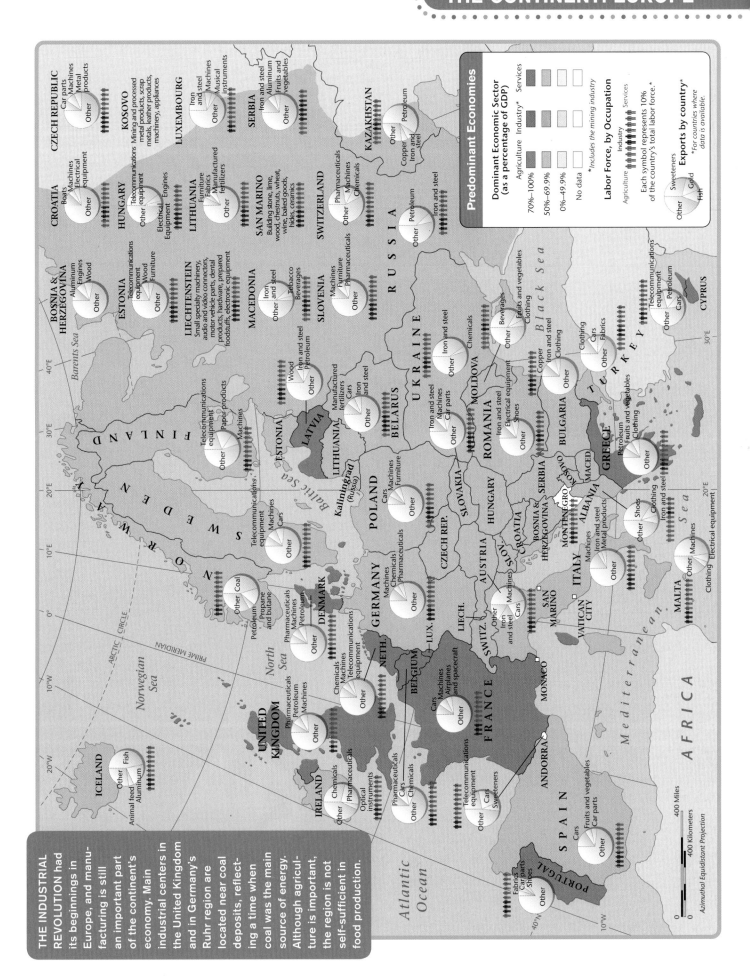

THE INDUSTRIAL REVOLUTION had its beginnings in Europe, and manufacturing is still an important part of the continent's economy. Main industrial centers in the United Kingdom and in Germany's Ruhr region are located near coal deposits, reflecting a time when coal was the main source of energy. Although agriculture is important, the region is not self-sufficient in food production.

European Union

In the years following World War II, the countries of Europe looked for ways to restore political stability to the continent while rebuilding their war-ravaged economies. The first step toward the European Union was taken in 1950 when France proposed creating common institutions to jointly govern coal and steel production in Europe. In 1951 France, West Germany, Italy, Belgium, Netherlands, and Luxembourg created the European Coal and Steel Community with the goal of bringing former adversaries together. In 1957 the Treaty of Rome established the European Economic Community (EEC), which removed trade barriers among member countries. In 1965 that organization joined with other countries of Europe to form the European Community (EC).

The Maastricht Treaty, signed in 1992 and effective in 1993, established today's European Union (EU) and paved the way for a common foreign policy and a single European currency—the euro. The euro now circulates in 12 member countries and will expand to others as strict economic and financial standards are met. The treaty also established the groundwork for the open flow of people, products, and services among member countries. In 1995 three more countries joined the EU, bringing the membership to 15. But in May 2004, the EU almost doubled in size with the admission of 10 countries to membership: Estonia, Latvia, Lithuania, Poland, Czech Republic, Slovakia, Hungary, Cyprus, Slovenia, and Malta. In 2007 the addition of Bulgaria and Romania raised membership to 27 countries. Three additional countries—Croatia, the former Yugoslav Republic of Macedonia, and Turkey—have applied for membership.

⇑ EUROPEAN UNION LEADERS hold a press conference at European Council headquarters in Brussels, Belgium. The Council, made up of ministers from member states, is the main decision-making body of the European Union. It passes laws, sets economic policies, and enters into international agreements between the European Union and non-EU countries.

THE CONTINENT: EUROPE

ASIA

ICELAND

Norwegian Sea

Faroe Islands (Denmark)

Shetland Islands

Orkney Islands

N O R W A Y

S W E D E N

F I N L A N D
1995

Atlantic Ocean

European Union

Member country
Newly admitted country
Candidate country
Other European country
1957 Year of admission

ESTONIA 2004

LATVIA 2004

Baltic Sea

LITHUANIA 2004

Kaliningrad (Russia)

R U S S I A

North Sea

1995

DENMARK 1973

BELARUS

KAZAKHSTAN

UNITED KINGDOM 1973

IRELAND 1973

NETHERLANDS 1957

BELGIUM 1957

LUXEMBOURG 1957

GERMANY (WEST) 1957 (EAST) 1990

POLAND 2004

U K R A I N E

CZECH REP. 2004

LIECH.

SLOVAKIA 2004

MOLDOVA

Bay of Biscay

F R A N C E 1957

SWITZ.

AUSTRIA 1995

HUNGARY 2004

SLOVENIA 2004

CROATIA

ROMANIA 2007

Europe Asia

Black Sea

GEORGIA

PORTUGAL 1986

S P A I N 1986

ANDORRA

MONACO

SAN MARINO

BOSN. & HERZG.

SERBIA

MONT.

KOS.

BULGARIA 2007

T U R K E Y

A S I A

Corsica (France)

VATICAN CITY

ITALY 1957

MACED.

ALBANIA

Gibraltar (U.K.)

Sardinia (Italy)

Balearic Is. (Spain)

Mediterranean Sea

GREECE 1981

Sicily

Crete

A F R I C A

MALTA 2004

CYPRUS 2004

Asia Africa

0   400 Miles
0   400 Kilometers
Azimuthal Equidistant Projection

EU IN THE GLOBAL ECONOMY

With a total population of almost 500 million, the European Union (EU) is a major player in the global economy. The EU leads all countries in total exports and is surpassed only by the United States in imports. More than one-fifth of the EU's exports go to the United States, while its leading import partners are China, the United States, and Russia. The EU's main exports include machinery, motor vehicles, airplanes, plastics, chemicals, and pharmaceuticals.

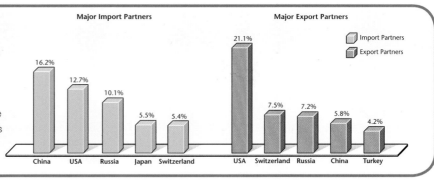

Major Import Partners

Import Partners
Export Partners

China 16.2%
USA 12.7%
Russia 10.1%
Japan 5.5%
Switzerland 5.4%

Major Export Partners

USA 21.1%
Switzerland 7.5%
Russia 7.2%
China 5.8%
Turkey 4.2%

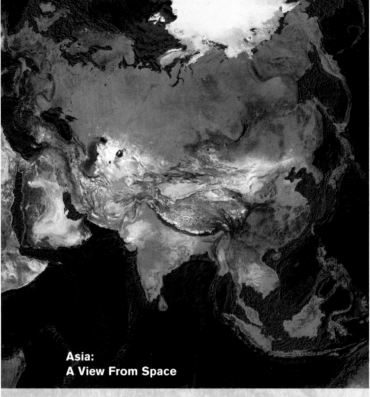

Asia:
A View From Space

From the frozen shores of the Arctic Ocean to the equatorial islands of Indonesia, Asia stretches across 90 degrees of latitude. From the Ural Mountains to the Pacific Ocean it covers more than 150 degrees of longitude. Here, three of history's great culture hearths emerged in the valleys of the Tigris and Euphrates, the Indus, and the Yellow (Huang) Rivers. Today, Asia is home to more than 60 percent of Earth's people and some of the world's fastest growing economies.

Terraced rice fields on Bali, Indonesia

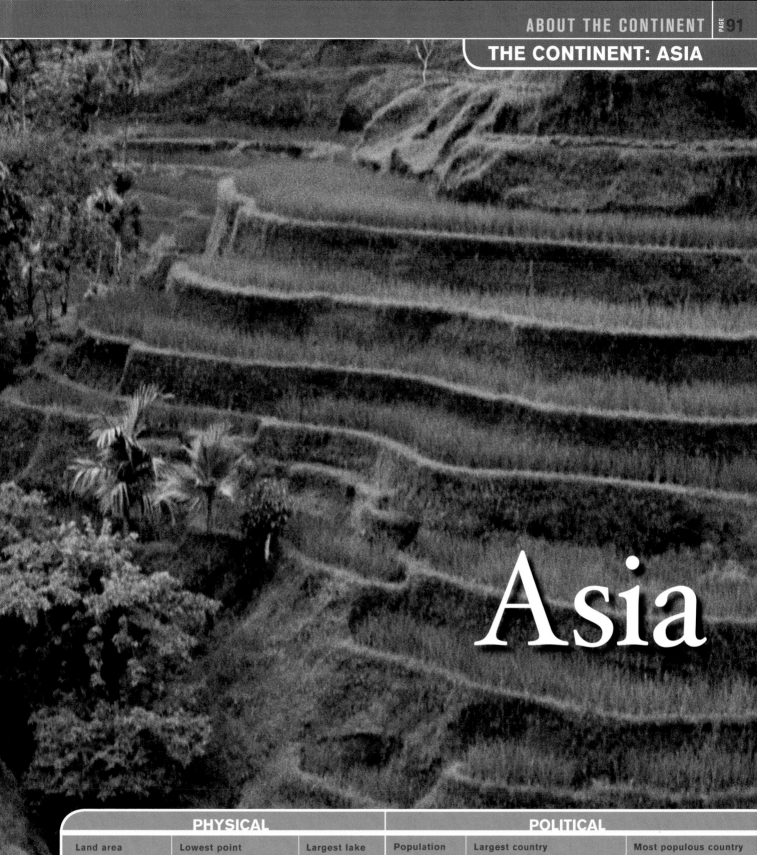

THE CONTINENT: ASIA

Asia

PHYSICAL			POLITICAL		
Land area 17,208,000 sq mi (44,570,000 sq km)	Lowest point Dead Sea, Israel-Jordan -1,380 ft (-421 m)	Largest lake entirely in Asia Lake Baikal 12,200 sq mi (31,500 sq km)	Population 4,009,521,000	Largest country entirely in Asia China 3,705,405 sq mi (9,596,960 sq km)	Most populous country China Pop. 1,348,317,000
Highest point Mount Everest, China-Nepal 29,035 ft (8,850 m)	Longest river Yangtze (Chang), China 3,964 mi (6,380 km)		Number of independent countries 46 (excluding Russia)	Smallest country Maldives 115 sq mi (298 sq km)	Least populous country Maldives Pop. 304,000

THE CONTINENT: ASIA

ASIA'S PHYSICAL characteristics are impressive. It boasts the world's highest peak (Mount Everest), the deepest lake (Lake Baikal), and 30 percent of Earth's land area. Diversity also marks the Asian landscape, from the dry deserts of the Arabian Peninsula to the frozen tundra of Siberia to steamy rain forests in Borneo.

A commonly accepted division between Asia and Europe—marked here by a maroon, dashed line—is formed by the Ural Mountains, Ural River, Caspian Sea, Caucasus Mountains, and the Black Sea with its outlets, the Bosporus and Dardanelles.

Physical

▲ Highest point
▼ Lowest point
+ Other mountain peak

AUSTRALIA

New Guinea

Moluccas

INDONESIA

Celebes (Sulawesi)

Borneo

Java

Java Sea

Sumatra

Arafura Sea

Philippine Islands

Mindanao

Luzon

Taiwan

Ryukyu Islands

Pacific Ocean

East China Sea

South China Sea

Hainan

Malay Peninsula

Indochina Peninsula

Mekong

Salween

Andaman Sea

Andaman Is.

Nicobar Is.

Bay of Bengal

Sri Lanka

Maldive Islands

Deccan Plateau

Indian Ocean

Arabian Sea

Socotra

Gulf of Aden

Gulf of Oman

Persian Gulf

Arabian Peninsula

Red Sea

AFRICA

Zagros Mountains

▼ Dead Sea -1,380 ft (-421 m) Lowest point in Asia

Tigris

Euphrates

Asia-Africa boundary

Asia Minor

Black Sea

Mediterranean Sea

EUROPE

Caspian Sea

Europe Asia

Aral Sea

The Steppes

Amu Darya

Syr Darya

Ural Mountains

West Siberian Plain

Ob

Irtysh

Yenisey

Angara

Lena

Central Siberian Plateau

Verkhoyansk Range

Taymyr Peninsula

Laptev Sea

Kara Sea

Arctic Ocean

North Pole

East Siberian Sea

Chukchi Peninsula

Kamchatka Peninsula

Kuril Islands

Sea of Okhotsk

Sakhalin

Hokkaido

Honshu

JAPAN

Sea of Japan (East Sea)

Amur

Lake Baikal -5,371 ft (-1,637 m) World's deepest lake

Mongolian Plateau

Gobi

Altay Mountains

Tian Shan

+ K2 (Godwin Austen) 28,250 ft (8,611 m)

Kunlun Mountains

Plateau of Tibet

HIMALAYA

Hindu Kush

Indus

Ganges

Brahmaputra

▲ Mt. Everest 29,035 ft (8,850 m) World's highest point

Great Indian Desert

North China Plain

Yellow Sea

Huang (Yellow)

Yangtze (Chang)

TROPIC OF CANCER

EQUATOR

800 Miles
800 Kilometers
0

Two-point Equidistant Projection

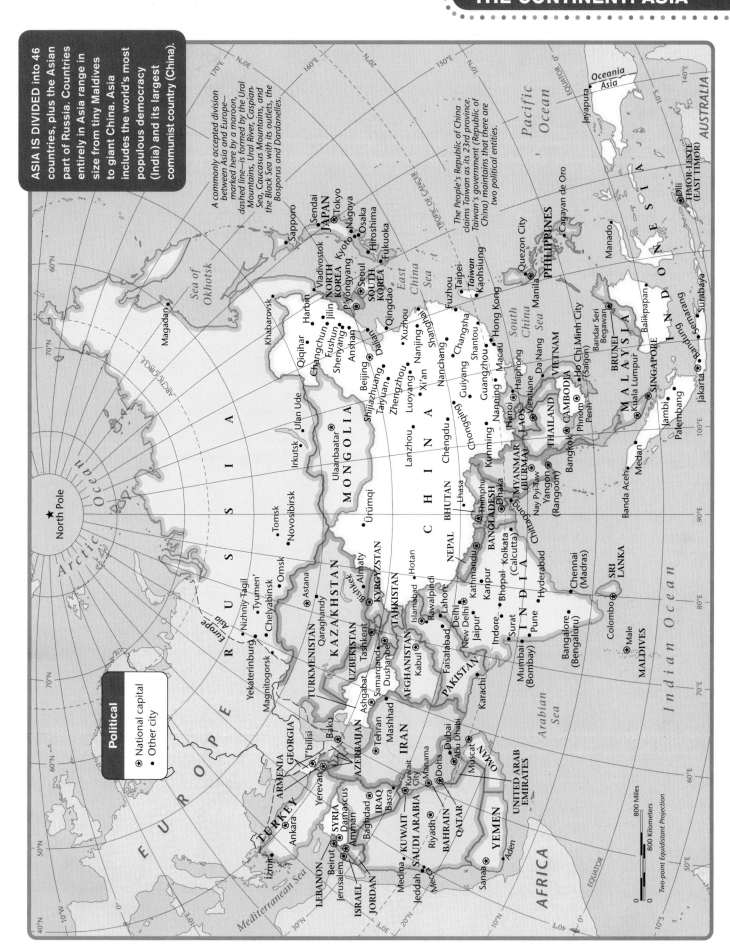

ASIA IS DIVIDED into 46 countries, plus the Asian part of Russia. Countries entirely in Asia range in size from tiny Maldives to giant China. Asia includes the world's most populous democracy (India) and its largest communist country (China).

A commonly accepted division between Asia and Europe—marked here by a maroon, dashed line—is formed by the Ural Mountains, Ural River, Caspian Sea, Caucasus Mountains, and the Black Sea with its outlets, the Bosporus and Dardanelles.

The People's Republic of China claims Taiwan as its 23rd province. Taiwan's government (Republic of China) maintains that there are two political entities.

Political
- ⊛ National capital
- • Other city

Two-point Equidistant Projection

800 Miles
800 Kilometers

THE CONTINENT: ASIA

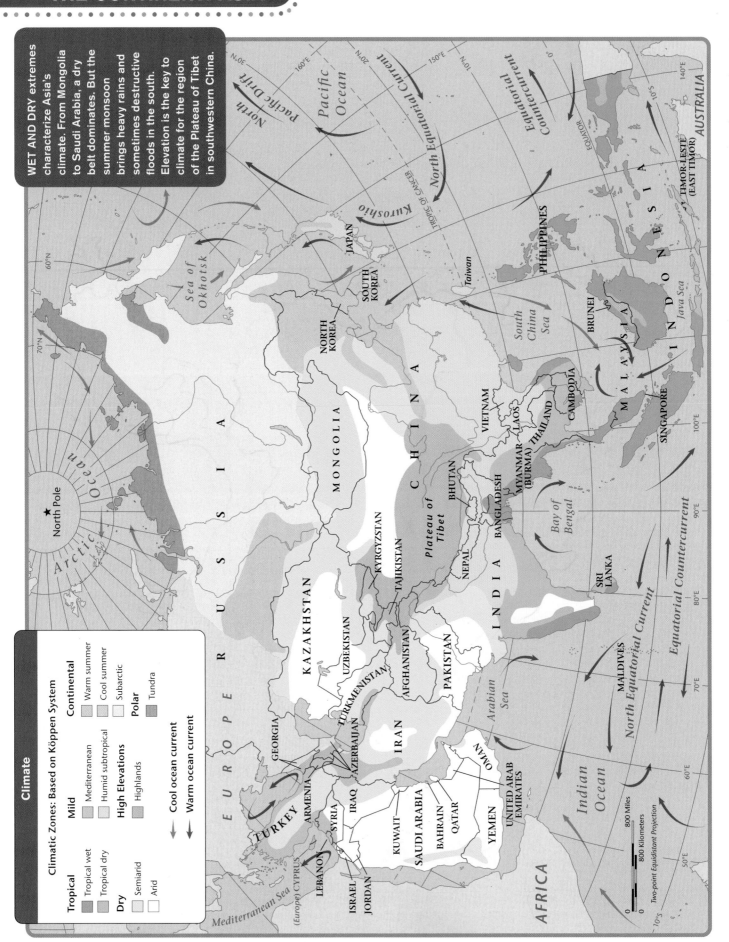

WET AND DRY extremes characterize Asia's climate. From Mongolia to Saudi Arabia, a dry belt dominates. But the summer monsoon brings heavy rains and sometimes destructive floods in the south. Elevation is the key to climate for the region of the Plateau of Tibet in southwestern China.

Climate

Climatic Zones: Based on Köppen System

Tropical
- Tropical wet
- Tropical dry

Dry
- Semiarid
- Arid

Mild
- Mediterranean
- Humid subtropical

High Elevations
- Highlands

Continental
- Warm summer
- Cool summer
- Subarctic

Polar
- Tundra

→ Cool ocean current
→ Warm ocean current

800 Miles
800 Kilometers
Two-point Equidistant Projection

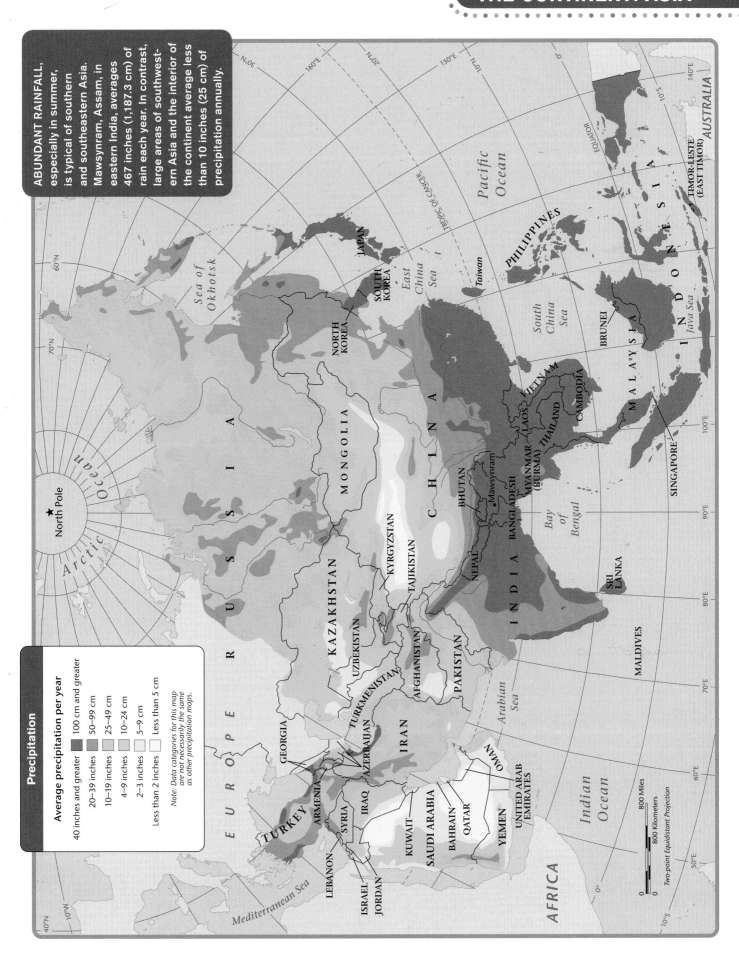

ABUNDANT RAINFALL, especially in summer, is typical of southern and southeastern Asia. Mawsynram, Assam, in eastern India, averages 467 inches (1,187.3 cm) of rain each year. In contrast, large areas of southwestern Asia and the interior of the continent average less than 10 inches (25 cm) of precipitation annually.

Precipitation

Average precipitation per year

- 40 inches and greater — 100 cm and greater
- 20–39 inches — 50–99 cm
- 10–19 inches — 25–49 cm
- 4–9 inches — 10–24 cm
- 2–3 inches — 5–9 cm
- Less than 2 inches — Less than 5 cm

Note: Data categories for this map are not necessarily the same as other precipitation maps.

North Pole

Arctic Ocean

Sea of Okhotsk

EUROPE

RUSSIA

KAZAKHSTAN

MONGOLIA

CHINA

JAPAN

NORTH KOREA

SOUTH KOREA

East China Sea

Pacific Ocean

South China Sea

Taiwan

PHILIPPINES

BRUNEI

MALAYSIA

INDONESIA

TIMOR-LESTE (EAST TIMOR)

AUSTRALIA

SINGAPORE

VIETNAM

LAOS

THAILAND

CAMBODIA

MYANMAR (BURMA)

BANGLADESH

BHUTAN

NEPAL

Mawsynram

INDIA

SRI LANKA

MALDIVES

Bay of Bengal

Arabian Sea

Indian Ocean

PAKISTAN

AFGHANISTAN

TAJIKISTAN

KYRGYZSTAN

UZBEKISTAN

TURKMENISTAN

IRAN

IRAQ

AZERBAIJAN

ARMENIA

GEORGIA

TURKEY

SYRIA

LEBANON

ISRAEL

JORDAN

SAUDI ARABIA

KUWAIT

BAHRAIN

QATAR

UNITED ARAB EMIRATES

OMAN

YEMEN

Mediterranean Sea

AFRICA

TROPIC OF CANCER

EQUATOR

800 Miles

800 Kilometers

Two-point Equidistant Projection

MORE THAN ONE-THIRD of Earth's people live in two Asian countries: China and India. Although most of the continent's people live in rural areas, it has 11 metropolitan areas with populations greater than 10 million people.

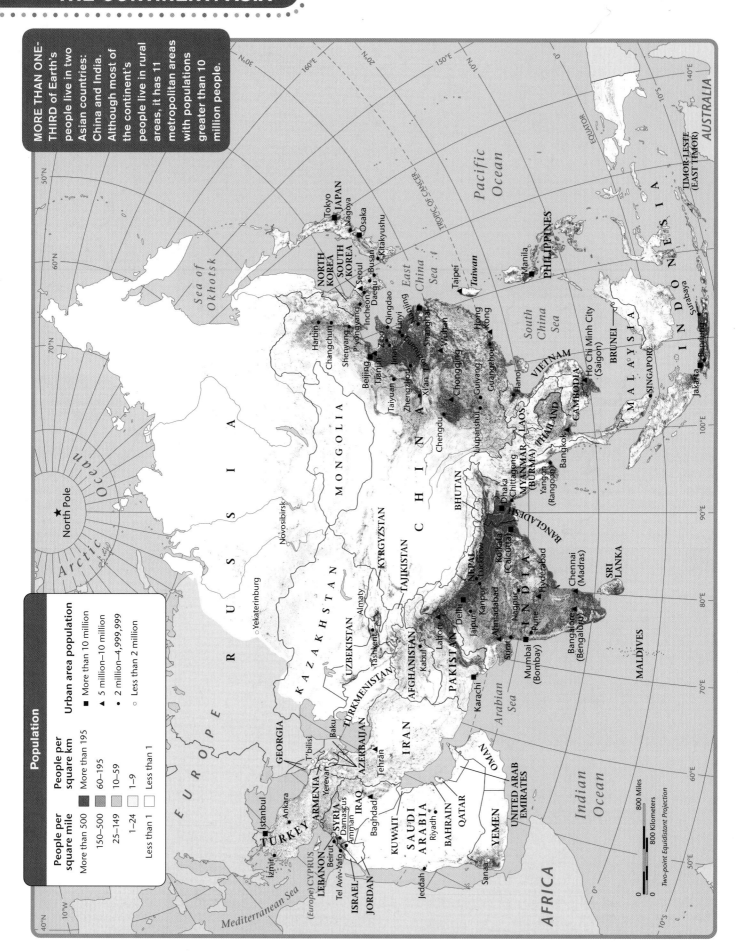

Population

People per square mile	People per square km
More than 500	More than 195
150–500	60–195
25–149	10–59
1–24	1–9
Less than 1	Less than 1

Urban area population

- ■ More than 10 million
- ▲ 5 million–10 million
- ● 2 million–4,999,999
- ○ Less than 2 million

800 Miles

800 Kilometers

Two-point Equidistant Projection

THE CONTINENT: ASIA

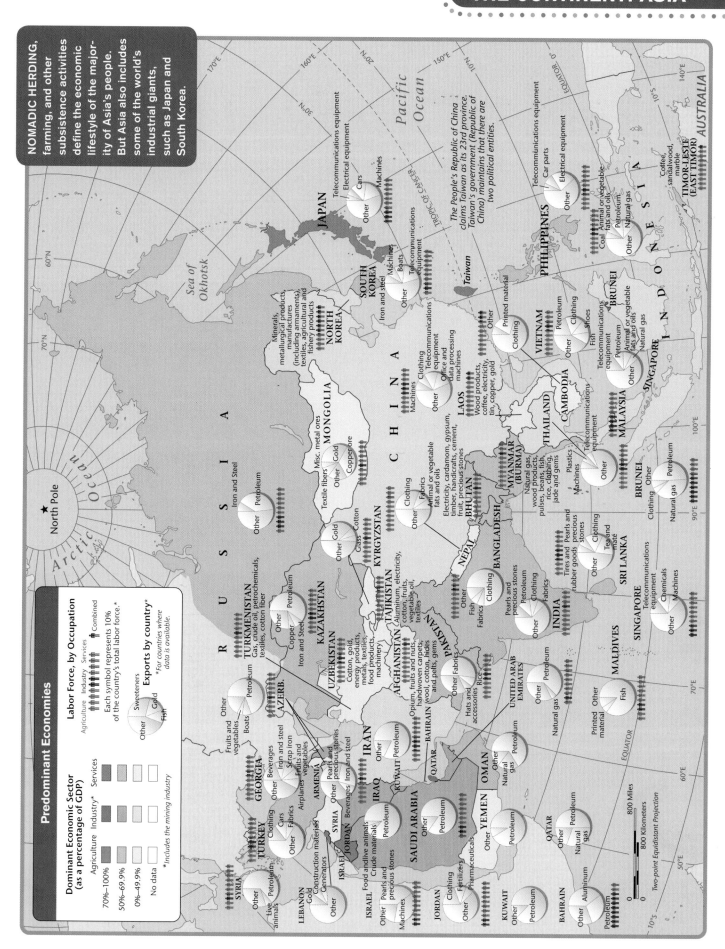

NOMADIC HERDING, farming, and other subsistence activities define the economic lifestyle of the majority of Asia's people. But Asia also includes some of the world's industrial giants, such as Japan and South Korea.

Predominant Economies

Dominant Economic Sector
(as a percentage of GDP)

Agriculture	Industry*	Services
70%–100%		
50%–69.9%		
0%–49.9%		
No data		

*Includes the mining industry

Labor Force, by Occupation

Agriculture Industry Services Combined

Each symbol represents 10% of the country's total labor force.*

Exports by country*

Sweeteners
Gold
Fish
Other

*For countries where data is available.

The People's Republic of China claims Taiwan as its 23rd province. Taiwan's government (Republic of China) maintains that there are two political entities.

Pacific Ocean

Arctic Ocean

North Pole

Sea of Okhotsk

RUSSIA

MONGOLIA

CHINA

JAPAN
Telecommunications equipment
Electrical equipment
Cars
Machines
Other

SOUTH KOREA
Iron and steel
Machines
Boats
Telecommunications equipment
Other

NORTH KOREA
Minerals, metallurgical products, manufactures (including armaments), textiles, agricultural and fishery products

Iron and Steel
Petroleum
Other

Misc. metal ores
Gold
Copper ore
Other

Textile fibers
Gold
Other
Coal
Cotton

KYRGYZSTAN

TAJIKISTAN
Aluminum, electricity, cotton, fruits, vegetable oil, textiles

Clothing
Other
Fabrics
Animal or vegetable fats and oils

LAOS
Wood products, coffee, electricity, tin, copper, gold
Electricity, cardamom, gypsum, timber, handicrafts, cement, fruit, precious stones

Office and data processing machines
Clothing
Telecommunications equipment
Other
Machines

VIETNAM
Petroleum
Clothing
Shoes
Fish
Other

PHILIPPINES
Telecommunications equipment
Car parts
Electrical equipment
Petroleum
Natural gas
Other

BRUNEI
Animal or vegetable fats and oils
Natural gas
Petroleum
Other

Coal
Animal or vegetable fats and oils
Petroleum
Other

INDONESIA

TIMOR-LESTE (EAST TIMOR)
Coffee, sandalwood, marble

AUSTRALIA

SINGAPORE
Telecommunications equipment
Clothing
Other

MALAYSIA
Telecommunications equipment
Other

THAILAND
Telecommunications equipment
Printed material
Other

CAMBODIA
Clothing
Other

MYANMAR (BURMA)
Natural gas, wood products, pulses, beans, fish, rice, clothing, jade and gems
Plastics
Machines

BANGLADESH
Clothing
Petroleum
Fabrics
Other
Fish

BHUTAN

NEPAL
Other
Fabrics
Clothing

INDIA
Tires and rubber goods
Pearls and precious stones
Clothing
Fabrics
Tea and maté
Other

Pearls and precious stones

SRI LANKA
Telecommunications equipment
Clothing
Chemicals
Machines
Other

MALDIVES
Printed material
Fish
Other

PAKISTAN
Rice
Other
Fabrics

AFGHANISTAN
Opium, fruits and nuts, handwoven carpets, wool, cotton, hides and pelts, gems

KAZAKHSTAN
Petroleum
Copper
Iron and Steel
Other

TURKMENISTAN
Gas, crude oil, petrochemicals, textiles, cotton fiber

UZBEKISTAN
Cotton, gold, energy products, metals, textiles, food products, machinery

AZERB.
Petroleum
Other

GEORGIA
Fruits and vegetables
Boats
Beverages
Iron and steel
Scrap iron
Fruits and vegetables
Other

ARMENIA
Airplanes
Pearls and precious stones
Iron and steel
Other
Beverages

IRAN
Petroleum
Other

IRAQ
Petroleum
Other

KUWAIT
Petroleum
Other

SAUDI ARABIA
Petroleum
Other

YEMEN
Petroleum
Other

OMAN
Petroleum
Natural gas
Other

QATAR
Petroleum
Natural gas
Other

UNITED ARAB EMIRATES
Petroleum
Natural gas
Other

BAHRAIN
Petroleum
Aluminum
Other

SYRIA
Petroleum
Other
Live animals

LEBANON
Gold
Pearls and precious stones
Other

ISRAEL
Food and live animals
Crude materials
Pearls and precious stones
Machines

JORDAN
Clothing
Fertilizers
Pharmaceuticals
Other

TURKEY
Clothing
Cars
Fabrics
Other

Construction materials
Generators

EQUATOR

TROPIC OF CANCER

Taiwan

0   800 Miles
0   800 Kilometers
Two-point Equidistant Projection

GLOBAL CONTAINER PORTS: FACTS & FIGURES

Largest World Container Ports
(by volume – million tons)

Shanghai	443.0 MT
Singapore	423.3 FT
Rotterdam	376.6 MT
Ningbo	272.4 MT
Tianjin	245.1 MT
Guangzhou	241.7 MT
Hong Kong	230.1 MT
Busan	217.2 RT
South Louisiana	192.5 MT

MT=Metric Ton; FT=Freight Ton; RT=Revenue Ton

Leading U.S. Container Trade Partners
(exports by volume – metric tons)

China	19,950,429
Taiwan	8,204,783
Japan	7,980,335
South Korea	6,160,397
Hong Kong	3,704,075
Belgium	3,036,484
India	2,642,381
Indonesia	2,241,680
Brazil	2,191,802

Leading U.S. Container Trade Partners
(imports by volume – metric tons)

China	52,072,462
Brazil	5,320,929
Japan	5,234,186
South Korea	4,057,291
Taiwan	4,008,774
Germany	3,971,391
India	3,524,941
Thailand	3,318,148

Largest Container Shipping Companies
(by TEU capacity)*

A.P. Moller-Maersk Group	Denmark
Mediterranean Shipping Company S.A.	Italy
CMA CGM S.A.	France
Evergreen Marine Corp.	Taiwan
Hapag-Lloyd	Germany
China Shipping Container Lines	China
American President Lines Ltd.	U.S.A.
Hanjin-Senator	Korea/Germany
China Ocean Shipping Co.	China

*TEU is the standard unit for describing a ship's cargo carrying capacity, or a shipping terminal's cargo handling capacity.

East Asia Ports

Since the mid-20th century the world's economy has expanded to a truly global scale, made possible, in large part, by the growth of containerized shipping. The first container ship, a converted oil tanker, set sail from Newark, New Jersey, in 1956 carrying 58 containers. Today, more than 4,000 container vessels move manufactured goods cheaply and efficiently among ports around the world.

Container ships range in size up to 1,300 feet (396 m) long and 180 feet (55 m) wide—bigger than four football fields. The capacity of a container ship is measured in TEUs—a unit of measure equivalent to a 20-foot standard container. A large container vessel can carry more than 10,000 20-foot containers, each loaded with as much as 100 tons of cargo. Container ports are equipped with giant cranes, more than 400 feet (122 m) tall and weighing as much as 2,000 tons, that can move 30 to 40 containers on and off a ship each hour. With six of the world's busiest container ports, containerized shipping has played an important role in Asia's economic boom.

⇧ WAIGAOQIAO TERMINAL, Shanghai Port's largest container terminal, appears as a colorful mosaic when viewed from above. Shanghai leads all container ports in tonnage handled, moving more than 400 million tons of goods and material each year.

⇧ SHIPPING CONTAINERS are stacked high above trucks moving through the busy port of Busan, which opened in 2004, 280 miles (450 km) southeast of South Korea's capital, Seoul.

⇧ OLD MEETS NEW in the harbor of Ho Chi Minh City, Vietnam. Vendors sail their traditional sampan near a giant container vessel in this newly built Southeast Asian container port.

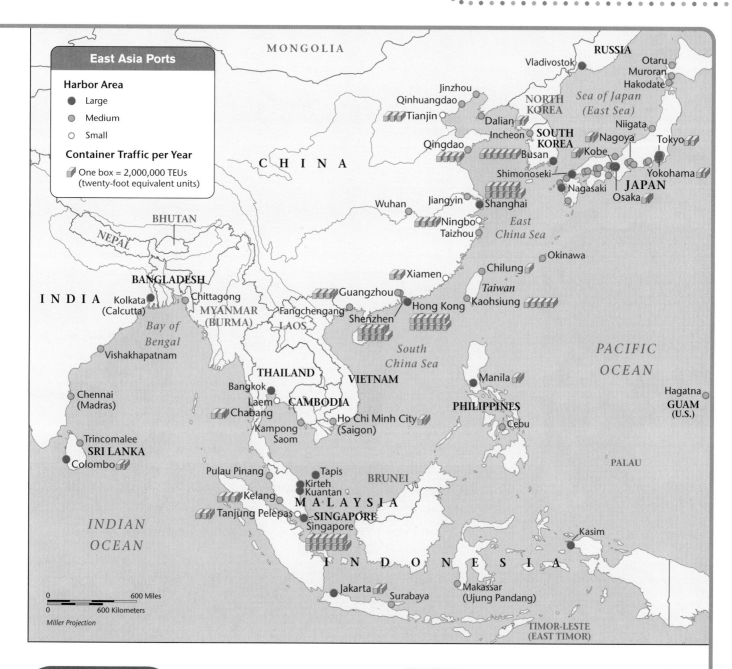

East Asia Ports

Harbor Area
- ● Large
- ● Medium
- ○ Small

Container Traffic per Year

🗳 One box = 2,000,000 TEUs (twenty-foot equivalent units)

MONGOLIA

RUSSIA
Vladivostok
Otaru
Muroran
Hakodate
Jinzhou
NORTH
KOREA
Qinhuangdao
Sea of Japan
(East Sea)
Tianjin
Dalian
Niigata
Incheon
SOUTH
KOREA
Nagoya
Tokyo
C H I N A
Qingdao
Busan
Kobe
Yokohama
Shimonoseki
JAPAN
Nagasaki
Osaka

BHUTAN
NEPAL
Wuhan
Jiangyin
Shanghai
East
China Sea
Ningbo
Taizhou

BANGLADESH
Chilung
Xiamen
I N D I A
Kolkata
(Calcutta)
Chittagong
MYANMAR
(BURMA)
Fangchengang
Guangzhou
Taiwan
Kaohsiung
Okinawa

LAOS
Hong Kong
Shenzhen
PACIFIC
OCEAN

Bay of
Bengal
Vishakhapatnam
South
China Sea
THAILAND
VIETNAM
Manila
Chennai
(Madras)
Bangkok
CAMBODIA
PHILIPPINES
Hagatna
GUAM
(U.S.)
Laem
Chabang
Ho Chi Minh City
(Saigon)
Cebu
Kampong
Saom
Trincomalee
SRI LANKA
Colombo
PALAU
Pulau Pinang
Tapis
BRUNEI
Kirteh
Kuantan
Kelang
M A L A Y S I A
Kasim
INDIAN
OCEAN
Tanjung Pelepas
SINGAPORE
Singapore
I N D O N E S I A

0   600 Miles
0   600 Kilometers
Miller Projection

Jakarta
Surabaya
Makassar
(Ujung Pandang)

TIMOR-LESTE
(EAST TIMOR)

CONTAINER TRAFFIC

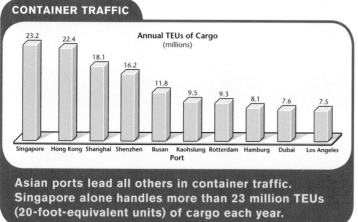

Annual TEUs of Cargo
(millions)

Port	TEUs
Singapore	23.2
Hong Kong	22.4
Shanghai	18.1
Shenzhen	16.2
Busan	11.8
Kaohsiung	9.5
Rotterdam	9.3
Hamburg	8.1
Dubai	7.6
Los Angeles	7.5

Asian ports lead all others in container traffic. Singapore alone handles more than 23 million TEUs (20-foot-equivalent units) of cargo each year.

⬆ CONTAINER CRANES line this waterway in Hong Kong, one of the busiest international container ports in the world.

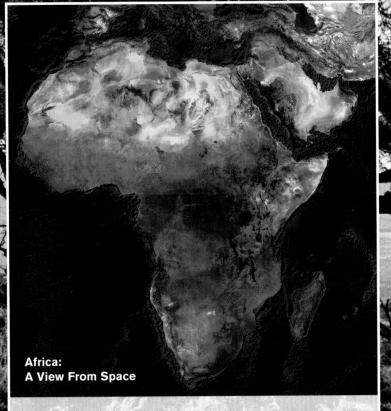

**Africa:
A View From Space**

From space, Africa appears divided into three regions: the north, dominated by the Sahara, the largest hot desert in the world; a central green band of rain forests and tropical grasslands; and more dry land to the south. Africa may actually be dividing: the Great Rift Valley, running from the Red Sea through the volcanic Afar Triangle to the southern lake district, may split apart the continent.

PHYSICAL

Land area	Lowest point	Largest lake
11,608,000 sq mi (30,065,000 sq km)	Lake Assai, Djibouti -512 ft (-156 m)	Victoria 26,800 sq mi (69,500 sq km)
Highest point Kilimanjaro, Tanzania 19,340 ft (5,895 m)	Longest river Nile 4,241 mi (6,825 km)	

POLITICAL

Population	Largest country	Most populous country
943,758,000	Sudan 967,500 sq mi (2,505,813 sq km)	Nigeria Pop. 144,430,000
Number of independent countries 53	Smallest country Seychelles 176 sq mi (455 sq km)	Least populous country Seychelles Pop. 86,000

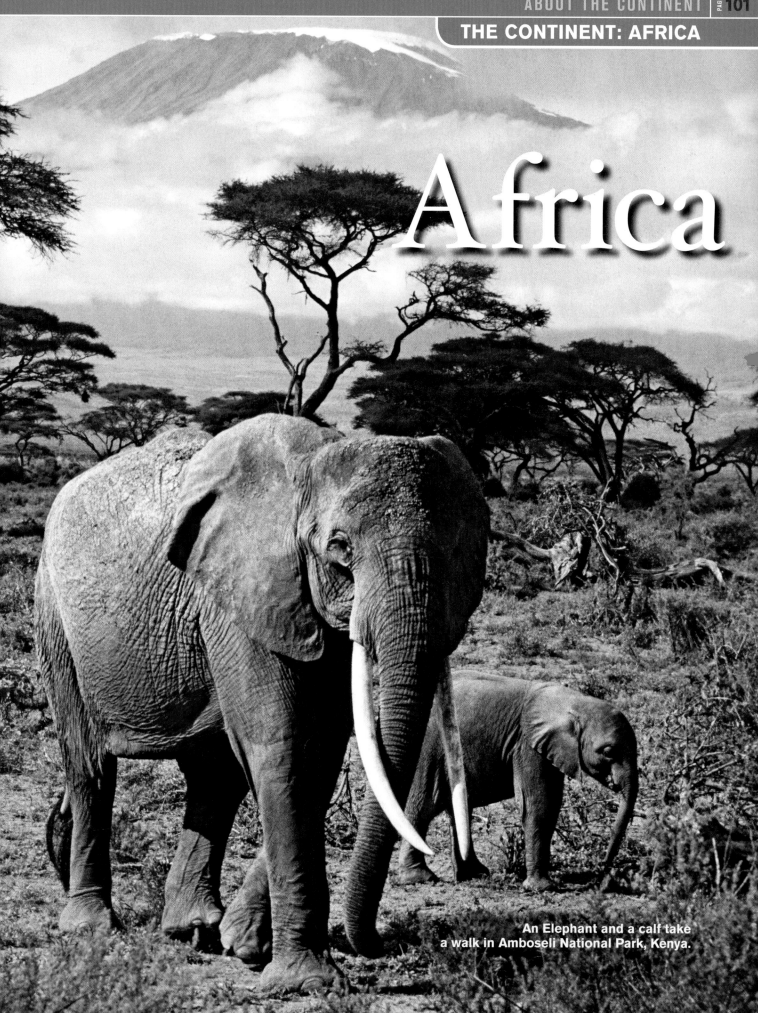

Africa

An Elephant and a calf take
a walk in Amboseli National Park, Kenya.

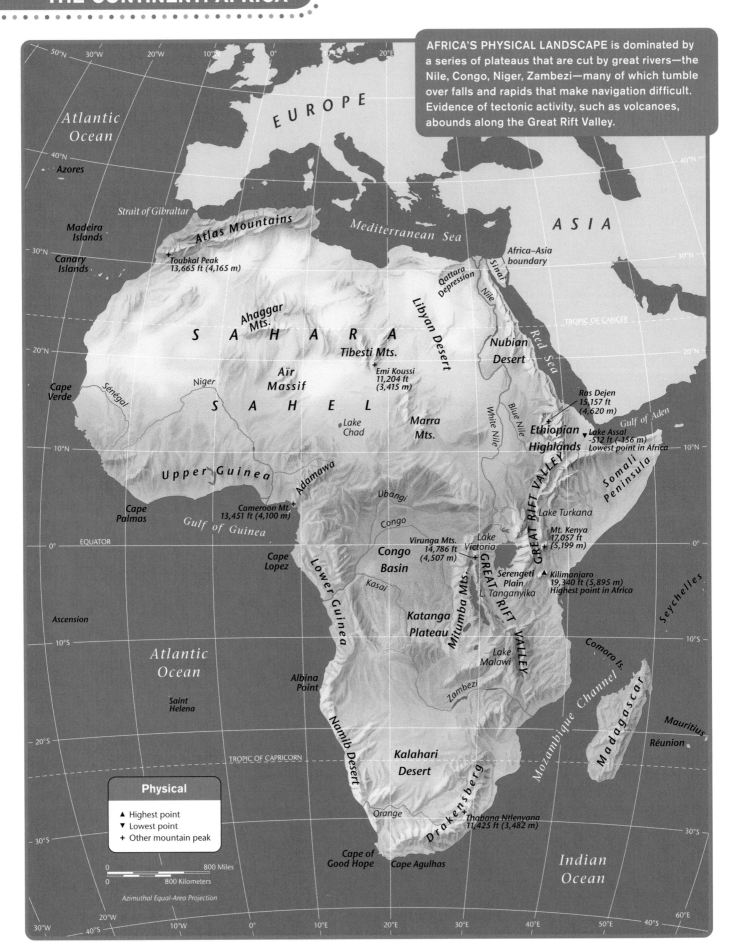

AFRICA'S PHYSICAL LANDSCAPE is dominated by a series of plateaus that are cut by great rivers—the Nile, Congo, Niger, Zambezi—many of which tumble over falls and rapids that make navigation difficult. Evidence of tectonic activity, such as volcanoes, abounds along the Great Rift Valley.

EUROPE

ASIA

Atlantic Ocean

Azores

Madeira Islands

Canary Islands

Cape Verde

Cape Palmas

Ascension

Atlantic Ocean

Saint Helena

Strait of Gibraltar

Atlas Mountains

Toubkal Peak 13,665 ft (4,165 m)

Mediterranean Sea

Ahaggar Mts.

S A H A R A

Aïr Massif

S A H E L

Niger

Sénégal

Tibesti Mts.

Emi Koussi 11,204 ft (3,415 m)

Libyan Desert

Qattara Depression

Nile

Sinai

Africa–Asia boundary

TROPIC OF CANCER

Nubian Desert

Red Sea

Lake Chad

Marra Mts.

White Nile

Blue Nile

Ras Dejen 15,157 ft (4,620 m)

Gulf of Aden

Ethiopian Highlands

Lake Assal -512 ft (-156 m) Lowest point in Africa

Upper Guinea

Adamawa

Cameroon Mt. 13,451 ft (4,100 m)

Gulf of Guinea

Ubangi

Congo

Somali Peninsula

Lake Turkana

Mt. Kenya 17,057 ft (5,199 m)

EQUATOR

Cape Lopez

Lower Guinea

Kasai

Congo Basin

Virunga Mts. 14,786 ft (4,507 m)

Lake Victoria

Serengeti Plain

L. Tanganyika

Kilimanjaro 19,340 ft (5,895 m) Highest point in Africa

GREAT RIFT VALLEY

Mitumba Mts.

Katanga Plateau

Seychelles

Albina Point

Namib Desert

Lake Malawi

Zambezi

Comoro Is.

Mozambique Channel

Madagascar

Mauritius

Réunion

TROPIC OF CAPRICORN

Kalahari Desert

Drakensberg

Orange

Thabana Ntlenyana 11,425 ft (3,482 m)

Cape of Good Hope

Cape Agulhas

Indian Ocean

Physical

▲ Highest point
▼ Lowest point
+ Other mountain peak

0   800 Miles
0   800 Kilometers

Azimuthal Equal-Area Projection

THE CONTINENT: AFRICA

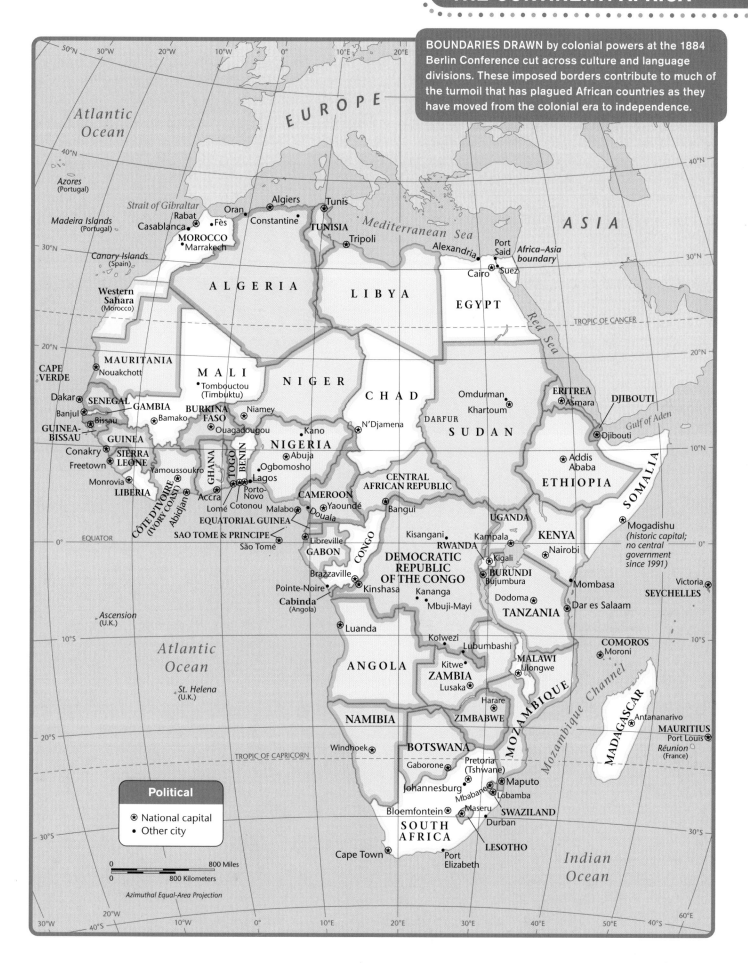

BOUNDARIES DRAWN by colonial powers at the 1884 Berlin Conference cut across culture and language divisions. These imposed borders contribute to much of the turmoil that has plagued African countries as they have moved from the colonial era to independence.

EUROPE

ASIA

Atlantic Ocean

Azores (Portugal)

Madeira Islands (Portugal)

Strait of Gibraltar

Rabat
Casablanca
Fès
Marrakech
MOROCCO

Oran
Constantine
Algiers

Tunis
TUNISIA
Tripoli

Mediterranean Sea

Alexandria
Port Said
Cairo
Suez
Africa–Asia boundary

Canary Islands (Spain)

Western Sahara (Morocco)

ALGERIA

LIBYA

EGYPT

Red Sea

TROPIC OF CANCER

CAPE VERDE

MAURITANIA
Nouakchott

MALI

Tombouctou (Timbuktu)

NIGER

CHAD

Omdurman
Khartoum

ERITREA
Asmara

DJIBOUTI
Djibouti

Gulf of Aden

Dakar
SENEGAL
GAMBIA
Banjul
Bissau
GUINEA-BISSAU
GUINEA

Niamey
Bamako
BURKINA FASO
Ouagadougou

Kano

N'Djamena

DARFUR

SUDAN

Conakry
SIERRA LEONE
Freetown
Yamoussoukro

NIGERIA
Abuja
Ogbomosho
Lagos
Porto-Novo
Cotonou
GHANA
TOGO
BENIN

CENTRAL AFRICAN REPUBLIC

Addis Ababa

ETHIOPIA

SOMALIA

Monrovia
LIBERIA
CÔTE D'IVOIRE (IVORY COAST)
Accra
Abidjan
Lomé

Malabo
EQUATORIAL GUINEA
SAO TOME & PRINCIPE
São Tomé

CAMEROON
Yaoundé
Douala

Bangui

UGANDA
Kampala
Kisangani

KENYA
Nairobi

Mogadishu (historic capital; no central government since 1991)

EQUATOR

Libreville
GABON
CONGO
Brazzaville
Pointe-Noire

DEMOCRATIC REPUBLIC OF THE CONGO
Kinshasa
Kananga
Mbuji-Mayi

RWANDA
Kigali
BURUNDI
Bujumbura

Dodoma

Mombasa
Dar es Salaam

Victoria
SEYCHELLES

Ascension (U.K.)

Cabinda (Angola)

Luanda

Kolwezi

TANZANIA

St. Helena (U.K.)

Atlantic Ocean

ANGOLA

Lubumbashi
Kitwe
ZAMBIA
Lusaka

Harare

COMOROS
Moroni

MALAWI
Lilongwe

MOZAMBIQUE

Mozambique Channel

MADAGASCAR
Antananarivo

MAURITIUS
Port Louis
Réunion (France)

NAMIBIA

ZIMBABWE

TROPIC OF CAPRICORN

Windhoek

BOTSWANA
Gaborone

Pretoria (Tshwane)
Johannesburg
Mbabane
Lobamba
Maputo

SWAZILAND

Bloemfontein
Maseru
LESOTHO
Durban

SOUTH AFRICA

Cape Town

Port Elizabeth

Indian Ocean

Political

⊛ National capital
• Other city

0 ___ 800 Miles
0 ___ 800 Kilometers

Azimuthal Equal-Area Projection

THE CONTINENT: AFRICA

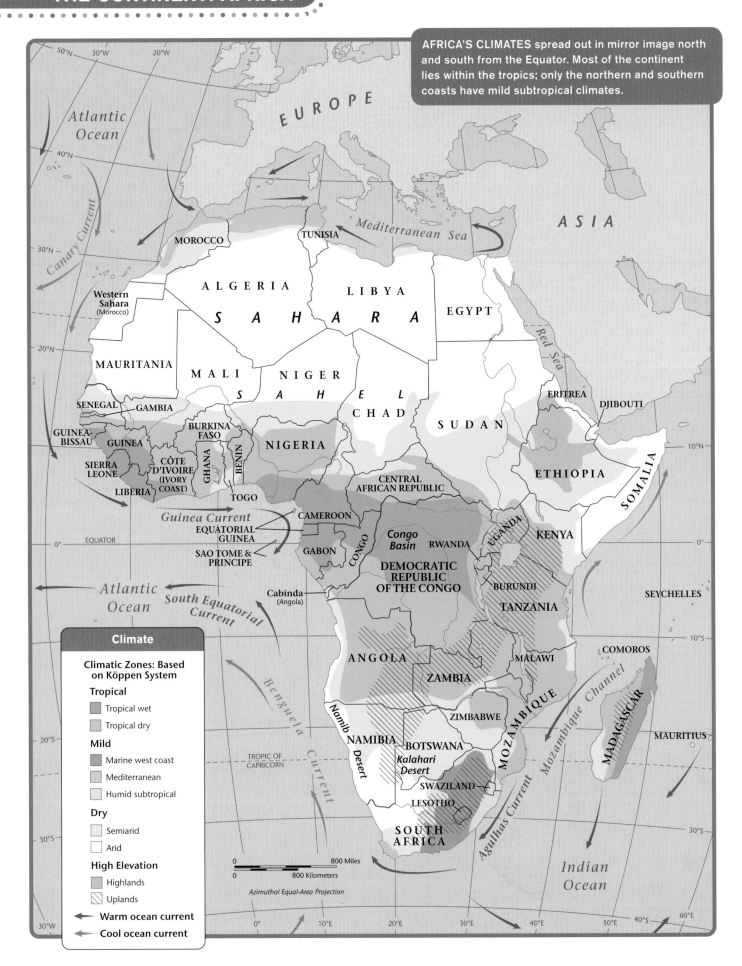

AFRICA'S CLIMATES spread out in mirror image north and south from the Equator. Most of the continent lies within the tropics; only the northern and southern coasts have mild subtropical climates.

Atlantic Ocean

EUROPE

ASIA

Canary Current

Mediterranean Sea

MOROCCO

TUNISIA

Western Sahara (Morocco)

ALGERIA

LIBYA

EGYPT

SAHARA

Red Sea

MAURITANIA

MALI

NIGER

S A H E L

SENEGAL

GAMBIA

CHAD

SUDAN

ERITREA

DJIBOUTI

GUINEA-BISSAU

GUINEA

BURKINA FASO

NIGERIA

SIERRA LEONE

CÔTE D'IVOIRE (IVORY COAST)

GHANA

BENIN

TOGO

LIBERIA

ETHIOPIA

SOMALIA

CENTRAL AFRICAN REPUBLIC

Guinea Current

CAMEROON

EQUATORIAL GUINEA

SAO TOME & PRINCIPE

GABON

CONGO

Congo Basin

RWANDA

UGANDA

KENYA

EQUATOR

Atlantic Ocean

South Equatorial Current

Cabinda (Angola)

DEMOCRATIC REPUBLIC OF THE CONGO

BURUNDI

TANZANIA

SEYCHELLES

COMOROS

ANGOLA

MALAWI

ZAMBIA

MOZAMBIQUE

Mozambique Channel

MADAGASCAR

MAURITIUS

Benguela Current

ZIMBABWE

Namib Desert

NAMIBIA

BOTSWANA

TROPIC OF CAPRICORN

Kalahari Desert

SWAZILAND

LESOTHO

SOUTH AFRICA

Agulhas Current

Indian Ocean

Climate

Climatic Zones: Based on Köppen System

Tropical
- Tropical wet
- Tropical dry

Mild
- Marine west coast
- Mediterranean
- Humid subtropical

Dry
- Semiarid
- Arid

High Elevation
- Highlands
- Uplands

← Warm ocean current

← Cool ocean current

0   800 Miles
0   800 Kilometers

Azimuthal Equal-Area Projection

THE CONTINENT: AFRICA

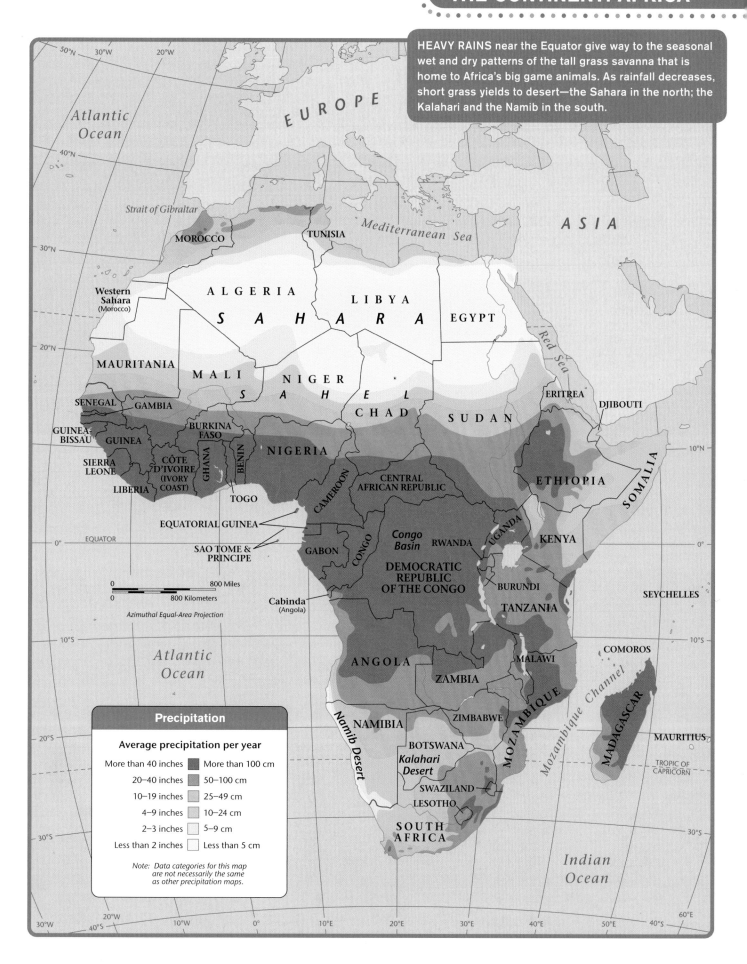

HEAVY RAINS near the Equator give way to the seasonal wet and dry patterns of the tall grass savanna that is home to Africa's big game animals. As rainfall decreases, short grass yields to desert—the Sahara in the north; the Kalahari and the Namib in the south.

Atlantic Ocean

EUROPE

ASIA

Strait of Gibraltar

Mediterranean Sea

MOROCCO

TUNISIA

Western Sahara (Morocco)

ALGERIA

LIBYA

EGYPT

SAHARA

Red Sea

MAURITANIA

MALI

NIGER

S A H E L

ERITREA

DJIBOUTI

SENEGAL

GAMBIA

CHAD

SUDAN

GUINEA-BISSAU

GUINEA

BURKINA FASO

SIERRA LEONE

CÔTE D'IVOIRE (IVORY COAST)

GHANA

BENIN

NIGERIA

LIBERIA

TOGO

EQUATORIAL GUINEA

SAO TOME & PRINCIPE

CAMEROON

CENTRAL AFRICAN REPUBLIC

ETHIOPIA

SOMALIA

EQUATOR

GABON

CONGO

Congo Basin

RWANDA

UGANDA

KENYA

DEMOCRATIC REPUBLIC OF THE CONGO

BURUNDI

SEYCHELLES

Cabinda (Angola)

TANZANIA

Atlantic Ocean

COMOROS

ANGOLA

MALAWI

ZAMBIA

MOZAMBIQUE

Mozambique Channel

MADAGASCAR

MAURITIUS

Namib Desert

NAMIBIA

ZIMBABWE

TROPIC OF CAPRICORN

BOTSWANA

Kalahari Desert

SWAZILAND

LESOTHO

SOUTH AFRICA

Indian Ocean

0 800 Miles
0 800 Kilometers

Azimuthal Equal-Area Projection

Precipitation

Average precipitation per year

More than 40 inches	More than 100 cm
20–40 inches	50–100 cm
10–19 inches	25–49 cm
4–9 inches	10–24 cm
2–3 inches	5–9 cm
Less than 2 inches	Less than 5 cm

Note: Data categories for this map are not necessarily the same as other precipitation maps.

THE CONTINENT: AFRICA

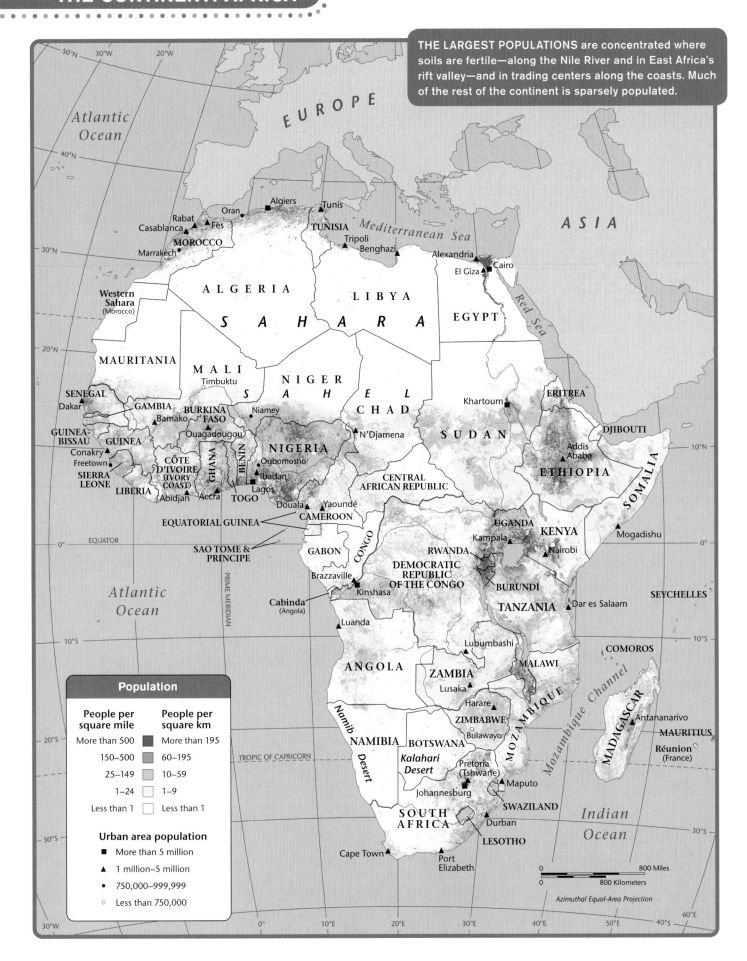

THE LARGEST POPULATIONS are concentrated where soils are fertile—along the Nile River and in East Africa's rift valley—and in trading centers along the coasts. Much of the rest of the continent is sparsely populated.

Atlantic Ocean

EUROPE

ASIA

Mediterranean Sea

Oran
Algiers
Tunis
Rabat
Casablanca Fès
MOROCCO
Marrakech
TUNISIA
Tripoli
Benghazi
Alexandria
El Giza Cairo

Western Sahara (Morocco)

ALGERIA

LIBYA

EGYPT

Red Sea

S A H A R A

MAURITANIA

M A L I
Timbuktu

N I G E R

S A H E L

C H A D

Khartoum

ERITREA

SENEGAL
Dakar
GAMBIA
GUINEA-BISSAU
Conakry
Freetown
SIERRA LEONE
LIBERIA

Bamako
BURKINA FASO
Ouagadougou
Niamey
CÔTE D'IVOIRE (IVORY COAST)
GHANA
Abidjan
Accra
BENIN
TOGO
Ogbomosho
Ibadan
Lagos

NIGERIA

N'Djamena

S U D A N

DJIBOUTI

Addis Ababa

ETHIOPIA

SOMALIA

GUINEA

CENTRAL AFRICAN REPUBLIC

Douala Yaoundé
CAMEROON
EQUATORIAL GUINEA

EQUATOR

SAO TOME & PRINCIPE

GABON

CONGO

Brazzaville
Kinshasa
Cabinda (Angola)

DEMOCRATIC REPUBLIC OF THE CONGO

RWANDA
BURUNDI

UGANDA
Kampala

KENYA
Nairobi

Mogadishu

SEYCHELLES

PRIME MERIDIAN

Atlantic Ocean

Luanda

TANZANIA
Dar es Salaam

Indian Ocean

Lubumbashi

ANGOLA

ZAMBIA
Lusaka

MALAWI

COMOROS

Mozambique Channel

Namib Desert

Harare
ZIMBABWE
Bulawayo

MOZAMBIQUE

MADAGASCAR
Antananarivo
MAURITIUS
Réunion (France)

NAMIBIA

BOTSWANA

Kalahari Desert

TROPIC OF CAPRICORN

Pretoria (Tshwane)
Maputo

Johannesburg

SWAZILAND

SOUTH AFRICA

Durban

LESOTHO

Cape Town

Port Elizabeth

Population

People per square mile	People per square km
More than 500	More than 195
150–500	60–195
25–149	10–59
1–24	1–9
Less than 1	Less than 1

Urban area population

■ More than 5 million

▲ 1 million–5 million

• 750,000–999,999

○ Less than 750,000

0   800 Miles
0   800 Kilometers

Azimuthal Equal-Area Projection

THE CONTINENT: AFRICA

AFRICA'S ECONOMY depends heavily on the export of cash crops, such as coffee, cacao (chocolate), peanuts, and palm oil; of minerals, including precious metals, such as gold and platinum; of gemstones, especially diamonds; and of industrial metals, such as chromite and manganese. Manufacturing is limited.

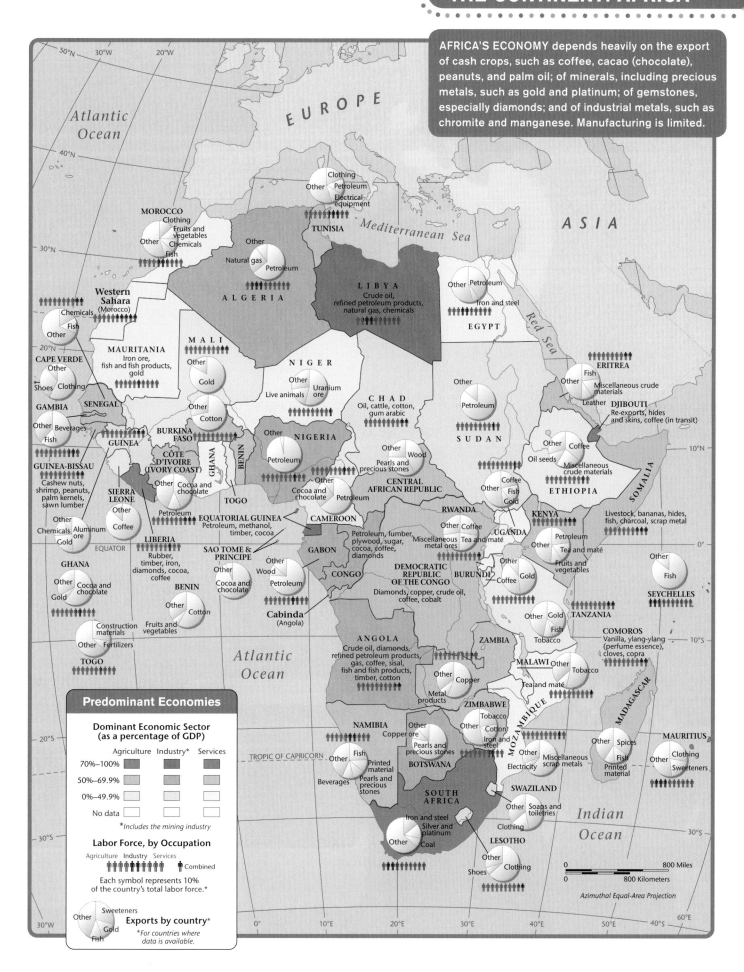

EUROPE

ASIA

Atlantic Ocean

Mediterranean Sea

Red Sea

Indian Ocean

Atlantic Ocean

TUNISIA — Clothing, Petroleum, Electrical equipment, Other

MOROCCO — Clothing, Fruits and vegetables, Chemicals, Fish, Other

ALGERIA — Other, Natural gas, Petroleum

LIBYA Crude oil, refined petroleum products, natural gas, chemicals

EGYPT — Other, Petroleum, Iron and steel

Western Sahara (Morocco) — Chemicals, Fish, Other

MAURITANIA Iron ore, fish and fish products, gold

MALI — Other, Gold

NIGER — Other, Live animals, Uranium ore

CHAD Oil, cattle, cotton, gum arabic

SUDAN — Other, Petroleum

ERITREA — Fish, Miscellaneous crude materials, Leather, Other

DJIBOUTI Re-exports, hides and skins, coffee (in transit)

CAPE VERDE — Other, Shoes, Clothing

SENEGAL — Other, Cotton

BURKINA FASO

ETHIOPIA — Other, Coffee, Oil seeds, Miscellaneous crude materials

SOMALIA Livestock, bananas, hides, fish, charcoal, scrap metal

GAMBIA — Other, Beverages, Fish

GUINEA-BISSAU Cashew nuts, shrimp, peanuts, palm kernels, sawn lumber

GUINEA

NIGERIA — Other, Petroleum

CENTRAL AFRICAN REPUBLIC — Other, Wood, Pearls and precious stones

CÔTE D'IVOIRE (IVORY COAST) — Other, Cocoa and chocolate

GHANA

BENIN

TOGO

KENYA — Other, Coffee, Fish, Gold

RWANDA — Other, Coffee

UGANDA — Coffee, Tea and maté

SEYCHELLES — Other, Fish

SIERRA LEONE — Other, Coffee

LIBERIA Rubber, timber, iron, diamonds, cocoa, coffee

EQUATORIAL GUINEA Petroleum, methanol, timber, cocoa

CAMEROON — Other, Cocoa and chocolate, Petroleum

GABON — Other, Wood, Petroleum

CONGO

DEMOCRATIC REPUBLIC OF THE CONGO Diamonds, copper, crude oil, coffee, cobalt. — Petroleum, lumber, plywood, sugar, cocoa, coffee, diamonds. Miscellaneous metal ores

BURUNDI — Coffee, Gold

TANZANIA — Other, Gold, Fish

COMOROS Vanilla, ylang-ylang (perfume essence), cloves, copra

SAO TOME & PRINCIPE — Other, Cocoa and chocolate

GHANA — Other, Cocoa and chocolate, Gold

BENIN — Other, Cotton, Fruits and vegetables

TOGO — Other, Construction materials, Fertilizers

Cabinda (Angola) — Other, Petroleum

ANGOLA Crude oil, diamonds, refined petroleum products, gas, coffee, sisal, fish and fish products, timber, cotton

ZAMBIA — Other, Copper, Metal products

MALAWI — Other, Tobacco, Tea and maté

MOZAMBIQUE — Other, Electricity, Miscellaneous scrap metals

MADAGASCAR — Other, Spices, Fish, Printed material

MAURITIUS — Other, Clothing, Sweeteners

ZIMBABWE — Other, Tobacco, Cotton, Iron and steel

NAMIBIA — Other, Copper ore, Pearls and precious stones, Fish

BOTSWANA — Other, Beverages, Printed material, Pearls and precious stones

SWAZILAND — Other, Soaps and toiletries

SOUTH AFRICA — Other, Iron and steel, Silver and platinum, Coal

LESOTHO — Other, Shoes, Clothing

Predominant Economies

Dominant Economic Sector (as a percentage of GDP)

	Agriculture	Industry*	Services
70%–100%			
50%–69.9%			
0%–49.9%			
No data			

*Includes the mining industry

Labor Force, by Occupation

Agriculture Industry Services   Combined

Each symbol represents 10% of the country's total labor force.*

Exports by country* — Other, Sweeteners, Gold, Fish

*For countries where data is available.

Azimuthal Equal-Area Projection

0 — 800 Miles
0 — 800 Kilometers

THE CONTINENT: AFRICA

PROTECTED AREAS: FACTS & FIGURES

Forest loss:
9.9 million acres
(4 million ha) each year

Main causes: logging, subsistence agriculture, fuelwood collection

Highest rate:
Nigeria: 11.1 percent each year

Greatest loss: Nigeria, Sudan

Threatened species:

Mammals	779
Birds	638
Reptiles	181
Fish	1,184
Plants	2,312

Selected species at risk:
African elephants, black rhinoceros, eastern chimpanzees, gazelles, hippopotamus, lemurs, mountain gorillas, mountain zebras

Protected areas in Africa:
More than 772,000 square miles
(2 million sq km)

Land protected in Sub-Saharan Africa: 5.9 percent

Countries with highest percent of land protected:

Botswana	18.1%
Equatorial Guinea	16.8%
Tanzania	14.6%
Congo	14.1%

Protected Areas

Africa is home to many different animals. Some are familiar, such as giraffes and rhinoceros; others are rare. All are part of Earth's valuable storehouse of biodiversity, but many are at risk due to a variety of pressures. Natural changes, such as periodic drought, may put stress on both plant and animal populations, but human activity is the main threat. Africa's human population is growing on average at a rate of 2.4 percent each year. Converting land for agricultural use, hunting animals for food, and cutting trees for fuel, as well as expanding commercial logging and building roads have led to loss of natural habitat for many of Africa's animals. Some, such as the mountain gorilla, are even at risk of extinction.

To reverse this trend of biodiversity loss, many countries have created protected areas (see map at right), which include nature reserves, wilderness areas, and national parks. Protected areas allow animals to live in a natural environment. They also provide a source of income for African countries, many of which are very poor, as tourists come on photo safaris to view these unique animals.

⇧ ENDANGERED. A silverback mountain gorilla in Rwanda watches intently. Native to the Virunga Mountains of central Africa, only about 700 mountain gorillas remain in the wild.

⇦ STANDING TALL. At an average height of more than 18 feet (5.7 m), giraffes are the world's tallest mammal. This giraffe stands on the grassy plain of Kenya's Masai Mara.

BIODIVERSITY THREATENED

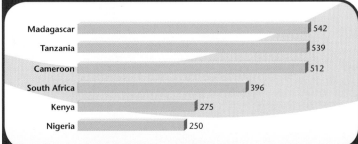

Madagascar	542
Tanzania	539
Cameroon	512
South Africa	396
Kenya	275
Nigeria	250

Madagascar, an island country off the southeast coast, leads all countries in Africa in numbers of species that are critically endangered, endangered, or vulnerable.

THE CONTINENT: AFRICA

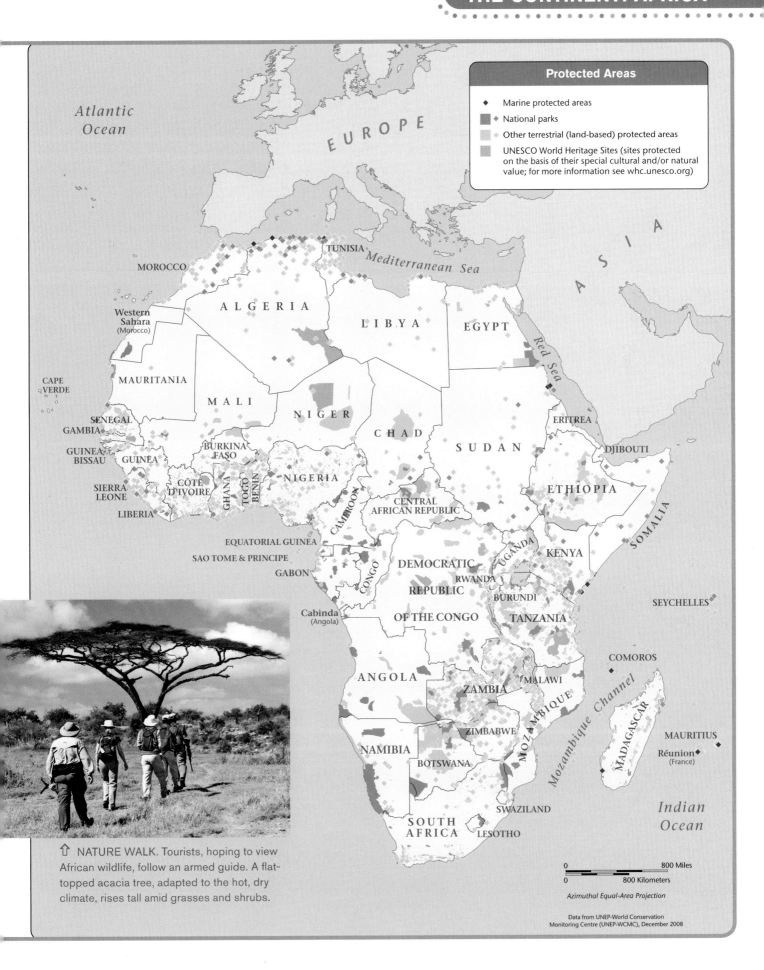

Protected Areas

◆ Marine protected areas

◆ National parks

Other terrestrial (land-based) protected areas

UNESCO World Heritage Sites (sites protected on the basis of their special cultural and/or natural value; for more information see whc.unesco.org)

Atlantic Ocean

EUROPE

ASIA

MOROCCO

TUNISIA

Mediterranean Sea

Western Sahara (Morocco)

ALGERIA

LIBYA

EGYPT

Red Sea

CAPE VERDE

MAURITANIA

MALI

NIGER

CHAD

SUDAN

ERITREA

DJIBOUTI

SENEGAL

GAMBIA

GUINEA-BISSAU

GUINEA

BURKINA FASO

NIGERIA

ETHIOPIA

SIERRA LEONE

CÔTE D'IVOIRE

GHANA

TOGO

BENIN

CAMEROON

CENTRAL AFRICAN REPUBLIC

SOMALIA

LIBERIA

EQUATORIAL GUINEA

SAO TOME & PRINCIPE

GABON

CONGO

DEMOCRATIC REPUBLIC OF THE CONGO

UGANDA

RWANDA

BURUNDI

KENYA

TANZANIA

SEYCHELLES

Cabinda (Angola)

ANGOLA

ZAMBIA

MALAWI

COMOROS

ZIMBABWE

NAMIBIA

BOTSWANA

MOZAMBIQUE

Mozambique Channel

MADAGASCAR

MAURITIUS

Réunion (France)

SWAZILAND

SOUTH AFRICA

LESOTHO

Indian Ocean

⬆ NATURE WALK. Tourists, hoping to view African wildlife, follow an armed guide. A flat-topped acacia tree, adapted to the hot, dry climate, rises tall amid grasses and shrubs.

0 — 800 Miles
0 — 800 Kilometers

Azimuthal Equal-Area Projection

Data from UNEP-World Conservation Monitoring Centre (UNEP-WCMC), December 2008

Australia:
A View From Space

Smallest of Earth's great landmasses, Australia is the only one that is both a continent and a country. It is part of the greater region of Oceania, which includes New Zealand, the eastern part of New Guinea, and hundreds of smaller islands scattered across the Pacific Ocean. Although Hawai'i is politically part of the United States, geographically and culturally it is part of Oceania.

Ayers Rock in the evening light, Uluru, Australia

THE REGION: AUSTRALIA, NEW ZEALAND & OCEANIA

Australia, New Zealand & Oceania

PHYSICAL			POLITICAL		
Area and population totals are for the independent countries in the region only.	Highest point Mount Wilhelm, Papua New Guinea 14,793 ft (4,509 m)	Longest river Murray-Darling, Australia 2,310 mi (3,718 km)	Population 34,569,000	Largest country Australia 2,969,906 sq mi (7,692,024 sq km)	Most populous country Australia Pop. 21,000,000
Land area 3,278,062 sq mi (8,490,180 sq km)	Lowest point Lake Eyre, Australia -52 ft (-16 m)	Largest lake Lake Eyre, Australia 3,430 sq mi (8,884 sq km)	Number of independent countries 14	Smallest country Nauru 8 sq mi (21 sq km)	Least populous country Tuvalu Pop. 10,000

THE REGION: AUSTRALIA, NEW ZEALAND & OCEANIA

PHYSICAL CONTRASTS mark Oceania. Flat, arid land dominates most of Australia. Rain forest covers eastern New Guinea, and the snow-covered Southern Alps soar above New Zealand's South Island. Most of the remaining islands in this region are coral atolls or, like the Hawai'ian Islands, are volcanic in origin.

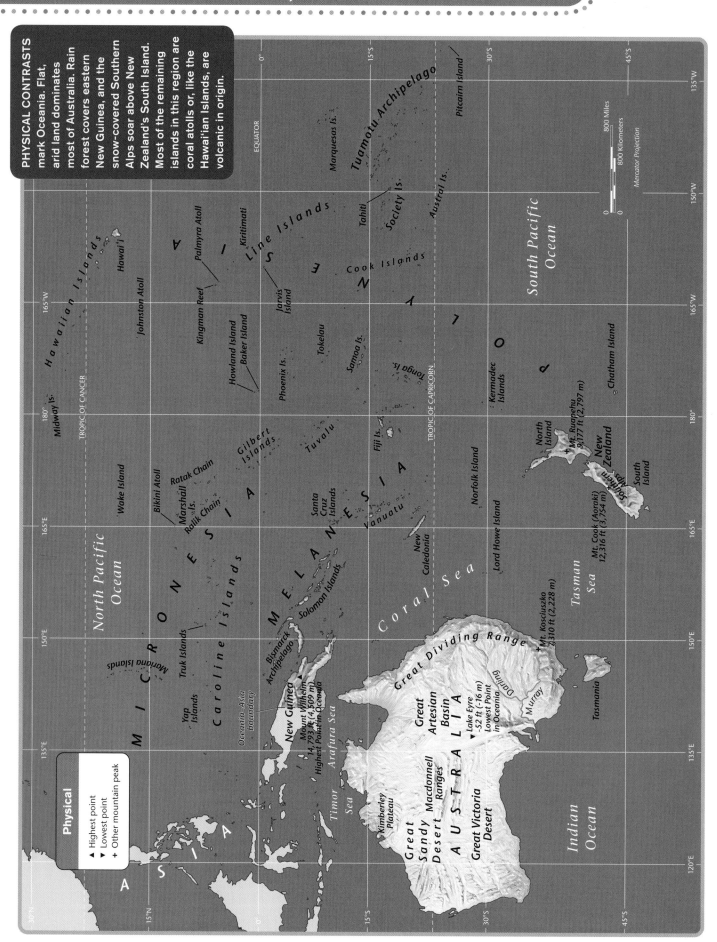

Physical
- ▲ Highest point
- ▶ Lowest point
- + Other mountain peak

800 Miles
800 Kilometers
Mercator Projection

EQUATOR
TROPIC OF CANCER
TROPIC OF CAPRICORN

North Pacific Ocean
South Pacific Ocean
Indian Ocean

Hawaiian Islands
Hawai'i
Midway Is.
Johnston Atoll
Palmyra Atoll
Kingman Reef
Kiritimati
Line Islands
Jarvis Island
Howland Island
Baker Island
Phoenix Is.
Tokelau
Samoa Is.
Marquesas Is.
Tuamotu Archipelago
Tahiti
Society Is.
Austral Is.
Cook Islands
Pitcairn Island

POLYNESIA
MICRONESIA
MELANESIA

Mariana Islands
Yap Islands
Truk Islands
Caroline Islands
Wake Island
Bikini Atoll
Ratak Chain
Marshall Is.
Ralik Chain
Gilbert Islands
Tuvalu
Fiji Is.
Tonga Is.
Santa Cruz Islands
Vanuatu
New Caledonia
Kermadec Islands
Norfolk Island
Lord Howe Island

Bismarck Archipelago
New Guinea
Mount Wilhelm 14,793 ft (4,509 m) Highest Point in Oceania
Oceania–Asia boundary
Solomon Islands

Timor Sea
Arafura Sea
Coral Sea
Tasman Sea

ASIA

AUSTRALIA
Great Sandy Desert
Kimberley Plateau
Macdonnell Ranges
Great Victoria Desert
Great Artesian Basin
Lake Eyre -52 ft (-16 m) Lowest Point in Oceania
Great Dividing Range
Mt. Kosciuszko 7,310 ft (2,228 m)
Darling
Murray
Tasmania

New Zealand
North Island
South Island
Mt. Ruapehu 9,177 ft (2,797 m)
Mt. Cook (Aoraki) 12,316 ft (3,754 m)
Southern Alps
Chatham Island

THE REGION: AUSTRALIA, NEW ZEALAND & OCEANIA

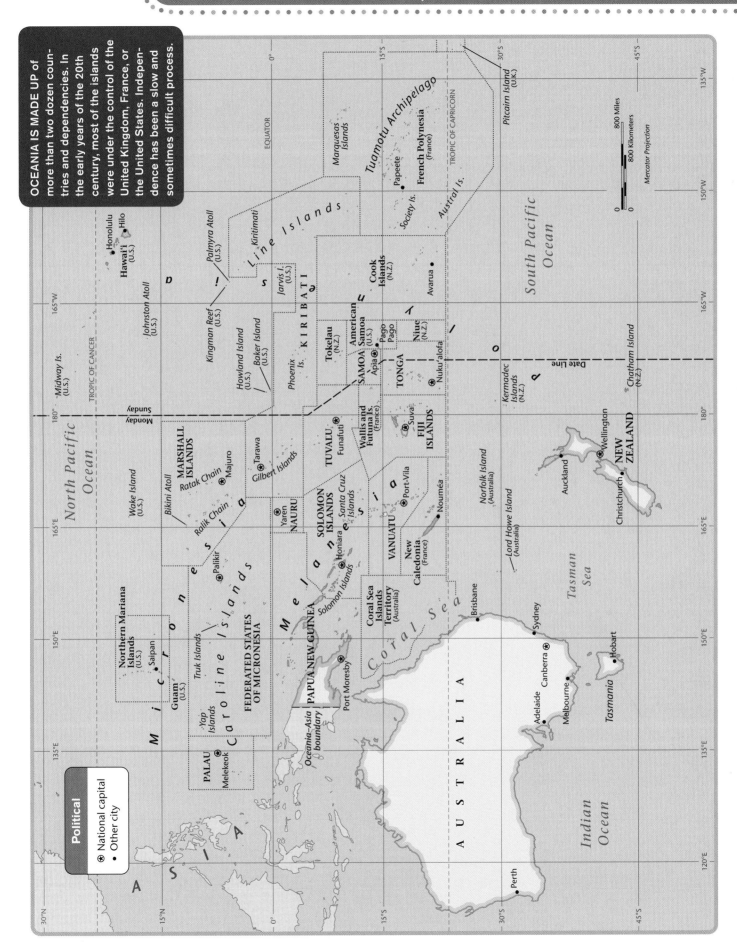

OCEANIA IS MADE UP of more than two dozen countries and dependencies. In the early years of the 20th century, most of the islands were under the control of the United Kingdom, France, or the United States. Independence has been a slow and sometimes difficult process.

800 Miles
800 Kilometers
Mercator Projection

Honolulu • Hilo
Hawai'i (U.S.)

Midway Is. (U.S.)

TROPIC OF CANCER

North Pacific Ocean

Wake Island (U.S.)

Johnston Atoll (U.S.)

Palmyra Atoll (U.S.)

Line Islands

Kiritimati

Marquesas Islands

Tuamotu Archipelago

TROPIC OF CAPRICORN

Papeete
Society Is.
French Polynesia (France)

Austral Is.

Pitcairn Island (U.K.)

South Pacific Ocean

Kingman Reef (U.S.)

Jarvis I. (U.S.)

Cook Islands (N.Z.)

Avarua

Howland Island (U.S.)

Baker Island (U.S.)

Phoenix Is.

KIRIBATI

Tokelau (N.Z.)

American Samoa

Pago Pago

Niue (N.Z.)

Nuku'alofa

Kermadec Islands (N.Z.)

Chatham Island (N.Z.)

SAMOA
Apia ⊛

TONGA ⊛

Date Line

EQUATOR

TROPIC OF CANCER

Sunday
Monday

MARSHALL ISLANDS
Ratak Chain
Bikini Atoll
Majuro

Rolik Chain

Palikir ⊛

Tarawa
Gilbert Islands

Yaren
NAURU

TUVALU
Funafuti ⊛

Wallis and Futuna Is. (France)

Suva ⊛
FIJI ISLANDS

Wellington ⊛
NEW ZEALAND

Auckland

Christchurch

Micronesia

Northern Mariana Islands (U.S.)
Saipan

Guam (U.S.)

Truk Islands

FEDERATED STATES OF MICRONESIA

Caroline Islands

Yap Islands

PALAU
Melekeok ⊛

Melanesia

PAPUA NEW GUINEA

Port Moresby ⊛

Oceania-Asia boundary

Solomon Islands

SOLOMON ISLANDS
Honiara ⊛

Santa Cruz Islands

VANUATU
Port-Vila ⊛

New Caledonia (France)
Nouméa

Coral Sea Islands Territory (Australia)

Coral Sea

Norfolk Island (Australia)

Lord Howe Island (Australia)

Tasman Sea

Brisbane
Sydney
Canberra ⊛
Adelaide
Melbourne
Hobart
Tasmania

AUSTRALIA

Perth

Indian Ocean

ASIA

Political
⊛ National capital
• Other city

THE REGION: AUSTRALIA, NEW ZEALAND & OCEANIA

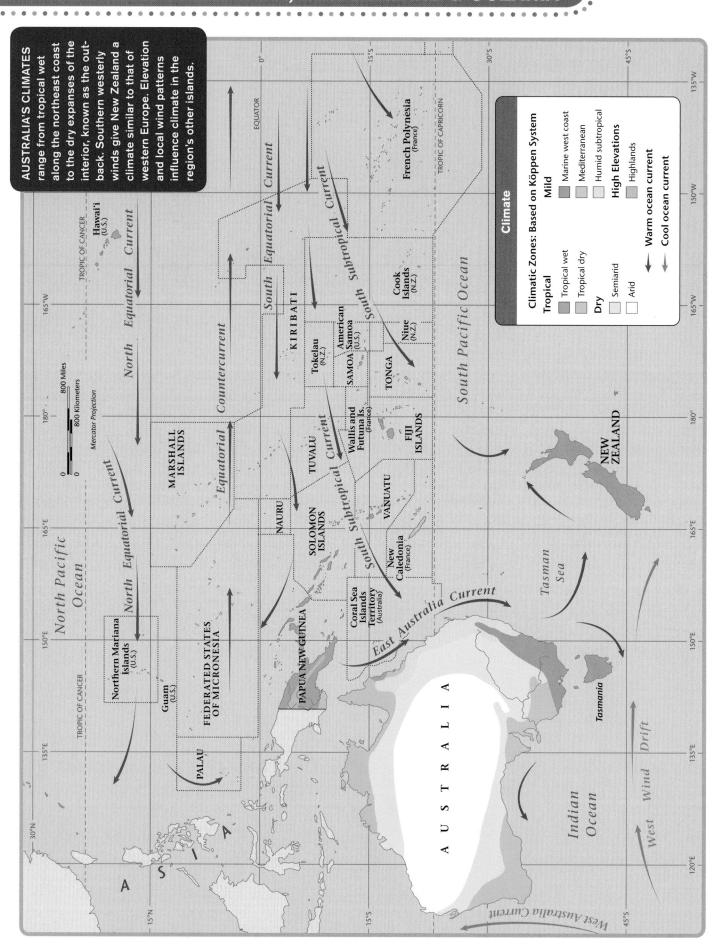

AUSTRALIA'S CLIMATES range from tropical wet along the northeast coast to the dry expanses of the interior, known as the outback. Southern westerly winds give New Zealand a climate similar to that of western Europe. Elevation and local wind patterns influence climate in the region's other islands.

Climate

Climatic Zones: Based on Köppen System

Tropical
- Tropical wet
- Tropical dry

Dry
- Semiarid
- Arid

Mild
- Marine west coast
- Mediterranean
- Humid subtropical

High Elevations
- Highlands

→ Warm ocean current
→ Cool ocean current

800 Miles
800 Kilometers
Mercator Projection

North Pacific Ocean

TROPIC OF CANCER

Hawai'i (U.S.)

North Equatorial Current

North Equatorial Current

Equatorial Countercurrent

South Equatorial Current

South Subtropical Current

French Polynesia (France)

TROPIC OF CAPRICORN

South Pacific Ocean

Cook Islands (N.Z.)

Niue (N.Z.)

KIRIBATI

Tokelau (N.Z.)

American Samoa (U.S.)

SAMOA

TONGA

Wallis and Futuna Is. (France)

FIJI ISLANDS

TUVALU

South Subtropical Current

VANUATU

NAURU

SOLOMON ISLANDS

New Caledonia (France)

South Subtropical Current

Coral Sea Islands Territory (Australia)

PAPUA NEW GUINEA

East Australia Current

Tasman Sea

NEW ZEALAND

Tasmania

MARSHALL ISLANDS

Northern Mariana Islands (U.S.)

Guam (U.S.)

FEDERATED STATES OF MICRONESIA

PALAU

TROPIC OF CANCER

A S I A

AUSTRALIA

Indian Ocean

West Wind Drift

West Australia Current

THE REGION: AUSTRALIA, NEW ZEALAND & OCEANIA

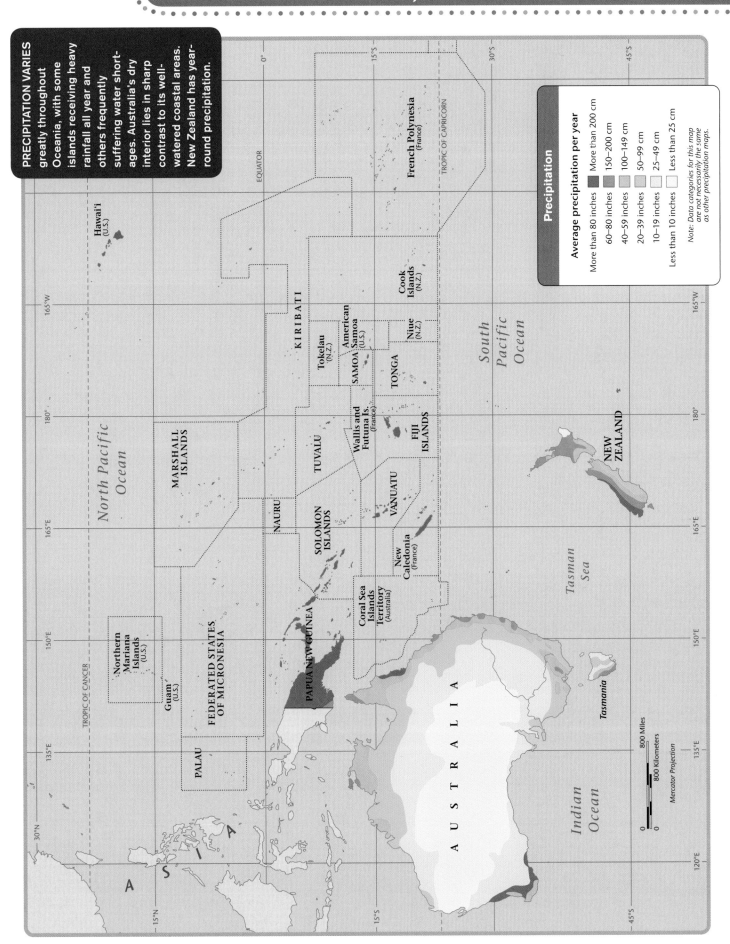

PRECIPITATION VARIES greatly throughout Oceania, with some islands receiving heavy rainfall all year and others frequently suffering water shortages. Australia's dry interior lies in sharp contrast to its well-watered coastal areas. New Zealand has year-round precipitation.

Precipitation

Average precipitation per year

- More than 200 cm — More than 80 inches
- 150–200 cm — 60–80 inches
- 100–149 cm — 40–59 inches
- 50–99 cm — 20–39 inches
- 25–49 cm — 10–19 inches
- Less than 25 cm — Less than 10 inches

Note: Data categories for this map are not necessarily the same as other precipitation maps.

Hawai'i (U.S.)

French Polynesia (France)

Cook Islands (N.Z.)

North Pacific Ocean

KIRIBATI

Tokelau (N.Z.)

American Samoa (U.S.)

SAMOA

Niue (N.Z.)

TONGA

MARSHALL ISLANDS

TUVALU

Wallis and Futuna Is. (France)

FIJI ISLANDS

South Pacific Ocean

NAURU

VANUATU

SOLOMON ISLANDS

New Caledonia (France)

NEW ZEALAND

PAPUA NEW GUINEA

Coral Sea Islands Territory (Australia)

Tasman Sea

Northern Mariana Islands (U.S.)

FEDERATED STATES OF MICRONESIA

Guam (U.S.)

PALAU

A S I A

A U S T R A L I A

Tasmania

Indian Ocean

Mercator Projection

800 Miles
800 Kilometers

EQUATOR

TROPIC OF CAPRICORN

TROPIC OF CANCER

THE REGION: AUSTRALIA, NEW ZEALAND & OCEANIA

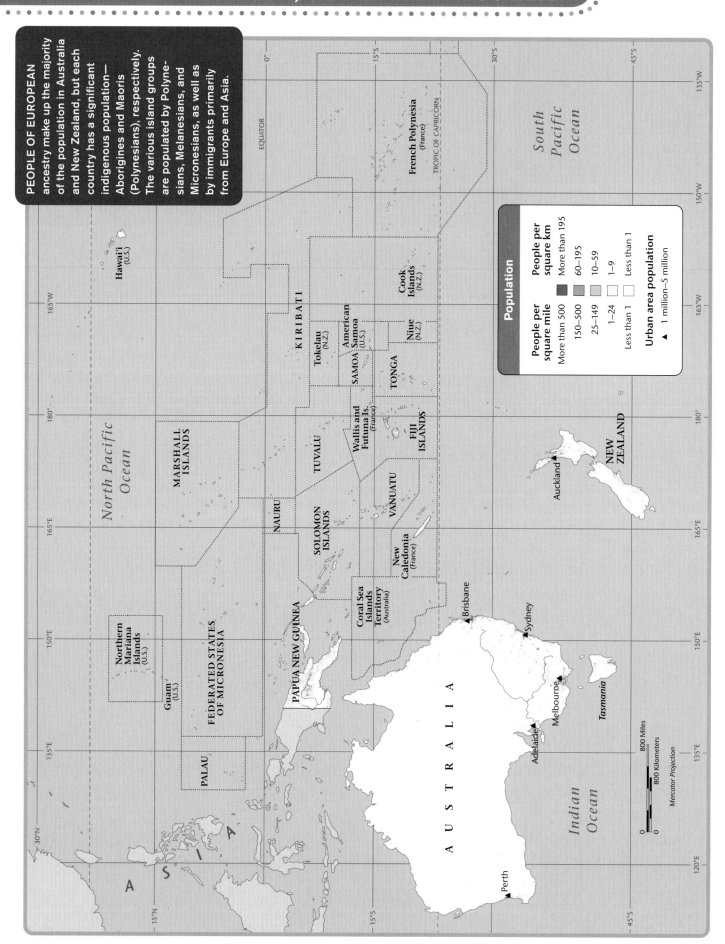

PEOPLE OF EUROPEAN ancestry make up the majority of the population in Australia and New Zealand, but each country has a significant indigenous population—Aborigines and Maoris (Polynesians), respectively. The various island groups are populated by Polynesians, Melanesians, and Micronesians, as well as by immigrants primarily from Europe and Asia.

Population

People per square mile

- More than 500
- 150–500
- 25–149
- 1–24
- Less than 1

People per square km

- More than 195
- 60–195
- 10–59
- 1–9
- Less than 1

Urban area population

- ▲ 1 million–5 million

Hawai'i (U.S.)

French Polynesia (France)

TROPIC OF CAPRICORN

EQUATOR

South Pacific Ocean

North Pacific Ocean

KIRIBATI

Cook Islands (N.Z.)

Tokelau (N.Z.)

American Samoa (U.S.)

SAMOA

Niue (N.Z.)

TONGA

MARSHALL ISLANDS

Wallis and Futuna Is. (France)

FIJI ISLANDS

TUVALU

VANUATU

NAURU

SOLOMON ISLANDS

New Caledonia (France)

NEW ZEALAND

Auckland

Northern Mariana Islands (U.S.)

Guam (U.S.)

FEDERATED STATES OF MICRONESIA

PALAU

PAPUA NEW GUINEA

Coral Sea Islands Territory (Australia)

Brisbane

Sydney

Melbourne

Tasmania

Adelaide

A S I A

A U S T R A L I A

Indian Ocean

Perth

800 Miles

800 Kilometers

Mercator Projection

THE REGION: AUSTRALIA, NEW ZEALAND & OCEANIA

PRIMARY ECONOMIC products make up much of the market in Oceania. New Zealand and Australia account for almost two-thirds of world wool exports and more than one-fifth of beef exports. Plantation agriculture, fishing, tourism, or mining form the economic base in most of the small island countries. For example, New Caledonia is a leading exporter of nickel, and Fiji exports sugar and gold.

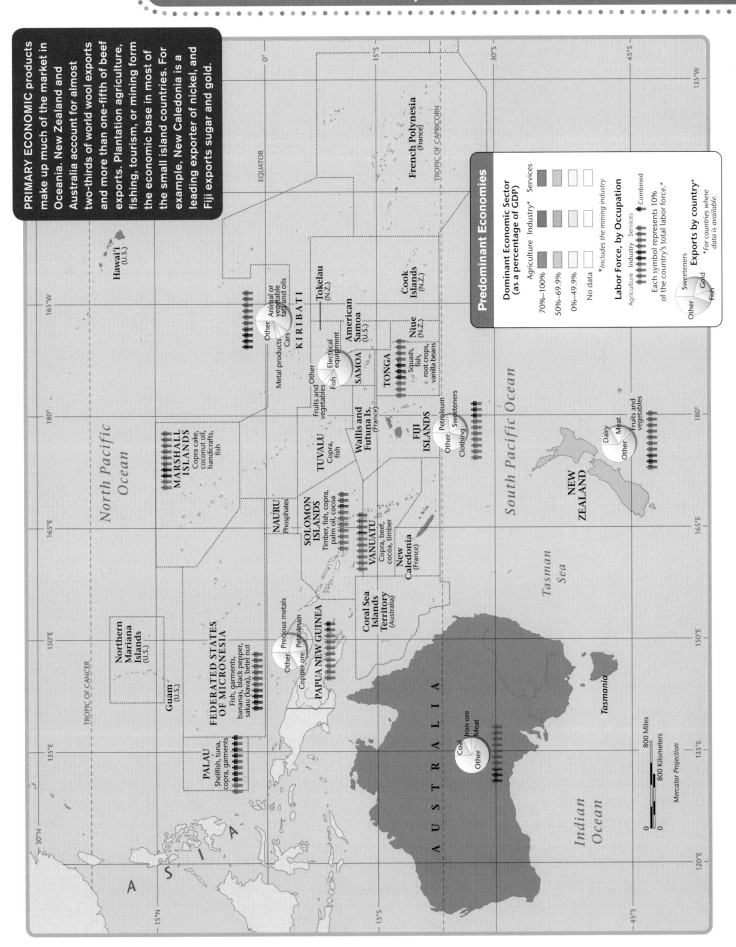

Predominant Economies

Dominant Economic Sector (as a percentage of GDP)

Agriculture Industry* Services

70%–100%
50%–69.9%
0%–49.9%
No data

*Includes the mining industry

Labor Force, by Occupation

Agriculture Industry Services Combined

Each symbol represents 10% of the country's total labor force.*

Exports by country*

*For countries where data is available.

Other / Sweeteners / Gold / Fish

Hawai'i (U.S.)

North Pacific Ocean

MARSHALL ISLANDS
Copra cake, coconut oil, handicrafts, fish

KIRIBATI
Animal or vegetable fats and oils / Cars / Other / Metal products

Tokelau (N.Z.)

American Samoa (U.S.)

SAMOA
Electrical equipment / Fish / Other

Cook Islands (N.Z.)

French Polynesia (France)

TROPIC OF CAPRICORN

Niue (N.Z.)

TONGA
Squash, fish, root crops, vanilla beans

TUVALU
Copra, fish / Fruits and vegetables

Wallis and Futuna Is. (France)

FIJI ISLANDS
Petroleum / Sweeteners / Other / Clothing

NAURU
Phosphates

SOLOMON ISLANDS
Timber, fish, copra, palm oil, cocoa

VANUATU
Copra, beef, cocoa, timber

New Caledonia (France)

Northern Mariana Islands (U.S.)

TROPIC OF CANCER

Guam (U.S.)

FEDERATED STATES OF MICRONESIA
Fish, garments, bananas, black pepper, sakau (kava), betel nut

PALAU
Shellfish, tuna, copra, garments

PAPUA NEW GUINEA
Precious metals / Other / Petroleum / Copper ore

Coral Sea Islands Territory (Australia)

South Pacific Ocean

NEW ZEALAND
Dairy / Meat / Other / Fruits and vegetables

Tasman Sea

A U S T R A L I A
Coal / Iron ore / Meat / Other

Tasmania

Indian Ocean

A S I A

EQUATOR

Mercator Projection

0   800 Miles
0   800 Kilometers

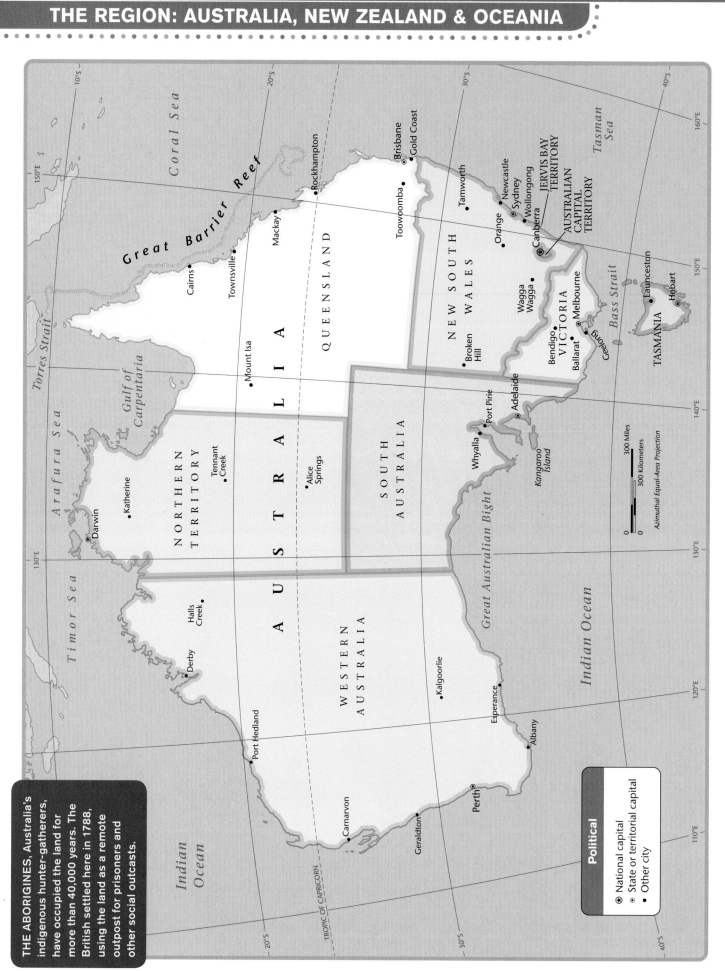

Coral Sea

Great Barrier Reef

Brisbane
Gold Coast

Rockhampton

Tamworth
Newcastle
Sydney
Wollongong
Canberra
JERVIS BAY
TERRITORY
AUSTRALIAN
CAPITAL
TERRITORY

Toowoomba

Mackay

NEW SOUTH WALES

Orange

Tasman Sea

Launceston
Hobart

Cairns

Townsville

QUEENSLAND

Wagga
Wagga

VICTORIA
Melbourne

Bass Strait

Torres Strait

Mount Isa

Broken
Hill

Bendigo
Ballarat
Geelong

TASMANIA

Arafura Sea

Gulf of
Carpentaria

Port Pirie
Adelaide

Whyalla

NORTHERN
TERRITORY

Tennant
Creek

AUSTRALIA

Alice
Springs

SOUTH
AUSTRALIA

Kangaroo
Island

300 Miles

300 Kilometers

Azimuthal Equal-Area Projection

Katherine

Great Australian Bight

Timor Sea

Darwin

Indian Ocean

Halls
Creek

Derby

WESTERN
AUSTRALIA

Kalgoorlie

Port Hedland

Esperance

Albany

Indian
Ocean

Carnarvon

Geraldton

Perth

TROPIC OF CAPRICORN

Political

⊛ National capital
◉ State or territorial capital
• Other city

THE REGION: AUSTRALIA, NEW ZEALAND & OCEANIA

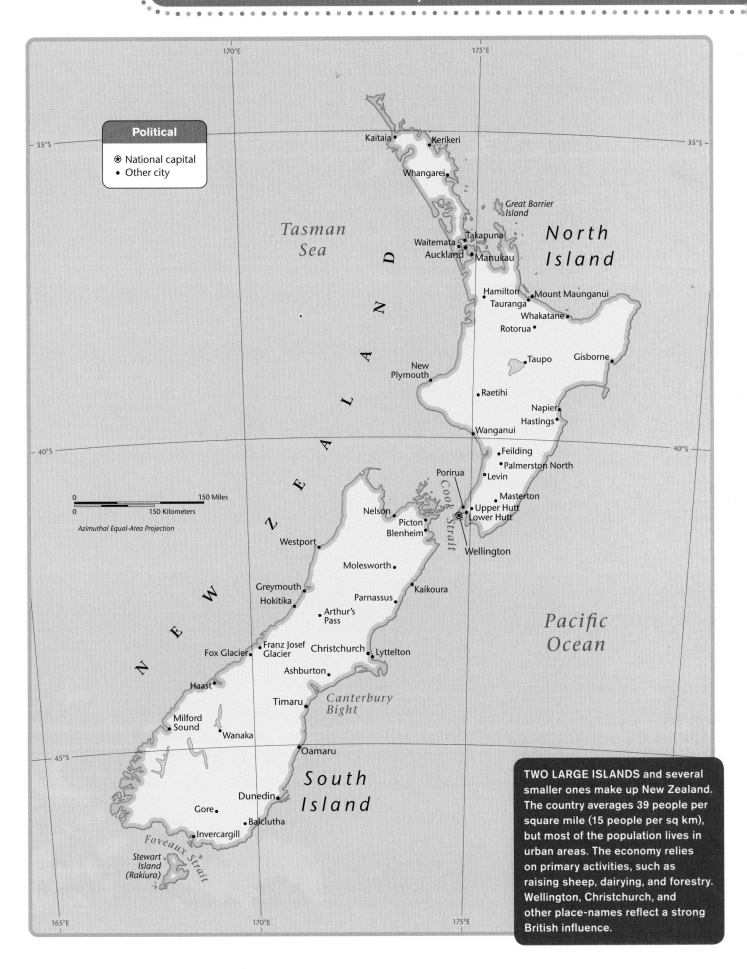

Political

⊛ National capital
• Other city

35°S

170°E   175°E

Kaitaia
Kerikeri
Whangarei

Tasman Sea

Great Barrier Island

North Island

Takapuna
Waitemata
Auckland Manukau

Hamilton Mount Maunganui
Tauranga
Whakatane
Rotorua

Taupo Gisborne

New Plymouth

Raetihi

Napier
Hastings

Wanganui

NEW ZEALAND

40°S

Feilding
Palmerston North
Porirua Levin
Masterton
Nelson Upper Hutt
Picton Lower Hutt
Blenheim

Westport

Molesworth

Greymouth Kaikoura
Hokitika Parnassus

Arthur's Pass

Fox Glacier Franz Josef Glacier Christchurch Lyttelton
Haast Ashburton

Milford Sound Timaru *Canterbury Bight*
Wanaka

Oamaru

South Island

Dunedin
Gore
Balclutha
Invercargill

Foveaux Strait

Stewart Island (Rakiura)

Cook Strait

Wellington

Pacific Ocean

150 Miles
0
0
150 Kilometers
Azimuthal Equal-Area Projection

165°E   170°E   175°E

TWO LARGE ISLANDS and several smaller ones make up New Zealand. The country averages 39 people per square mile (15 people per sq km), but most of the population lives in urban areas. The economy relies on primary activities, such as raising sheep, dairying, and forestry. Wellington, Christchurch, and other place-names reflect a strong British influence.

CORAL REEFS: SELECTED FACTS

Most coral reefs are between 5,000 and 10,000 years old, but some may have begun growing as much as 50 million years ago.

TYPES OF REEFS

FRINGING REEF –
near coastlines of islands and continents

BARRIER REEF –
parallel to a coastline but separated from it by deep lagoons

ATOLL –
ring of coral surrounding protected lagoons

PATCH REEF –
small, isolated reef growing up from a continental shelf

GROWING CONDITIONS

SUNLIGHT –
corals grow in shallow water

CLEAR WATER –
allows sunlight to penetrate

WARM WATER –
between 70° and 85°F (21° and 29°C)

CLEAN WATER –
pollution and sediments block sunlight and smother corals

SALT WATER –
a certain balance in the ratio of salt to water is necessary

Great Barrier Reef

Stretching like intricate necklaces along the edges of landmasses in the warm ocean waters of the tropics, coral reefs form one of nature's most complex ecosystems. Corals are tiny marine animals that thrive in shallow coastal waters of the tropics. One type of coral, called a "hard coral," produces a limestone skeleton. When the tiny animal dies, its stone-like skeleton is left behind. The accumulation of millions of these skeletons over thousands of years has produced the large reef formations found in many coastal waters of the tropics.

⬆ ANEMONE FISH swim among the waving polyps of one of the reef's sea anemones. These fish are specially adapted to live safely among the venom-filled tentacles that can inject a paralyzing neurotoxin into unsuspecting prey when disturbed.

Most coral reefs are found between 30 degrees N and 30 degrees S latitude in waters with a temperature between 70 and 85 degrees Fahrenheit (21 and 29 degrees Celsius). It is estimated that Earth's coral reefs cover 110,000 square miles (284,300 sq km). Coral reefs are important because they form a habitat for marine animals such as fish, sea turtles, lobsters, and starfish. They also protect fragile coastlines from damaging ocean waves and may be a source of valuable medicines.

The world's largest coral reef, the Great Barrier Reef, lies off the northeast coast of Australia (see large map). This reef, which is made up of more than 400 different types of coral and is home to more than 1,500 species of fish, is a popular tourist destination. People visit to snorkel and dive along the reef and view the great diversity of marine life living among the corals.

⇨ BRILLIANTLY COLORED CORALS and the fish that live among them attract divers and snorkelers to the Great Barrier Reef every year.

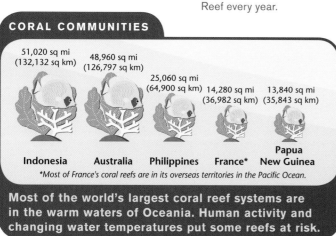

CORAL COMMUNITIES

51,020 sq mi (132,132 sq km) — Indonesia

48,960 sq mi (126,797 sq km) — Australia

25,060 sq mi (64,900 sq km) — Philippines

14,280 sq mi (36,982 sq km) — France*

13,840 sq mi (35,843 sq km) — Papua New Guinea

*Most of France's coral reefs are in its overseas territories in the Pacific Ocean.

Most of the world's largest coral reef systems are in the warm waters of Oceania. Human activity and changing water temperatures put some reefs at risk.

THE REGION: AUSTRALIA, NEW ZEALAND & OCEANIA

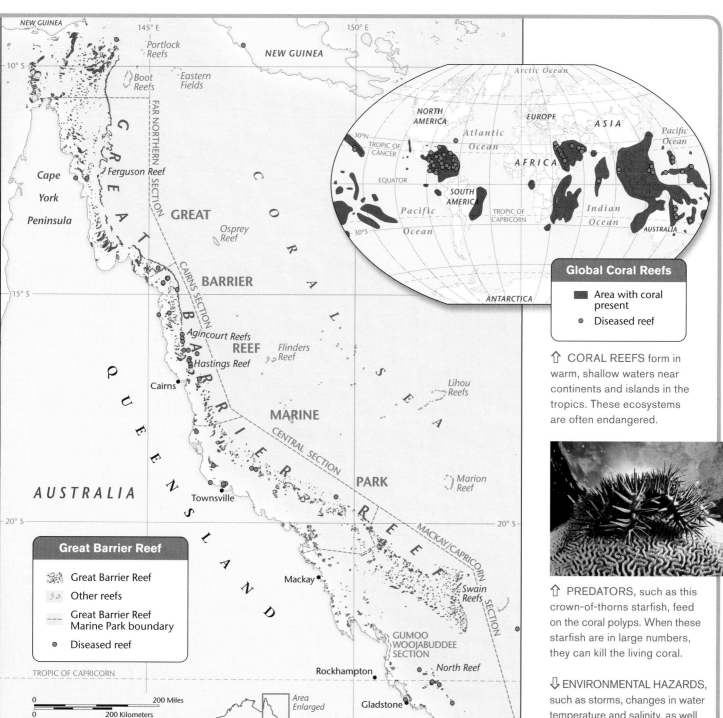

Global Coral Reefs

■ Area with coral present

● Diseased reef

⇧ CORAL REEFS form in warm, shallow waters near continents and islands in the tropics. These ecosystems are often endangered.

Great Barrier Reef

Great Barrier Reef

Other reefs

Great Barrier Reef Marine Park boundary

● Diseased reef

0 — 200 Miles
0 — 200 Kilometers
Mercator Projection

Area Enlarged
AUSTRALIA

⇧ PREDATORS, such as this crown-of-thorns starfish, feed on the coral polyps. When these starfish are in large numbers, they can kill the living coral.

⇩ ENVIRONMENTAL HAZARDS, such as storms, changes in water temperature and salinity, as well as pollution, put corals at risk.

⇧ THE GREAT BARRIER REEF stretches along the northeast coast of Australia for 1,429 miles (2,300 km), from the tip of the Cape York Peninsula to just north of Brisbane in the state of Queensland. The reef is actually a collection of more than 3,000 individual reef systems and is home to many different species of fish, mollusks, rays, dolphins, reptiles, and birds. There are even giant clams more than 120 years old. In addition, the reef is habitat for several endangered species, including the dugong (sea cow) and the green sea turtle. UNESCO recognized the Great Barrier Reef as a World Heritage Site in 1981.

Antarctica:
A View From Space

About 180 million years ago Antarctica broke away from the ancient super-continent Gondwana. Slowly the continent drifted to its present location at the southernmost point on Earth. Approximately 98 percent of the continent lies under permanent ice sheets that are nearly 3 miles (5 km) thick in places. It is estimated that if all of Antarctica's ice was to melt, the global ocean level would rise more than 200 feet (60 m).

A humpback whale swims by an iceberg off the coast of Antarctica .

THE CONTINENT: ANTARCTICA

PHYSICAL			POLITICAL		
Land area 5,100,000 sq mi (13,209,000 sq km)	**Lowest point** Bentley Subglacial Trench -8,383 ft (-2,555 m)	**Average precipitation on the polar plateau** Less than 2 in (5 cm) per year	**Population** There are no indigenous inhabitants, but there are both permanent and summer-only staffed research stations.	**Number of independent countries** 0	**Number of countries operating year-round research stations** 19
Highest point Vinson Massif 16,067 ft (4,897 m)	**Coldest place** Annual average temperature **Plateau Station** -70°F (-56.7°C)			**Number of countries claiming land** 7	**Number of year-round research stations** 45

Antarctica

THE CONTINENT: ANTARCTICA

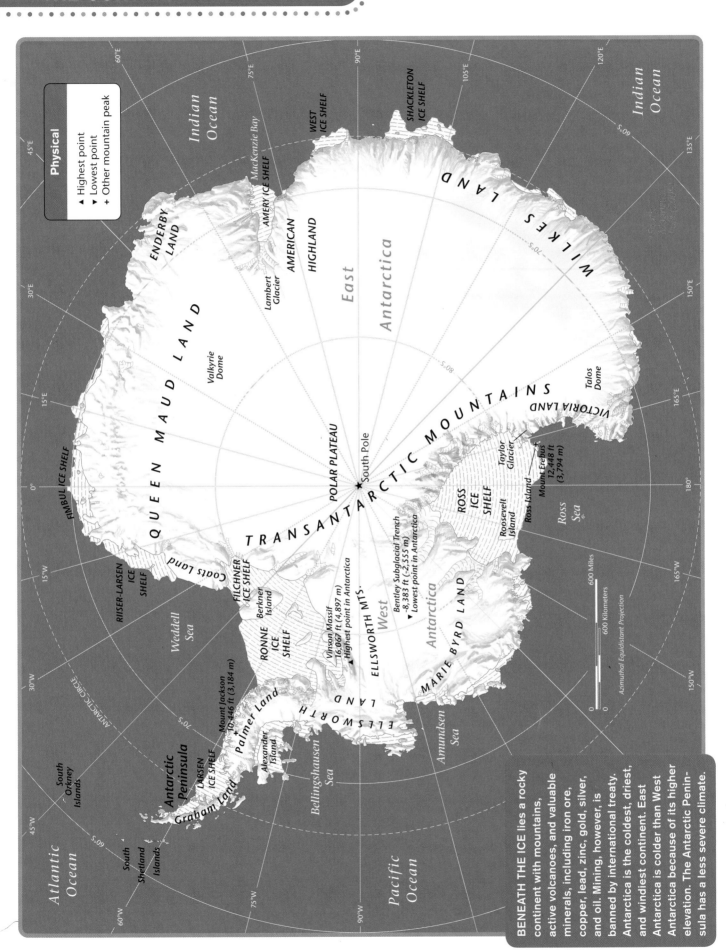

Physical
- ▲ Highest point
- ▶ Lowest point
- + Other mountain peak

Indian Ocean

Indian Ocean

WEST ICE SHELF

SHACKLETON ICE SHELF

MacKenzie Bay

AMERY ICE SHELF

ENDERBY LAND

AMERICAN HIGHLAND

Lambert Glacier

WILKES LAND

East Antarctica

Q U E E N   M A U D   L A N D

Valkyrie Dome

Talos Dome

VICTORIA LAND

FIMBUL ICE SHELF

POLAR PLATEAU

South Pole

T R A N S A N T A R C T I C   M O U N T A I N S

Taylor Glacier

Mount Erebus 12,448 ft (3,794 m)

Ross Island

ROSS ICE SHELF

Roosevelt Island

Ross Sea

RIISER-LARSEN ICE SHELF

Coats Land

FILCHNER ICE SHELF

Berkner Island

RONNE ICE SHELF

Weddell Sea

Bentley Subglacial Trench -8,383 ft (-2,555 m) ▶ Lowest point in Antarctica

Vinson Massif 16,067 ft (4,897 m) ▲ Highest point in Antarctica

ELLSWORTH MTS.

West Antarctica

MARIE BYRD LAND

Amundsen Sea

Mount Jackson 10,446 ft (3,184 m) +

Palmer Land

E L L S W O R T H   L A N D

Antarctic Peninsula

LARSEN ICE SHELF

Alexander Island

Graham Land

Bellingshausen Sea

South Orkney Islands

ANTARCTIC CIRCLE

South Shetland Islands

Atlantic Ocean

Pacific Ocean

600 Miles
600 Kilometers
Azimuthal Equidistant Projection

BENEATH THE ICE lies a rocky continent with mountains, active volcanoes, and valuable minerals, including iron ore, copper, lead, zinc, gold, silver, and oil. Mining, however, is banned by international treaty. Antarctica is the coldest, driest, and windiest continent. East Antarctica is colder than West Antarctica because of its higher elevation. The Antarctic Peninsula has a less severe climate.

THE CONTINENT: ANTARCTICA

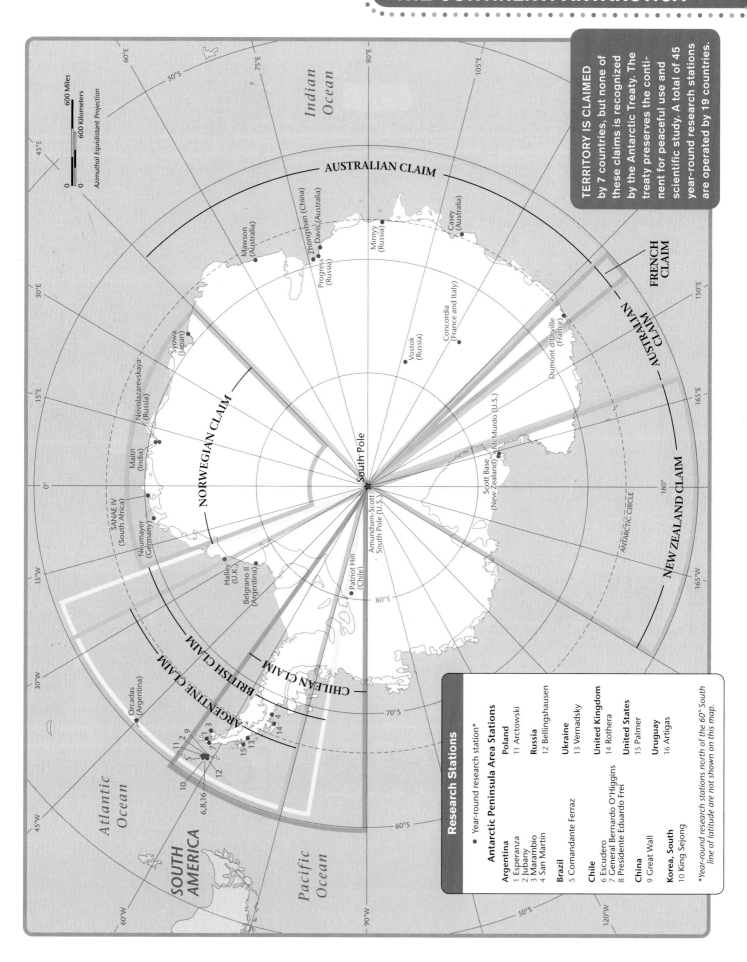

TERRITORY IS CLAIMED by 7 countries, but none of these claims is recognized by the Antarctic Treaty. The treaty preserves the continent for peaceful use and scientific study. A total of 45 year-round research stations are operated by 19 countries.

600 Miles
600 Kilometers
Azimuthal Equidistant Projection

Indian Ocean

AUSTRALIAN CLAIM

Mawson (Australia)
Zhongshan (China)
Davis (Australia)
Progress (Russia)
Casey (Australia)
Mirnyy (Russia)
Concordia (France and Italy)
Vostok (Russia)
Dumont d'Urville (France)

FRENCH CLAIM
AUSTRALIAN CLAIM

Syowa (Japan)
Novolazarevskaya (Russia)
Maitri (India)
Neumayer (Germany)
SANAE IV (South Africa)

NORWEGIAN CLAIM

McMurdo (U.S.)
Scott Base (New Zealand)
Amundsen-Scott South Pole (U.S.)

South Pole

NEW ZEALAND CLAIM

ANTARCTIC CIRCLE

Halley (U.K.)
Belgrano II (Argentina)
Patriot Hill (Chile)

BRITISH CLAIM
ARGENTINE CLAIM
CHILEAN CLAIM

Orcadas (Argentina)

11 2 9
1 3
5 7
12
6,8,16
15 13
4
14
10

80°S

70°S

60°S

50°S

Atlantic Ocean

SOUTH AMERICA

Pacific Ocean

Research Stations

• Year-round research station*

Antarctic Peninsula Area Stations

Argentina
1 Esperanza
2 Jubany
3 Marambio
4 San Martín

Brazil
5 Comandante Ferraz

Chile
6 Escudero
7 General Bernardo O'Higgins
8 Presidente Eduardo Frei

China
9 Great Wall

Korea, South
10 King Sejong

Poland
11 Arctowski

Russia
12 Bellingshausen

Ukraine
13 Vernadsky

United Kingdom
14 Rothera

United States
15 Palmer

Uruguay
16 Artigas

*Year-round research stations north of the 60° South line of latitude are not shown on this map.

Flags & Stats

The following pages provide a quick glance at flags, facts, and figures for all 194 independent countries, listed in alphabetical order, that were recognized by the National Geographic Society in 2008. An independent country has a national government that is accepted as having the highest legal authority over the land and people within its boundaries.

The flags shown are national flags recognized by the United Nations. Each flag symbolizes the diverse cultures and histories of the respective country. The statistical data, which provide highlights of geography and demography, offer a brief overview of each country. Area figures include land as well as surface areas for inland bodies of water. Population figures are for mid-2007 as provided by the Population Reference Bureau of the United States. The languages listed are either the ones most commonly spoken within a country or official languages of a country. For example, not every language spoken in a specific country can be listed, but those shown are the most representative of that country.

Angola
Continent: Africa
Area: 481,354 sq mi (1,246,700 sq km)
Population: 16,293,000
Capital: Luanda 4,007,000
Language: Portuguese, Bantu and other African languages

Austria
Continent: Europe
Area: 32,378 sq mi (83,858 sq km)
Population: 8,315,000
Capital: Vienna 2,315,000
Language: German

Barbados
Continent: North America
Area: 166 sq mi (430 km)
Population: 278,000
Capital: Bridgetown 116,000
Language: English

Antigua and Barbuda
Continent: North America
Area: 171 sq mi (442 sq km)
Population: 86,000
Capital: St. John's 26,000
Language: English, local dialects

Azerbaijan
Continent: Europe/Asia
Area: 33,436 sq mi (86,600 sq km)
Population: 8,581,000
Capital: Baku 1,892,000
Language: Azerbaijani (Azeri)

Belarus
Continent: Europe
Area: 80,153 sq mi (207,595 sq km)
Population: 9,696,000
Capital: Minsk 1,806,000
Language: Belarusian, Russian

Argentina
Continent: South America
Area: 1,073,518 sq mi (2,780,400 sq km)
Population: 39,356,000
Capital: Buenos Aires 12,795,000
Language: Spanish, English, Italian, German, French

Bahamas
Continent: North America
Area: 5,382 sq mi (13,939 sq km)
Population: 334,000
Capital: Nassau 240,000
Language: English, Creole

Belgium
Continent: Europe
Area: 11,787 sq mi (30,528 sq km)
Population: 10,611,000
Capital: Brussels 1,743,000
Language: Dutch, French

Afghanistan
Continent: Asia
Area: 251,773 sq mi (652,090 sq km)
Population: 31,890,000
Capital: Kabul 3,324,000
Language: Afghan Persian (Dari), Pashto, Turkic languages, Baluchi, 30 minor languages

Algeria
Continent: Africa
Area: 919,595 sq mi (2,381,741 sq km)
Population: 34,104,000
Capital: Algiers 3,355,000
Language: Arabic, French, Berber dialects

Armenia
Continent: Asia
Area: 11,484 sq mi (29,743 sq km)
Population: 3,014,000
Capital: Yerevan 1,102,000
Language: Armenian

Bahrain
Continent: Asia
Area: 277 sq mi (717 sq km)
Population: 762,000
Capital: Manama 157,000
Language: Arabic, English, Farsi, Urdu

Belize
Continent: North America
Area: 8,867 sq mi (22,965 sq km)
Population: 311,000
Capital: Belmopan 16,000
Language: Spanish, Creole, Mayan dialects, English, Garifuna (Carib), German

Albania
Continent: Europe
Area: 11,100 sq mi (28,748 sq km)
Population: 3,174,000
Capital: Tirana 406,000
Language: Albanian, Greek, Vlach, Romani, Slavic dialects

Andorra
Continent: Europe
Area: 181 sq mi (468 sq km)
Population: 81,000
Capital: Andorra la Vella 24,000
Language: Catalan, French, Castilian, Portuguese

Australia
Continent: Australia/Oceania
Area: 2,969,906 sq mi (7,692,024 sq km)
Population: 21,000,000
Capital: Canberra 378,000
Language: English

Bangladesh
Continent: Asia
Area: 56,977 sq mi (147,570 sq km)
Population: 149,002,000
Capital: Dhaka 13,485,000
Language: Bangla (Bengali), English

Benin
Continent: Africa
Area: 43,484 sq mi (112,622 sq km)
Population: 9,033,000
Capital: Porto-Novo (constitutional) 257,000; Cotonou (seat of government) 762,000
Language: French, Fon, Yoruba, tribal languages

Bhutan
Continent: Asia
Area: 17,954 sq mi
(46,500 sq km)
Population: 896,000
Capital: Thimphu 83,000
Language: Dzongkha, Tibetan
dialects, Nepalese dialects

Brunei
Continent: Asia
Area: 2,226 sq mi
(5,765 sq km)
Population: 372,000
Capital: Bandar Seri Begawan
22,000
Language: Malay, English,
Chinese

Cameroon
Continent: Africa
Area: 183,569 sq mi
(475,442 sq km)
Population: 18,060,000
Capital: Yaoundé 1,610,000
Language: 24 major African
language groups, English,
French

Chile
Continent: South America
Area: 291,930 sq mi
(756,096 sq km)
Population: 16,598,000
Capital: Santiago 5,719,000
Language: Spanish

Costa Rica
Continent: North America
Area: 19,730 sq mi
(51,100 sq km)
Population: 4,477,000
Capital: San José 1,284,000
Language: Spanish, English

Bolivia
Continent: South America
Area: 424,164 sq mi
(1,098,581 sq km)
Population: 9,815,000
Capital: La Paz 1,590,000;
Sucre (legal) 243,000
Language: Spanish, Quechua,
Aymara

Bulgaria
Continent: Europe
Area: 42,855 sq mi
(110,994 sq km)
Population: 7,660,000
Capital: Sofia 1,186,000
Language: Bulgarian, Turkish,
Roma

Canada
Continent: North America
Area: 3,855,101 sq mi
(9,984,670 sq km)
Population: 32,943,000
Capital: Ottawa 1,143,000
Language: English, French

China
Continent: Asia
Area: 3,705,405 sq mi
(9,596,960 sq km)
Population: 1,348,317,000
Capital: Beijing 11,106,000
Language: Standard Chinese
or Mandarin, Yue, Wu, Minbei
dialects, minority languages

Côte d'Ivoire (Ivory Coast)
Continent: Africa
Area: 124,503 sq mi
(322,462 sq km)
Population: 20,237,000
Capital: Abidjan 3,801,000;
Yamoussoukro 669,000
Language: French, Dioula,
other native dialects

Bosnia and Herzegovina
Continent: Europe
Area: 19,741 sq mi
(51,129 sq km)
Population: 3,845,000
Capital: Sarajevo 377,000
Language: Bosnian, Croatian,
Serbian

Burkina Faso
Continent: Africa
Area: 105,869 sq mi
(274,200 sq km)
Population: 14,784,000
Capital: Ouagadougou
1,148,000
Language: French, native
African languages

Cape Verde
Continent: Africa
Area: 1,558 sq mi
(4,036 sq km)
Population: 494,000
Capital: Praia 125,000
Language: Portuguese, Crioulo

Colombia
Continent: South America
Area: 440,831 sq mi
(1,141,748 sq km)
Population: 46,156,000
Capital: Bogotá 7,764,000
Language: Spanish

Croatia
Continent: Europe
Area: 21,831 sq mi
(56,542 sq km)
Population: 4,448,000
Capital: Zagreb 689,000
Language: Croatian

Botswana
Continent: Africa
Area: 224,607 sq mi
(581,730 sq km)
Population: 1,753,000
Capital: Gaborone 224,000
Language: Setswana, Kalanga

Burundi
Continent: Africa
Area: 10,747 sq mi
(27,834 sq km)
Population: 8,508,000
Capital: Bujumbura 430,000
Language: Kirundi, French,
Swahili

Central African Republic
Continent: Africa
Area: 240,535 sq mi
(622,984 sq km)
Population: 4,343,000
Capital: Bangui 672,000
Language: French, Sangho,
tribal languages

Comoros
Continent: Africa
Area: 719 sq mi
(1,862 sq km)
Population: 711,000
Capital: Moroni 46,000
Language: Arabic, French,
Shikomoro

Cuba
Continent: North America
Area: 42,803 sq mi
(110,860 sq km)
Population: 11,248,000
Capital: Havana 2,178,000
Language: Spanish

Brazil
Continent: South America
Area: 3,300,169 sq mi
(8,547,403 sq km)
Population: 189,335,000
Capital: Brasília 3,594,000
Language: Portuguese

Cambodia
Continent: Asia
Area: 69,898 sq mi
(181,035 sq km)
Population: 14,364,000
Capital: Phnom Penh
1,465,000
Language: Khmer

Chad
Continent: Africa
Area: 495,755 sq mi
(1,284,000 sq km)
Population: 10,781,000
Capital: N'Djamena 987,000
Language: French, Arabic,
Sara, over 120 languages and
dialects

Congo
Continent: Africa
Area: 132,047 sq mi
(342,000 sq km)
Population: 3,801,000
Capital: Brazzaville 1,332,000
Language: French, Lingala,
Monokutuba, local languages

Cyprus
Continent: Europe
Area: 3,572 sq mi
(9,251 sq km)
Population: 1,023,000
Capital: Nicosia 233,000
Language: Greek, Turkish,
English

Czech Republic
(Czechia)
Continent: Europe
Area: 30,450 sq mi
(78,866 sq km)
Population: 10,305,000
Capital: Prague 1,162,000
Language: Czech

Dominican
Republic
Continent: North America
Area: 18,704 sq mi
(48,442 sq km)
Population: 9,366,000
Capital: Santo Domingo
2,154,000
Language: Spanish

Eritrea
Continent: Africa
Area: 46,774 sq mi
(121,144 sq km)
Population: 4,851,000
Capital: Asmara 600,000
Language: Afar, Arabic, Tigre,
Kunama, Tigrinya, other Cushitic
languages

France
Continent: Europe
Area: 210,026 sq mi
(543,965 sq km)
Population: 61,725,000
Capital: Paris 9,902,000
Language: French

Ghana
Continent: Africa
Area: 92,100 sq mi
(238,537 sq km)
Population: 22,995,000
Capital: Accra 2,120,000
Language: Asante, Ewe, Fante,
Boron, Dagomba, Dangme,
Dagarte, Akyem, Ga, English

Democratic Republic
of the Congo
Continent: Africa
Area: 905,365 sq mi
(2,344,885 sq km)
Population: 62,636,000
Capital: Kinshasa 7,851,000
Language: French, Lingala,
Kingwana, Kikongo, Tshiluba

Ecuador
Continent: South America
Area: 109,483 sq mi
(283,560 sq km)
Population: 13,473,000
Capital: Quito 1,697,000
Language: Spanish, Quechua,
other Amerindian languages

Estonia
Continent: Europe
Area: 17,462 sq mi
(45,227 sq km)
Population: 1,341,000
Capital: Tallinn 397,000
Language: Estonian, Russian

Gabon
Continent: Africa
Area: 103,347 sq mi
(267,667 sq km)
Population: 1,331,000
Capital: Libreville 576,000
Language: French, Fang,
Myene, Nzebi, Bapounou/
Eschira, Bandjabi

Greece
Continent: Europe
Area: 50,949 sq mi
(131,957 sq km)
Population: 11,189,000
Capital: Athens 3,242,000
Language: Greek

Denmark
Continent: Europe
Area: 16,640 sq mi
(43,098 sq km)
Population: 5,454,000
Capital: Copenhagen 1,086,000
Language: Danish, Faroese,
Greenlandic, German, English
as second language

Egypt
Continent: Africa
Area: 386,874 sq mi
(1,002,000 sq km)
Population: 73,418,000
Capital: Cairo 11,893,000
Language: Arabic, English,
French

Ethiopia
Continent: Africa
Area: 437,600 sq mi
(1,133,380 sq km)
Population: 77,127,000
Capital: Addis Ababa
3,102,000
Language: Amharic, Oromigna,
Tigrinya, Guaragigna, Somali

Gambia
Continent: Africa
Area: 4,361 sq mi
(11,295 sq km)
Population: 1,517,000
Capital: Banjul 407,000
Language: English, Mandinka,
Wolof, Fula, other indigenous
vernaculars

Grenada
Continent: North America
Area: 133 sq mi (344 sq km)
Population: 99,000
Capital: St. George's 32,000
Language: English, French
patois

Djibouti
Continent: Africa
Area: 8,958 sq mi
(23,200 sq km)
Population: 833,000
Capital: Djibouti 583,000
Language: French, Arabic,
Somali, Afar

El Salvador
Continent: North America
Area: 8,124 sq mi
(21,041 sq km)
Population: 6,877,000
Capital: San Salvador
1,433,000
Language: Spanish, Nahua

Fiji Islands
Continent: Australia/Oceania
Area: 7,095 sq mi
(18,376 sq km)
Population: 862,000
Capital: Suva 224,000
Language: English, Fijian,
Hindustani

Georgia
Continent: Europe/Asia
Area: 26,911 sq mi
(69,700 sq km)
Population: 4,524,000
Capital: T'bilisi 1,099,000
Language: Georgian, Russian,
Armenian, Azeri, Abkhaz

Guatemala
Continent: North America
Area: 42,042 sq mi
(108,889 sq km)
Population: 13,354,000
Capital: Guatemala City
1,025,000
Language: Spanish, 23 recog-
nized Amerindian languages

Dominica
Continent: North America
Area: 290 sq mi (751 sq km)
Population: 70,000
Capital: Roseau 14,000
Language: English, French
patois

Equatorial Guinea
Continent: Africa
Area: 10,831 sq mi
(28,051 sq km)
Population: 507,000
Capital: Malabo 96,000
Language: Spanish, French,
Fang, Bubi

Finland
Continent: Europe
Area: 130,558 sq mi
(338,145 sq km)
Population: 5,288,000
Capital: Helsinki 1,115,000
Language: Finnish, Swedish

Germany
Continent: Europe
Area: 137,847 sq mi
(357,022 sq km)
Population: 82,254,000
Capital: Berlin 3,405,000
Language: German

Guinea
Continent: Africa
Area: 94,926 sq mi
(245,857 sq km)
Population: 10,112,000
Capital: Conakry 1,494,000
Language: French, ethnic
languages

Guinea-Bissau
Continent: Africa
Area: 13,948 sq mi
(36,125 sq km)
Population: 1,695,000
Capital: Bissau 330,000
Language: Portuguese, Crioulo,
African languages

Iceland
Continent: Europe
Area: 39,769 sq mi
(103,000 sq km)
Population: 313,000
Capital: Reykjavík 192,000
Language: Icelandic, English,
Nordic languages, German

Ireland
Continent: Europe
Area: 27,133 sq mi
(70,273 sq km)
Population: 4,369,000
Capital: Dublin 1,060,000
Language: Irish (Gaelic),
English

Jordan
Continent: Asia
Area: 34,495 sq mi
(89,342 sq km)
Population: 5,728,000
Capital: Amman 1,064,000
Language: Arabic, English

Kuwait
Continent: Asia
Area: 6,880 sq mi
(17,818 sq km)
Population: 2,778,000
Capital: Kuwait 2,061,000
Language: Arabic, English

Guyana
Continent: South America
Area: 83,000 sq mi
(214,969 sq km)
Population: 763,000
Capital: Georgetown 133,000
Language: English, Amerindian
dialects, Creole, Hindustani,
Urdu

India
Continent: Asia
Area: 1,269,221 sq mi
(3,287,270 sq km)
Population: 1,131,883,000
Capital: New Delhi 15,926,000
(part of Delhi metropolitan area)
Language: Hindi, English,
212 other official languages

Israel
Continent: Asia
Area: 8,550 sq mi
(22,145 sq km)
Population: 7,347,000
Capital: Jerusalem 736,000
Language: Hebrew, Arabic,
English

Kazakhstan
Continent: Europe/Asia
Area: 1,049,155 sq mi
(2,717,300 sq km)
Population: 15,486,000
Capital: Astana 594,000
Language: Kazakh (Qazaq),
Russian

Kyrgyzstan
Continent: Asia
Area: 77,182 sq mi
(199,900 sq km)
Population: 5,216,000
Capital: Bishkek 837,000
Language: Kyrgyz, Uzbek,
Russian

Haiti
Continent: North America
Area: 10,714 sq mi
(27,750 sq km)
Population: 8,967,000
Capital: Port-au-Prince
2,002,000
Language: French, Creole

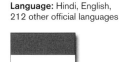

Indonesia
Continent: Asia
Area: 742,308 sq mi
(1,922,570 sq km)
Population: 231,627,000
Capital: Jakarta 9,143,000
Language: Bahasa Indonesia
(modified form of Malay),
English, Dutch, Javanese

Italy
Continent: Europe
Area: 116,345 sq mi
(301,333 sq km)
Population: 59,337,000
Capital: Rome 3,340,000
Language: Italian, German,
French, Slovene

Kenya
Continent: Africa
Area: 224,081 sq mi
(580,367 sq km)
Population: 36,914,000
Capital: Nairobi 3,011,000
Language: English, Kiswahili,
many indigenous languages

Laos
Continent: Asia
Area: 91,429 sq mi
(236,800 sq km)
Population: 5,862,000
Capital: Vientiane 746,000
Language: Lao, French,
English, various ethnic
languages

Honduras
Continent: North America
Area: 43,433 sq mi
(112,492 sq km)
Population: 7,106,000
Capital: Tegucigalpa 947,000
Language: Spanish, Amer-
indian dialects

Iran
Continent: Asia
Area: 636,296 sq mi
(1,648,000 sq km)
Population: 71,208,000
Capital: Tehran 7,875,000
Language: Persian, Turkic,
Kurdish, Luri, Baluchi, Arabic

Jamaica
Continent: North America
Area: 4,244 sq mi
(10,991 sq km)
Population: 2,680,000
Capital: Kingston 581,000
Language: English, English
patois

Kiribati
Continent: Australia/Oceania
Area: 313 sq mi (811 sq km)
Population: 96,000
Capital: Tarawa 42,000
Language: I-Kiribati, English

Latvia
Continent: Europe
Area: 24,938 sq mi
(64,589 sq km)
Population: 2,275,000
Capital: Riga 722,000
Language: Latvian, Russian,
Lithuanian

Hungary
Continent: Europe
Area: 35,919 sq mi
(93,030 sq km)
Population: 10,058,000
Capital: Budapest 1,675,000
Language: Hungarian

Iraq
Continent: Asia
Area: 168,754 sq mi
(437,072 sq km)
Population: 28,993,000
Capital: Baghdad 5,500,000
Language: Arabic, Kurdish,
Assyrian, Armenian

Japan
Continent: Asia
Area: 145,902 sq mi
(377,887 sq km)
Population: 127,730,000
Capital: Tokyo 35,676,000
Language: Japanese

Kosovo
Continent: Europe
Area: 4,203 sq mi
(10,887 sq km)
Population: 1,900,000
Capital: Pristina 600,000
Language: Albanian, Serbian,
Bosnian, Turkish, Roma

Lebanon
Continent: Asia
Area: 4,036 sq mi
(10,452 sq km)
Population: 3,921,000
Capital: Beirut 1,857,000
Language: Arabic, French,
English, Armenian

Lesotho
Continent: Africa
Area: 11,720 sq mi (30,355 sq km)
Population: 1,798,000
Capital: Maseru 212,000
Language: Sesotho, English, Zulu, Xhosa

Luxembourg
Continent: Europe
Area: 998 sq mi (2,586 sq km)
Population: 466,000
Capital: Luxembourg 84,000
Language: Luxembourgish, German, French

Maldives
Continent: Asia
Area: 115 sq mi (298 sq km)
Population: 304,000
Capital: Male 111,000
Language: Maldivian Dhivehi, English

Mauritius
Continent: Africa
Area: 788 sq mi (2,040 sq km)
Population: 1,261,000
Capital: Port Louis 150,000
Language: Creole, Bhojpuri, French

Mongolia
Continent: Asia
Area: 603,909 sq mi (1,564,116 sq km)
Population: 2,610,000
Capital: Ulaanbaatar 884,000
Language: Khalkha Mongol, Turkic, Russian

Liberia
Continent: Africa
Area: 43,000 sq mi (111,370 sq km)
Population: 3,750,000
Capital: Monrovia 1,165,000
Language: English, 20 ethnic languages

Macedonia
Continent: Europe
Area: 9,928 sq mi (25,713 sq km)
Population: 2,047,000
Capital: Skopje 480,000
Language: Macedonian, Albanian, Turkish

Mali
Continent: Africa
Area: 478,841 sq mi (1,240,192 sq km)
Population: 12,337,000
Capital: Bamako 1,494,000
Language: Bambara, French, numerous African languages

Mexico
Continent: North America
Area: 758,449 sq mi (1,964,375 sq km)
Population: 106,535,000
Capital: Mexico City 19,028,000
Language: Spanish, Mayan, Nahuatl, other indigenous languages

Montenegro
Continent: Europe
Area: 5,415 sq mi (14,026 sq km)
Population: 626,000
Capital: Podgorica 142,000
Language: Serbian (Ijekavian dialect), Bosnian, Albanian, Croatian

Libya
Continent: Africa
Area: 679,362 sq mi (1,759,540 sq km)
Population: 6,160,000
Capital: Tripoli 2,188,000
Language: Arabic, Italian, English

Madagascar
Continent: Africa
Area: 226,658 sq mi (587,041 sq km)
Population: 18,252,000
Capital: Antananarivo 1,697,000
Language: English, French, Malagasy

Malta
Continent: Europe
Area: 122 sq mi (316 sq km)
Population: 407,000
Capital: Valletta 199,000
Language: Maltese, English

Micronesia
Continent: Australia/Oceania
Area: 271 sq mi (702 sq km)
Population: 108,000
Capital: Palikir 7,000
Language: English, Trukese, Pohnpeian, Yapese, other indigenous languages

Morocco
Continent: Africa
Area: 274,461 sq mi (710,850 sq km)
Population: 31,711,000
Capital: Rabat 1,705,000
Language: Arabic, Berber dialects, French

Liechtenstein
Continent: Europe
Area: 62 sq mi (160 sq km)
Population: 35,000
Capital: Vaduz 5,000
Language: German, Alemannic dialect

Malawi
Continent: Africa
Area: 45,747 sq mi (118,484 sq km)
Population: 13,070,000
Capital: Lilongwe 732,000
Language: Chichewa, Chinyanja, Chiyao, Chitumbuka

Marshall Islands
Continent: Australia/Oceania
Area: 70 sq mi (181 sq km)
Population: 67,000
Capital: Majuro 28,000
Language: Marshallese

Moldova
Continent: Europe
Area: 13,050 sq mi (33,800 sq km)
Population: 3,991,000
Capital: Chisinau 592,000
Language: Moldovan, Russian, Gagauz

Mozambique
Continent: Africa
Area: 308,642 sq mi (799,380 sq km)
Population: 20,359,000
Capital: Maputo 1,445,000
Language: Emakhuwa, Xichangana, Portuguese, Elomwe, Cisena, Echuwabo

Lithuania
Continent: Europe
Area: 25,212 sq mi (65,300 sq km)
Population: 3,376,000
Capital: Vilnius 543,000
Language: Lithuanian, Russian, Polish

Malaysia
Continent: Asia
Area: 127,355 sq mi (329,847 sq km)
Population: 27,160,000
Capital: Kuala Lumpur 1,448,000
Language: Bahasa Malaysia, English, Chinese, Tamil, Telugu, Malayalam, Panjabi, Thai

Mauritania
Continent: Africa
Area: 397,955 sq mi (1,030,700 sq km)
Population: 3,124,000
Capital: Nouakchott 673,000
Language: Arabic, Pulaar, Soninke, French, Hassaniya, Wolof

Monaco
Continent: Europe
Area: 0.8 sq mi (2.0 sq km)
Population: 33,000
Capital: Monaco 33,000
Language: French, English, Italian, Monegasque

Myanmar (Burma)
Continent: Asia
Area: 261,218 sq mi (676,552 sq km)
Population: 49,805,000
Capital: Nay Pyi Taw (administrative) 418,000; Yangon (Rangoon) (legislative) 4,088,000
Language: Burmese, minority ethnic languages

Namibia
Continent: Africa
Area: 318,261 sq mi (824,292 sq km)
Population: 2,074,000
Capital: Windhoek 313,000
Language: Afrikaans, German, English

Nicaragua
Continent: North America
Area: 50,193 sq mi (130,000 sq km)
Population: 5,620,000
Capital: Managua 920,000
Language: Spanish

Oman
Continent: Asia
Area: 119,500 sq mi (309,500 sq km)
Population: 2,706,000
Capital: Muscat 621,000
Language: Arabic, English, Baluchi, Urdu, Indian dialects

Paraguay
Continent: South America
Area: 157,048 sq mi (406,752 sq km)
Population: 6,126,000
Capital: Asunción 1,870,000
Language: Spanish, Guarani

Qatar
Continent: Asia
Area: 4,448 sq mi (11,521 sq km)
Population: 882,000
Capital: Doha 386,000
Language: Arabic, English commonly a second language

Nauru
Continent: Australia/Oceania
Area: 8 sq mi (21 sq km)
Population: 14,000
Capital: Yaren 10,000
Language: Nauruan, English

Niger
Continent: Africa
Area: 489,191 sq mi (1,267,000 sq km)
Population: 14,226,000
Capital: Niamey 915,000
Language: French, Hausa, Djerma

Pakistan
Continent: Asia
Area: 307,374 sq mi (796,095 sq km)
Population: 169,271,000
Capital: Islamabad
Language: Punjabi, Sindhi, Siraiki, Pashto, Urdu, Baluchi, Hindko, English

Peru
Continent: South America
Area: 496,224 sq mi (1,285,216 sq km)
Population: 27,903,000
Capital: Lima 8,007,000
Language: Spanish, Quechua, Aymara, minor Amazonian languages

Romania
Continent: Europe
Area: 92,043 sq mi (238,391 sq km)
Population: 21,550,000
Capital: Bucharest 1,940,000
Language: Romanian, Hungarian

Nepal
Continent: Asia
Area: 56,827 sq mi (147,181 sq km)
Population: 27,828,000
Capital: Kathmandu 895,000
Language: Nepali, Maithali, Bhojpuri, Tharu, Tamang, Newar, Magar

Nigeria
Continent: Africa
Area: 356,669 sq mi (923,768 sq km)
Population: 144,430,000
Capital: Abuja 1,579,000
Language: English, Hausa, Yoruba, Igbo (Ibo), Fulani

Palau
Continent: Australia/Oceania
Area: 189 sq mi (489 sq km)
Population: 20,000
Capital: Melekeok NA
Language: Palauan, Filipino, English, Chinese

Philippines
Continent: Asia
Area: 115,831 sq mi (300,000 sq km)
Population: 88,706,000 Filipino(s)
Capital: Manila 11,100,000
Language: Filipino (based on Tagalog), English

Russia
Continent: Europe/Asia
Area: 6,592,850 sq mi (17,075,400 sq km)
Population: 141,681,000
Capital: Moscow 10,452,000
Language: Russian, many minority languages

Netherlands
Continent: Europe
Area: 16,034 sq mi (41,528 sq km)
Population: 16,368,000
Capital: Amsterdam 1,031,000
Language: Dutch, Frisian

North Korea
Continent: Asia
Area: 46,540 sq mi (120,538 sq km)
Population: 23,301,000
Capital: Pyongyang 3,301,000
Language: Korean

Panama
Continent: North America
Area: 29,157 sq mi (75,517 sq km)
Population: 3,340,000
Capital: Panama City 1,280,000
Language: Spanish, English

Poland
Continent: Europe
Area: 120,728 sq mi (312,685 sq km)
Population: 38,109,000
Capital: Warsaw 1,707,000
Language: Polish

Rwanda
Continent: Africa
Area: 10,169 sq mi (26,338 sq km)
Population: 9,347,000
Capital: Kigali 852,000
Language: Kinyarwanda, French, English, Kiswahili

New Zealand
Continent: Australia/Oceania
Area: 104,454 sq mi (270,534 sq km)
Population: 4,184,000
Capital: Wellington 366,000
Language: English, Maori

Norway
Continent: Europe
Area: 125,004 sq mi (323,758 sq km)
Population: 4,702,000
Capital: Oslo 834,000
Language: Bokmal Norwegian, Nynorsk Norwegian, Sami

Papua New Guinea
Continent: Australia/Oceania
Area: 178,703 sq mi (462,840 sq km)
Population: 6,331,000
Capital: Port Moresby 299,000
Language: Melanesian Pidgin, 820 indigenous languages

Portugal
Continent: Europe
Area: 35,655 sq mi (92,345 sq km)
Population: 10,667,000
Capital: Lisbon 2,811,000
Language: Portuguese, Mirandese

Samoa
Continent: Australia/Oceania
Area: 1,093 sq mi (2,831 sq km)
Population: 187,000
Capital: Apia 43,000
Language: Samoan (Polynesian), English

San Marino
Continent: Europe
Area: 24 sq mi (61 sq km)
Population: 31,000
Capital: San Marino 4,000
Language: Italian

Seychelles
Continent: Africa
Area: 176 sq mi (455 sq km)
Population: 86,000
Capital: Victoria 26,000
Language: Creole, English

Solomon Islands
Continent: Australia/Oceania
Area: 10,954 sq mi
(28,370 sq km)
Population: 495,000
Capital: Honiara 66,000
Language: Melanesian pidgin,
120 indigenous languages

Sri Lanka
Continent: Asia
Area: 25,299 sq mi
(65,525 sq km)
Population: 20,087,000
Capital: Colombo 656,000
Language: Sinhala, Tamil

Suriname
Continent: South America
Area: 63,037 sq mi
(163,265 sq km)
Population: 503,000
Capital: Paramaribo 252,000
Language: Dutch, English,
Sranang Tongo, Hindustani,
Javanese

Sao Tome and Principe
Continent: Africa
Area: 386 sq mi (1,001 sq km)
Population: 155,000
Capital: São Tomé 58,000
Language: Portuguese

Sierra Leone
Continent: Africa
Area: 27,699 sq mi
(71,740 sq km)
Population: 5,335,000
Capital: Freetown 826,000
Language: English, Mende,
Temne, Krio

Somalia
Continent: Africa
Area: 246,201 sq mi
(637,657 sq km)
Population: 9,119,000
Capital: Mogadishu 1,450,000
Language: Somali, Arabic,
Italian, English

St. Kitts and Nevis
Continent: North America
Area: 104 sq mi (269 sq km)
Population: 47,000
Capital: Basseterre 13,000
Language: English

Swaziland
Continent: Africa
Area: 6,704 sq mi
(17,363 sq km)
Population: 1,133,000
Capital: Mbabane (administrative) 78,000; Lobamba
(legislative and royal) NA
Language: English, siSwati

Saudi Arabia
Continent: Asia
Area: 756,985 sq mi
(1,960,582 sq km)
Population: 27,601,000
Capital: Riyadh 4,462,000
Language: Arabic

Singapore
Continent: Asia
Area: 255 sq mi (660 sq km)
Population: 4,634,000
Capital: Singapore 4,634,000
Language: Mandarin, English,
Malay, Hokkien, Cantonese,
Teochew, Tamil

South Africa
Continent: Africa
Area: 470,693 sq mi
(1,219,090 sq km)
Population: 47,867,000
Capital: Pretoria 1,336,000;
Bloemfontein 417,000; Cape
Town 3,211,000
Language: IsiZulu, IsiXhosa

St. Lucia
Continent: North America
Area: 238 sq mi (616 sq km)
Population: 170,000
Capital: Castries 14,000
Language: English, French
patois

Sweden
Continent: Europe
Area: 173,732 sq mi
(449,964 sq km)
Population: 9,146,000
Capital: Stockholm 1,264,000
Language: Swedish, small
Sami- and Finnish-speaking
minorities

Senegal
Continent: Africa
Area: 75,955 sq mi
(196,722 sq km)
Population: 12,379,000
Capital: Dakar 2,603,000
Language: French, Wolof,
Pulaar, Jola, Mandinka

Slovakia
Continent: Europe
Area: 18,932 sq mi
(49,035 sq km)
Population: 5,396,000
Capital: Bratislava 424,000
Language: Slovak, Hungarian

South Korea
Continent: Asia
Area: 38,321 sq mi
(99,250 sq km)
Population: 48,456,000
Capital: Seoul 9,799,000
Language: Korean, English

St. Vincent and the Grenadines
Continent: North America
Area: 150 sq mi (389 sq km)
Population: 111,000
Capital: Kingstown 26,000
Language: English, French
patois

Switzerland
Continent: Europe
Area: 15,940 sq mi
(41,284 sq km)
Population: 7,532,000
Capital: Bern 337,000
Language: German, French,
Italian, Romansh

Serbia
Continent: Europe
Area: 29,913 sq mi
(77,474 sq km)
Population: 7,625,000
Capital: Belgrade 1,100,000
Language: Serbian, Hungarian,
Albanian

Slovenia
Continent: Europe
Area: 7,827 sq mi
(20,273 sq km)
Population: 2,014,000
Capital: Ljubljana 244,000
Language: Slovene, Serbo-
Croatian

Spain
Continent: Europe
Area: 195,363 sq mi
(505,988 sq km)
Population: 45,332,000
Capital: Madrid 5,567,000
Language: Castilian Spanish,
Catalan, Galician, Basque

Sudan
Continent: Africa
Area: 967,500 sq mi
(2,505,813 sq km)
Population: 38,560,000
Capital: Khartoum 4,762,000
Language: Arabic, Nubian,
Ta Bedawie, many diverse
dialects of Nilotic, Nilo-Hamitic,
Sudanic languages, English

Syria
Continent: Asia
Area: 71,498 sq mi
(185,180 sq km)
Population: 19,929,000
Capital: Damascus 2,467,000
Language: Arabic, Kurdish,
Armenian, Aramaic, Circassian;
French and English somewhat
understood

Tajikistan
Continent: Asia
Area: 55,251 sq mi
(143,100 sq km)
Population: 7,133,000
Capital: Dushanbe 553,000
Language: Tajik, Russian

Tonga
Continent: Australia/Oceania
Area: 289 sq mi (748 sq km)
Population: 101,000
Capital: Nuku'alofa 25,000
Language: Tongan, English

Tuvalu
Continent: Australia/Oceania
Area: 10 sq mi (26 sq km)
Population: 10,000
Capital: Funafuti 5,000
Language: Tuvaluan, English,
Samoan, Kiribati

United States
Continent: North America
Area: 3,794,083 sq mi
(9,826,630 sq km)
Population: 302,200,000
Capital: Washington, D.C.
4,338,000
Language: English, Spanish,
other Indo-European languages

Venezuela
Continent: South America
Area: 352,144 sq mi
(912,050 sq km)
Population: 27,483,000
Capital: Caracas 2,986,000
Language: Spanish, numerous
indigenous dialects

Tanzania
Continent: Africa
Area: 364,900 sq mi
(945,087 sq km)
Population: 38,738,000
Capital: Dar es Salaam
2,930,000; Dodoma 83,000
Language: Swahili, Kiunguja,
English, Arabic, local languages

**Trinidad and
Tobago**
Continent: North America
Area: 1,980 sq mi (5,128 sq km)
Population: 1,387,000
Capital: Port-of-Spain 54,000
Language: English, Caribbean
Hindustani, French, Spanish,
Chinese

Uganda
Continent: Africa
Area: 93,104 sq mi
(241,139 sq km)
Population: 28,530,000
Capital: Kampala 1,420,000
Language: English, Ganda,
other local languages, Swahili,
Arabic

Uruguay
Continent: South America
Area: 68,037 sq mi
(176,215 sq km)
Population: 3,324,000
Capital: Montevideo 1,514,000
Language: Spanish

Vietnam
Continent: Asia
Area: 127,844 sq mi
(331,114 sq km)
Population: 85,134,000
Capital: Hanoi 4,377,000
Language: Vietnamese, English,
French, Chinese, Khmer

Thailand
Continent: Asia
Area: 198,115 sq mi
(513,115 sq km)
Population: 65,706,000
Capital: Bangkok 6,706,000
Language: Thai, English, ethnic
dialects

Tunisia
Continent: Africa
Area: 63,170 sq mi
(163,610 sq km)
Population: 10,225,000
Capital: Tunis 746,000
Language: Arabic, French

Ukraine
Continent: Europe
Area: 233,090 sq mi
(603,700 sq km)
Population: 46,505,000
Capital: Kiev 2,705,000
Language: Ukrainian, Russian

Uzbekistan
Continent: Asia
Area: 172,742 sq mi
(447,400 sq km)
Population: 26,499,000
Capital: Tashkent 2,184,000
Language: Uzbek, Russian,
Tajik

Yemen
Continent: Asia
Area: 207,286 sq mi
(536,869 sq km)
Population: 22,389,000
Capital: Sanaa 2,008,000
Language: Arabic

Timor-Leste (East Timor)
Continent: Asia
Area: 5,640 sq mi
(14,609 sq km)
Population: 1,048,000
Capital: Dili 159,000
Language: Tetum, Portuguese,
Indonesian, English, indigenous
languages

Turkey
Continent: Europe/Asia
Area: 300,948 sq mi
(779,452 sq km)
Population: 73,967,000
Capital: Ankara 3,715,000
Language: Turkish, Kurdish,
Dimli (Zaza), Azeri, Kabardian,
Gagauz

**United Arab
Emirates**
Continent: Asia
Area: 30,000 sq mi
(77,700 sq km)
Population: 4,424,000
Capital: Abu Dhabi 604,000
Language: Arabic, Persian,
English, Hindi, Urdu

Vanuatu
Continent: Australia/Oceania
Area: 1 4,707 sq mi
(2,190 sq km)
Population: 235,000
Capital: Port-Vila 40,000
Language: over 100 local
languages, pidgin (known as
Bislama or Bichelama)

Zambia
Continent: Africa
Area: 290,586 sq mi
(752,614 sq km)
Population: 11,477,000
Capital: Lusaka 1,328,000
Language: English, Bemba, Ka-
onda, Lozi, Lunda, Luvale, about
70 other indigenous languages

Togo
Continent: Africa
Area: 21,925 sq mi
(56,785 sq km)
Population: 6,585,000
Capital: Lomé 1,451,000
Language: French, Ewe, Mina,
Kabye, Dagomba

Turkmenistan
Continent: Asia
Area: 188,456 sq mi
(488,100 sq km)
Population: 5,409,000
Capital: Ashgabat 744,000
Language: Turkmen, Russian,
Uzbek

United Kingdom
Continent: Europe
Area: 93,788 sq mi
(242,910 sq km)
Population: 60,967,000
Capital: London 8,566,000
Language: English, Welsh,
Scottish form of Gaelic

Vatican City
Continent: Europe
Area: 0.2 sq mi (0.4 sq km)
Population: 798
Capital: Vatican City 798
Language: Italian, Latin, French

Zimbabwe
Continent: Africa
Area: 150,872 sq mi
(390,757 sq km)
Population: 13,349,000
Capital: Harare 1,572,000
Language: English, Shona,
Sindebele, numerous minor
tribal dialects

Glossary

Note: Terms defined within the main body of the atlas text are not listed below.

Arid climate type of dry climate in which annual precipitation is often less than 10 inches (25 cm); experiences great daily variations in day-night temperatures (pp. 20–21)

Asylum a place where a person can go to find safety; to offer asylum means to offer protection in a safe country to people who fear being persecuted or who have been persecuted in their own country (pp. 34–35)

Bathymetry measurement of depth at various places in the ocean or other body of water (p. 11)

Biodiversity biological diversity in an environment as indicated by numbers of different species of plants and animals (pp. 28, 108)

Boreal forest *see* northern coniferous forest

Boundary line established by people to separate one political or mapped area from another; physical features, such as mountains and rivers, or latitude and longitude lines sometimes act as boundaries (p. 10)

Breadbasket a geographic region that is a principal source of grain (p. 64)

Canadian Shield region containing the oldest rock in North America; areas are exposed in much of eastern Canada and some bordering U.S. regions (pp. 56, 62)

Civil war war between opposing groups of citizens of the same country (p. 53)

Coastal plain any comparatively level land of low elevation that borders the ocean (p. 64)

Continental climate midlatitude climate zone occurring on large land-masses in the Northern Hemisphere and character-ized by great variations of temperature, both season-ally and between day and night; continental cool summer climates are influenced by nearby colder sub-arctic climates; continental warm summer climates are influenced by nearby mild or dry climates (pp. 20–21)

Coordinated Universal Time (UTC) the basis for the current worldwide system of civil (versus military) time determined by highly precise atomic clocks; also known as Universal Time; formerly known as Greenwich Mean Time (p. 13)

Culture hearth center from which major cultural traditions spread and are adopted by people in a wide geographic area (p. 90)

Cybercafé a café that has a collection of computers that customers can use to access the Internet (p. 50)

Degraded forest a for-ested area severely damaged by overharvesting, repeated fires, overgrazing, poor man-agement practices, or other abuse that delays or prevents forest regrowth (p. 28)

Demography the statistical study of human populations, especially with reference to size and density, distribution, and vital statistics (p. 126)

Desert and dry shrub vegetation region with either hot or cold tempera-tures that annually receives 10 inches (25 cm) or less of precipitation (pp. 24–25)

Ecosystem term for classifying Earth's natural communities according to how all things in an environment, such as a forest or a coral reef, interact with each other (pp. 10, 15, 68, 79, 120)

Fault break in Earth's crust along which move-ment up, down, or sideways occurs (pp. 16–17)

Flooded grassland wetland dominated by grasses and covered by water (pp. 24–25)

Fossil fuel a fuel, such as coal, petroleum, and natural gas, derived from the remains of ancient plants and animals (p. 46)

Geothermal energy heat energy generated within Earth (p. 47)

Glacier large, slow-moving mass of ice that forms over time from snow (p. 54)

Global warming a theory about the increase of Earth's average global temperature due to a buildup of so-called greenhouse gases, such as carbon dioxide and meth-ane, released by human activities (p. 29)

Globalization the purposeful spread of activities, technology, goods, and values through-out the world through the expansion of global links, such as trade, media, and the Internet (p. 48)

Gondwana name given to the southern part of the supercontinent Pangaea; made up of what we now call Africa, South America, Australia, Antarctica, and India (p. 16)

Greenwich Mean Time *see* Coordinated Universal Time

Gross domestic product (GDP) the gross national product excluding the value of net income earned abroad (p. 42)

Gross national product (GNP) the total value of the goods and services produced by the residents of a nation during a specified period (as a year) (p. 42)

Groundwater water, primarily from rain or melted snow, that collects beneath Earth's surface, in saturated soil or in underground reservoirs, or aquifers, and that supplies springs and wells (p. 27)

Guerrilla a person who engages in irregular warfare, especially as a member of an independent unit carrying out harass-ment and sabotage (p. 52)

Hemisphere one-half of the globe; the Equator divides Earth into Northern and Southern Hemispheres; the prime meridian and the 180 degree meridian divide it into Eastern and Western Hemispheres (p. 5)

Highland/upland climate region associated with mountains or plateaus that varies depending on elevation, latitude, continental location, and exposure to sun and wind; in general, temperature decreases and precipitation increases with elevation (pp. 20–21)

Host country the country where a refugee first goes to find asylum (p. 34)

Hot spot in geology, an extremely hot region beneath the lithosphere that tends to stay relatively stationary while plates of Earth's outer crust move over it; environmentally, an ecological trouble spot (pp. 12, 28)

Humid subtropical climate region charac-terized by hot summers, mild to cool winters, and year-round pre-cipitation that is heaviest in summer; generally located on the south-eastern margins of continents (pp. 20–21)

Ice cap climate one of two kinds of polar climate; summer temperatures rarely rise above freezing and what little precipitation occurs is mostly in the form of snow (pp. 20–21)

Indigenous native to or occurring naturally in a specific area or environ-ment (p. 116)

Infiltration process that occurs in the water, or hydrologic, cycle when gravity causes surface water to seep down through the soil (p. 26)

Internally displaced person (IDP) a person who has fled his or her home to escape armed con-flict, generalized violence, human rights abuses, or natural or man-made disasters; unlike a refugee, such a person has not crossed an international border but remains in his or her own country (p. 34)

Landform physical feature shaped by uplifting, weathering, and erosion; mountains, plateaus, hills, and plains are the four major types (p. 22)

Language family group of languages that share a common ancestry (pp. 38–39)

Latin America cultural region generally considered to include Mexico, Central America, South America, and the West Indies; Portuguese and Spanish are the principal languages (pp. 36–37)

Llanos extensive, mostly treeless grasslands in the Orinoco River basin of northern South America (p. 72)

Lowlands fairly level land at a lower elevation than surrounding areas (p. 14)

Mangrove vegetation tropical trees and shrubs with dense root systems that grow in tidal mud flats and extend coastlines by trapping soil (pp. 24–25)

Marginal land land that has little value for growing crops or for commercial or residential development (p. 28)

Marine west coast type of mild climate common on the west coasts of continents in midlatitude regions; characterized by small variations in annual temperature range and wet, foggy winters (pp. 20–21)

Median age midpoint of a population's age; half the population is older than this age; half is younger (p. 33)

Mediterranean climate type of mild climate common on the west coasts of continents, named for the dominant climate along the Mediterranean coast; characterized by mild, rainy winters and hot, dry summers (pp. 20–21)

Mediterranean shrub low-growing, mostly small-leaved evergreen vegetation, such as chaparral, that thrives in Mediterranean climate regions (pp. 24–25)

Melanesia one of three major island groups that make up Oceania; includes the Fiji Islands, New Guinea, Vanuatu, the Solomon Islands, and New Caledonia (pp. 112–113)

Melanesian indigenous to Melanesia (p. 116)

Microclimate climate of a very limited area that varies from the overall climate of the surrounding region (p. 22)

Micronesia one of three major island groups that make up Oceania; made up of some 2,000 mostly coral islands, including Guam, Kiribati, the Mariana Islands, Palau, and the Federated States of Micronesia (pp. 112–113)

Micronesian indigenous to Micronesia (p. 116)

Monsoon seasonal change in the direction of the prevailing winds, which causes wet and dry seasons in some tropical areas (p. 94)

Mountain grassland vegetation region characterized by clumps of long grass that grow beyond the limit of forests at high elevations (pp. 24–25)

Nonrenewable resources elements of the natural environment, such as metals, minerals, and fossil fuels, that form within Earth by geological processes over millions of years and thus cannot readily be replaced (pp. 46–47)

Northern coniferous forest vegetation region composed primarily of cone-bearing, needle-leafed or scale-leafed evergreen trees that grow in regions with long winters and moderate to high annual precipitation; also called boreal forest or taiga (pp. 24–25)

Oceania name for the widely scattered islands of Polynesia, Micronesia, and Melanesia; often includes Australia and New Zealand (pp. 110–121)

Pampas temperate grassland primarily in Argentina between the Andes and the Atlantic Ocean; one of the richest agricultural regions in the world (pp. 70, 72)

Patagonia cool, windy, arid plateau region primarily in southern Argentina between the Andes and the Atlantic Ocean (p. 72)

Per capita the total national income divided by the number of people in the nation (p. 27)

Plain large area of relatively flat land; one of the four major kinds of landforms (p. 18)

Plate tectonics study of the interaction of slabs of Earth's crust as molten rock within Earth causes them to slowly move across the surface (pp. 16–17)

Plateau large, relatively flat area that rises above the surrounding landscape; one of the four major kinds of landforms (pp. 18–19)

Polar climates climates that occur at very high latitudes; generally too cold to support tree growth; include tundra and ice cap (pp. 20–21)

Polynesia one of three major regions in Oceania made up mostly of volcanic and coral islands, including the Hawai'ian and the Society Islands, Samoa, and French Polynesia (pp. 112–113)

Polynesian indigenous to Polynesia (p. 116)

Predominant economy main type of work that most people do to meet their wants and needs in a particular country (pp. 44–45, 61, 77, 87, 97, 107, 117)

Province land governed as a political or administrative unit of a country or empire; Canadian provinces, like U.S. states, have substantial powers of self-government (p. 63)

Rain forest see Tropical moist broadleaf forest

Renewable fresh water water that is replenished naturally, but the supply of which can be endangered by overuse and pollution (p. 26)

River basin area drained by a single river and its tributaries (p. 72)

Rural pertaining to the countryside, where most of the economic activity centers on agriculture-related work (pp. 36–37)

Sahel in Africa the semi-arid region of short, tropical grassland that lies between the dry Sahara and the humid savanna and that is prone to frequent droughts (p. 104)

Sampan a flat-bottomed skiff used in eastern Asia and usually propelled by two short oars (p. 98)

Savanna tropical tall grassland with scattered low trees (pp. 24–25)

Selva Portuguese word referring to tropical rain forests, especially in the Amazon Basin (p. 78)

Semiarid dry climate region that experiences great daily variation in day-night temperatures; receives enough rainfall to support grasslands (pp. 20–21)

Silt mineral particles that are larger than grains of clay but smaller than grains of sand (p. 78)

Stateless people those who have no recognized country (p. 35)

Steppe Slavic word referring to relatively flat, mostly treeless, temperate grass-lands that stretch across much of central Europe and central Asia (p. 92)

Subarctic climate region characterized by short, cool, sometimes freezing summers and long, bitter-cold winters; most precipitation falls in summer (pp. 20–21)

Subtropical climate region between tropical and continental climates characterized by distinct seasons but with milder temperatures than continental climates (pp. 20–21)

Suburb a residential area on the outskirts of a town or city (p. 36)

Sunbelt area of rapid population and economic growth south of the 37th parallel in the United States; its mild climate is attractive to retirees and a general absence of labor unions has drawn manufacturing to the region (p. 60)

Taiga see Northern coniferous forest

Temperate broadleaf forest vegetation region with distinct seasons and dependable rainfall; predominant species include oak, maple, and beech, all of which lose their leaves in the cold season (pp. 24–25)

Temperate coniferous forest vegetation region that has mild winters with heavy precipitation; made up of mostly evergreen, needleleaf trees that bear seeds in cones (pp. 24–25)

Temperate grassland vegetation region where grasses are dominant and the climate is characterized by hot summers, cold winters, and moderate rainfall (pp. 24–25)

Territory land under the jurisdiction of a country but that is not a state or a province (p. 57)

Tropical coniferous forest vegetation region that occurs in a cooler climate than tropical rain forests; has distinct wet and dry seasons; made up of mostly evergreen trees with seed-bearing cones (pp. 24–25)

Tropical dry climate region characterized by year-round high temperatures and sufficient precipitation to support savannas (pp. 20–21)

Tropical dry forest vegetation region that has distinct wet and dry seasons and a cooler climate than tropical moist forests; has shorter trees than rain forests and many shed their leaves in the dry season (pp. 24–25)

Tropical grassland and savanna vegetation region characterized by scattered individual trees; occurs in warm or hot climates with annual rainfall of 20 to 50 inches (50–130 cm) (pp. 24–25)

Tropical moist broad-leaf forest vegetation region occurring mostly in a belt between the Tropic of Cancer and the Tropic of Capricorn in areas that have at least 80 inches (200 cm) of rain annually and an average annual temperature of 80°F (20°C) (pp. 24–25, 78–79)

Tropical wet climate region characterized by year-round warm temperatures and rainfall ranging from 60 to 150 inches (150–400 cm) annually (pp. 20–21)

Troposphere region of Earth's atmosphere closest to the surface; where weather occurs (p. 5)

Tundra vegetation region at high latitudes and high elevations characterized by cold temperatures, low vegetation, and a short growing season (pp. 24–25)

Tundra climate region with one or more months of temperatures slightly above freezing when the ground is free of snow (pp. 20–21)

Twenty-foot-equivalent unit (TEU) the standard unit for describing a ship's cargo carrying capacity, or a shipping terminal's cargo handling capacity. A standard forty-foot (40 x 8 x 8 feet) container equals two TEUs (each 20 x 8 x 8 feet) (pp. 98–99)

Universalizing religion one that attempts to appeal to all people rather than to just those in a particular region or place (p. 40)

Upland climate see Highland/upland climate

Urban pertaining to a town or city, where most of the economic activity is not based on agriculture (pp. 36–37)

Urban agglomeration a group of several cities and/or towns and their suburbs (p. 37)

Watershed a region or area bounded peripherally by a divide and draining ultimately to a particular watercourse or body of water (pp. 26–27)

West Bank area bordering the west bank of the Jordan River that, according to a 1993 peace agreement between Israelis and Palestinians, has limited Palestinian autonomy; its future is subject to ongoing negotiations between these groups (p. 35)

Web Sites

Activities and lessons using maps: http://www.nationalgeographic.com/xpeditions/

Antarctica: http://www.nsf.gov/div/index.jsp?div=ANT

Cultural Diffusion: http://www2.geog.okstate.edu/users/lightfoot/lightfoot.html

Earth's Climates: http://www.worldclimate.com

Earth's Vegetation: http://www.earthobservatory.nasa.gov/Library/LandCover/

Environmental Hot Spots: http://earthtrends.wri.org/index.cfm

 Quiz for students: http://www.myfootprint.org/

Flags of the World: http://www.fotw.us/flags/index.html

Globalization: http://www.globalisationguide.org/

Map Projections: http://www.colorado.edu/geography/gcraft/notes/mapproj/mapproj.html

National Geographic Kids Atlases Homepage: http://www.nationalgeographic.com/kids-atlases/index.html

Natural Hazards:

 Earthquakes: http://earthquake.usgs.gov/

 Tsunamis: http://www.tsunami.noaa.gov

 Volcanoes: http://www.geo.mtu.edu/volcanoes/

Political World: http://www.cia.gov/cia/publications/factbook/index.html

Predominant World Economies: http://www.wto.org/english/res_e/statis_e/statis_e.htm

Reading Maps: http://egsc.usgs.gov/isb/pubs/teachers-packets/mapshow/mapshowindexpdf.html

http://leisure.ordnancesurvey.co.uk/leisure/tscontent/editorial/mapfacts/leaflets/map_reading_made_easy.pdf

Time Zones: http://tycho.usno.navy.mil/tzones.html

Types of Maps: http://erg.usgs.gov/isb/pubs/MapProjections/projections.html

World Cities: http://www.un.org/esa/population/publications/wup2003/WUP2003Report.pdf

World Conflicts: http://www.cnn.com/interactive/maps/world/fullpage.global.conflict/world.index.html

World Energy: http://www.bp.com/productlanding.do?categoryId=6929&contentId=7044622

World Food: http://www.cgiar.org/impact/research/index.html

World Languages: http://www.ethnologue.com/web.asp

 Interactive for students: http://www.ipl.org/div/kidspace/hello/

World Population: http://www.census.gov/ipc/www/idb/

World Refugees: http://www.unrefugees.org

World Religions: http://www.adherents.com/

World Water: http://water.usgs.gov

Thematic Index

Boldface indicates illustrations

Place-Name Index

Illustration Credits

Published by the National Geographic Society

John M. Fahey, Jr.
President and Chief Executive Officer

Gilbert M. Grosvenor
Chairman of the Board

Tim T. Kelly
President, Global Media Group

John Q. Griffin
President, Publishing

Nina D. Hoffman
Executive Vice President, President of Book Publishing Group

Prepared by the Book Division

Nancy Laties Feresten,
Vice President, Editor in Chief, Children's Books

Bea Jackson, *Director of Design and Illustrations, Children's Books*

Jennifer Emmett, *Executive Editor,
Reference and Solo, Children's Books*

Amy Shields, *Executive Editor, Series, Children's Books*

Carl Mehler, *Director of Maps*

Staff for this Book

Priyanka Lamichhane, *Project Editor*

David M. Seager, Ruth Thompson, *Art Directors*

Lori Renda, *Illustrations Editor*

Steven D. Gardner, Thomas L. Gray, Nicholas P. Rosenbach,
Map Editors

Matt Chwastyk, Steven D. Gardner, Gregory Ugiansky,
XNR Productions, *Map Research and Production*

Martha Sharma, *Writer and Chief Consultant*

Stuart Armstrong, *Graphics Illustrator*

Suzanne Patrick Fonda, *Release Editor*

Debbie Guthrie Haer, *Copy Editor*

Connie D. Binder, *Indexer*

Jennifer Thornton, *Managing Editor*

Grace Hill, *Associate Managing Editor*

Heidi Vincent, *Vice President,
Direct Response Sales and Marketing*

Jeff Reynolds, *Marketing Director, Children's Books*

R. Gary Colbert, *Production Director*

Lewis R. Bassford, *Production Manager*

Susan Borke, *Legal and Business Affairs*

Manufacturing and Quality Management

Christopher A. Liedel, *Chief Financial Officer*

Phillip L. Schlosser, *Vice President*

Chris Brown, *Technical Director*

Rachel Faulise, Nicole Elliott, and Monika Lynde,
Manufacturing Managers

Acknowledgements:
We are grateful for the assistance of
Richard W. Bullington, Jan D. Morris, Karla H. Tucker, and
Alfred L. Zebarth of NG Maps; the National Geographic Image
Collection; and Jo H. Tunstall, Robert W. Witt, and
Lyle Rosbotham, NG Book Division

Founded in 1888, the National Geographic Society is one of the largest nonprofit scientific and educational organizations in the world. It reaches more than 285 million people worldwide each month through its official journal, NATIONAL GEOGRAPHIC, and its four other magazines; the National Geographic Channel; television documentaries; radio programs; films; books; videos and DVDs; maps; and interactive media. National Geographic has funded more than 8,000 scientific research projects and supports an education program combating geographic illiteracy.

For more information, please call 1-800-NGS LINE (647-5463) or write to the following address:

NATIONAL GEOGRAPHIC SOCIETY
1145 17th Street N.W., Washington, D.C. 20036-4688 U.S.A.

Visit us online at www.nationalgeographic.com

For information about special discounts for bulk purchases, please contact National Geographic Books Special Sales: ngspecsales@ngs.org

For rights or permissions inquiries, please contact National Geographic Books Subsidiary Rights: ngbookrights@ngs.org

Teachers and librarians go to ngchildrensbooks.org

Published by the National Geographic Society
1145 17th Street N.W.
Washington, D.C. 20036-4688

The Library of Congress has cataloged the 2001 edition as follows:

National Geographic Society (U.S.)
National Geographic student atlas of the world.
p. cm.
Includes index and glossary.
ISBN 978-1-4263-0446-0 (pbk.)
ISBN 978-1-4263-0445-3 (hc.)
ISBN: 978-1-4263-0458-3 (library)
  1. Children's atlases. 2. Earth—remote-sensing images. 3. Physical
  geography—Maps for children. [1.Atlases.] I. Title: Student atlas
  of the world. II. Title.
G1021 .N42 2001
912—dc21   00-030006

Printed in the U.S.A.
09/CK=CML/1

Metric Conversion Tables

CONVERSION TO METRIC MEASURES

SYMBOL	WHEN YOU KNOW	MULTIPLY BY	TO FIND	SYMBOL
LENGTH				
in	inches	2.54	centimeters	cm
ft	feet	0.30	meters	m
yd	yards	0.91	meters	m
mi	miles	1.61	kilometers	km
AREA				
in^2	square inches	6.45	square centimeters	cm^2
ft^2	square feet	0.09	square meters	m^2
yd^2	square yards	0.84	square meters	m^2
mi^2	square miles	2.59	square kilometers	km^2
—	acres	0.40	hectares	ha
MASS				
oz	ounces	28.35	grams	g
lb	pounds	0.45	kilograms	kg
—	short tons	0.91	metric tons	t
VOLUME				
in^3	cubic inches	16.39	milliliters	mL
liq oz	liquid ounces	29.57	milliliters	mL
pt	pints	0.47	liters	L
qt	quarts	0.95	liters	L
gal	gallons	3.79	liters	L
ft^3	cubic feet	0.03	cubic meters	m^3
yd^3	cubic yards	0.76	cubic meters	m^3
TEMPERATURE				
°F	degrees Fahrenheit	5/9 after subtracting 32	degrees Celsius (centigrade)	°C

CONVERSION FROM METRIC MEASURES

SYMBOL	WHEN YOU KNOW	MULTIPLY BY	TO FIND	SYMBOL
LENGTH				
cm	centimeters	0.39	inches	in
m	meters	3.28	feet	ft
m	meters	1.09	yards	yd
km	kilometers	0.62	miles	mi
AREA				
cm^2	square centimeters	0.16	square inches	in^2
m^2	square meters	10.76	square feet	ft^2
m^2	square meters	1.20	square yards	yd^2
km^2	square kilometers	0.39	square miles	mi^2
ha	hectares	2.47	acres	—
MASS				
g	grams	0.04	ounces	oz
kg	kilograms	2.20	pounds	lb
t	metric tons	1.10	short tons	—
VOLUME				
mL	milliliters	0.06	cubic inches	in^3
mL	milliliters	0.03	liquid ounces	liq oz
L	liters	2.11	pints	pt
L	liters	1.06	quarts	qt
L	liters	0.26	gallons	gal
m^3	cubic meters	35.31	cubic feet	ft^3
m^3	cubic meters	1.31	cubic yards	yd^3
TEMPERATURE				
°C	degrees Celsius (centigrade)	9/5 then add 32	degrees Fahrenheit	°F